DEAR EVAN HANSEN
through the window

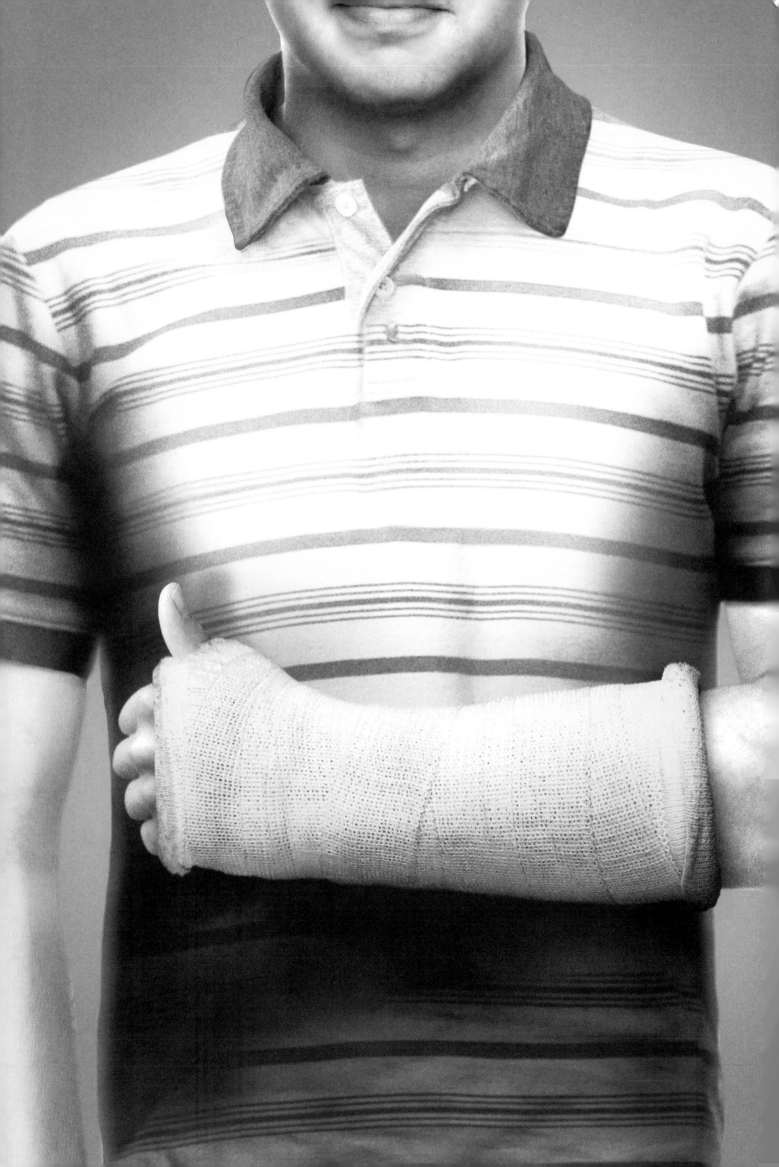

DEAR EVAN HANSEN

through the window

Book, music, lyrics, and annotations by
Steven Levenson, Benj Pasek & Justin Paul
As directed by Michael Greif

Interviews and text by Adam Green and Suzy Evans
Editorial contributions by Stacey Mindich

GRAND
CENTRAL
PUBLISHING

MELCHER
MEDIA

Designed by Paul Kepple, Max Vandenberg,
and Marissa Raybuck at
HEADCASE DESIGN
www.headcasedesign.com

GRAND CENTRAL PUBLISHING
Hachette Book Group
1290 Avenue of the Americas
New York, NY 10104
grandcentralpublishing.com
twitter.com/grandcentralpub

First Edition: November 2017

Grand Central Publishing is a division of Hachette
Book Group, Inc.

The Grand Central Publishing name and logo is a
trademark of Hachette Book Group, Inc.

The publisher is not responsible for websites (or
their content) that are not owned by the publisher.

The Hachette Speakers Bureau provides a wide
range of authors for speaking events. To find out
more, go to www.hachettespeakersbureau.com
or call (866) 376-6591.

This book was produced by
MELCHER MEDIA

PCN: 2017952636

ISBNs: 978-1538761915 (hardcover),
978-1538761908 (ebook)

Printed in Italy

10 9 8 7 6 5 4 3 2 1

CONTENTS

FOREWORD
by Michael Greif

AM A CAUTIOUS PERSON. I'M CAREFUL not to get ahead of myself or expect too much from the projects that I'm about to join. I believe that the work itself is its own reward—to find a way to depict the fascinating world that writers and composers are suggesting, the opportunity to join forces with the original imaginations and innovations of designers, choreographers, musical directors, and mostly to find ways to inspire, shape, or just marvel at the humanity and complexity that actors unearth as they breathe life into their characters.

But I was not cautious when I first encountered *Dear Evan Hansen*, then called the *Untitled P (Pasek)/P (Paul)/L (Levenson) Project*. I fell in love, hard. I thought the narrative, characters, and ideas that these three remarkable writers were choosing to explore were perfect for a musical and perfect for the moment. I knew that the emotional stakes would compel every character to sing about their aspirations and needs, and I knew I was in good company. I had met Stacey Mindich, and I could see she was serious and diligent and fiercely believed in this project. I had seen earlier works by Benj Pasek and Justin Paul; I read all of Steven Levenson's plays that I could get my hands on. As I began to work with these smart, extraordinary writers, I was impressed by their ambition, their rigor, their impatience (so right for their age), and was floored by their generosity, curiosity, and their ability to get into the heads and hearts of characters far beyond their experience and years.

No songs and very little actual dialogue remain these days from the *Untitled PPL Project* that I first encountered, but the spirit and the unique story of this unforgettable high school senior who fakes a friendship with a dead kid for all those complicated, unexpected, but completely believable and heartbreaking reasons does. It's been among the great pleasures of my life to witness and participate in the refining, retooling, and reprioritizing of that story alongside the most spectacular group of collaborators, who built the ideal visual and sonic world to ground the writers' creation.

And what a great privilege to see our fantastic actors—many of whom were in our very first reading and like me fell immediately in love (and turned down a lot of work along the way)—wrestle with the demands of their roles, cope with the changes and rewrites that got thrown their way, inspire the writers and me in unimagined ways, and triumph in creating complex, flawed, lovable, brave, authentic characters.

My very favorite aspect of *Dear Evan Hansen* is that you're able to clock the development from the time Evan, in a moment of intense peril, accidentally glances at an apple just sitting on the Murphys' dining room table. Cynthia transforms this "apple" into a cherished family memory she desperately needs to recall. Evan then fantasizes his perfect friendship scenario in Cynthia's orchard in a truly great song (which I'll always think of as "The Orchard Song"). Throughout the play, we watch that imagined landscape become an actual one that ultimately provides comfort and healing to some bruised and scarred people. In some ways, that evolution from theoretical to real feels like the very essence of artistic creation.

I've been very fortunate to have worked on some shows that have spoken directly to a new generation of theatergoers and have inspired an incredible group of theatermakers. I know that every night and for years to come imaginations will be sparked, hearts will be healed, and metaphorical orchards will be planted at the Music Box and every theater playing *Dear Evan Hansen*.

< The cast and creative team celebrate backstage at the 2017 Tony Awards after winning the award for Best Musical.

AT 6 P.M. ON A SWELTERING Tuesday in mid-June, a crowd of theatergoers is already lining up outside the Music Box Theatre, on West 45th Street, where the musical *Dear Evan Hansen* has been playing to sold-out houses since it opened on December 4, 2016. Despite the heat, the air is crisp with anticipation. Tonight's performance is the first since the show took home six Tony Awards, including Best Musical, at Radio City Music Hall two nights ago. On either side of the stage door, barricades have been set up to contain the throngs of fans of all ages who will gather to wait for the show's young star Ben Platt—fresh from his Best Performance by a Leading Actor in a Musical win at the Tonys—and his fellow cast members to emerge after the show. Some of the waiting fans have seen the musical multiple times, while others know it only from what they've watched online, and many have traveled from around the country to be here. They clutch *Playbills*, posters, or their self-made *Dear Evan Hansen* fan art, in the hope of scoring an autograph, a selfie, maybe even a conversation with one of the actors—any chance to connect and express how much the show means to them.

MEANWHILE, THE CAST, CREATIVE team, and crew of *Dear Evan Hansen* are assembled in an austere break room in the theater's basement. Packed shoulder to shoulder for a pre-show celebration hosted by lead producer Stacey Mindich, nearly everyone involved with the production is here, including Tony-winning songwriters Benj Pasek and Justin Paul, book writer Steven Levenson, orchestrator Alex Lacamoire, and co-star Rachel Bay Jones. (Director Michael Greif is at his daughter's high school graduation.) They're elated, if exhausted, after a frenetic awards season, capped by the emotional triumph at Radio City and the after-parties that went on until dawn. Amid the din of a dozen conversations—think a particularly loquacious family reunion—Platt, saving his voice, isn't saying much, even as he shuffles through the room in his slippers, freely dispensing hugs. Costumed in his character's now-iconic blue striped polo shirt, he matches the cake that Mindich custom-ordered for the occasion.

Mindich quiets everyone down. "It's been the most glorious, glorious two days, and it's been an embarrassment of riches," she begins, adding, "and Lin-Manuel kissed me!" As she thanks everyone for their contributions, she chronicles the history of the show: the initial idea that Pasek and Paul pitched her eight years earlier, the team of collaborators who joined them, and the celebration of this night. "You're all here because we are all Evan Hansen, and not just because we're all a little weird, but because I know that our hearts and our souls are all with this special show," she says. "I will never forget this. This has marked me and changed my life, and I know it has for all of you."

Paul makes a brief speech thanking Mindich for her steady hand through the stormy seas of the show's creation: "There were times when we felt very lost and didn't know what we were doing—or that we hated what we were doing—and then moments where everything was fine but we *thought* everything was terrible. But you always stayed the course, and you always believed in us."

Addressing the group, Levenson adds: "When all of you became involved, it became our responsibility to be equal to your talents and the gifts that you brought to the show. And that was really the thing that, for the last few years, spurred us to go above and beyond what we thought we were capable of. We owe that to the people in this room—you forced us to rise to your level."

When everyone turns expectantly to Pasek, he quickly says he doesn't have anything to add, before saying: "This is really a dream come true. And that's not a cliché—I mean, it is, but it doesn't feel like that right now. I've said that a lot in my life, and I haven't meant it, but I really do mean it now—I swear."

Soon, the production stage manager Judith Schoenfeld looks at her watch and calls, "Half hour." The actors dash to their dressing rooms, and the crew members scurry to their places. Mindich and the show's creative team head upstairs to join the extended *Dear Evan Hansen* family, including beaming agents and proud parents, to stand at the back of the theater and wait for the show to begin.

As soon as the lights begin to dim, the applause and the shouts of "Whoo!" start. A kaleidoscope of social media images flashes across the screens and monitors framing the stage, and the theater fills with a cacophony of voices from the internet. Suddenly, the images and the voices cut out and, center stage, a laptop opens, revealing Platt as Evan, his face bathed in its glow, a boy alone in the dark. A thunderous wave of applause and cheers greets him. It will be more than a minute before the noise dies down sufficiently for him to say his first line, "Dear Evan Hansen, Today is going to be a great day, and here's why." But even that reaction pales to the one that will follow Platt's performance of "Waving Through a Window," the show's—and his—signature song: an ecstatic roar and a standing ovation that one would be more likely to encounter at, say, a Beyoncé concert or a revival meeting than a Broadway musical.

Any list of unpromising ideas for a Broadway musical would have to include one whose hero is a lonely, depressive, pathologically shy teenage outsider so desperate to belong that he exploits a misunderstanding over the suicide of a classmate by pretending to have been his best friend. Add in the fact that he then rides the lie, even as it spirals out of his control, to high school popularity, social media stardom, a surrogate family, and the girl of his dreams, only to be forced, inevitably, to confront the truth and the pain he has caused—and the idea begins to sound downright catastrophic. But whether measured by its artistic achievement, critical reception, or box office success, by its gift for reaching a new generation of theatergoers, its ability to reflect and give voice to the experience of both adolescents and their parents, or the way, in an instance of life imitating art, it has united strangers from around the world through the internet, it is clear that *Dear Evan Hansen* has moved beyond Broadway success story to a cultural phenomenon.

PART OF THE SUCCESS OF *DEAR EVAN Hansen* certainly has something to do with the way it manages to tap into the zeitgeist: its canny use of social media as a plot device in an age when Facebook, Twitter, Instagram, Snapchat, and the prospect of platforms yet to be devised have become part of the fabric of our existence; its exploration of adolescent depression, anxiety, and suicide at a time when the topic is emerging out of shamed silence to become part of the national conversation. After an era marked by hit musical comedies of a decidedly irreverent, post-modern bent that simultaneously deconstructed and celebrated the form—from *Urinetown* and *The Producers* to *Avenue Q* and *The Book of Mormon*—*Dear Evan Hansen* arrived at a kind of post-ironic moment on

Broadway, with sophisticated audiences that hunger for shows combining full-throated sincerity with psychological realism, contemporary musical forms, and challenging, less obviously commercial subject matter. Consider that its immediate predecessors for the Best Musical Tony were *Fun Home*, a chamber piece about a lesbian cartoonist coming to terms with her sexuality and her gay father's suicide, and *Hamilton*, a multi-ethnic, hip-hop retelling of the founding of our country.

But the real secret of *Dear Evan Hansen*'s success lies in the extraordinary emotional bond that it creates with audiences night after night, allowing anyone who has ever been a teenager or a parent or a sibling—or has experienced the loneliness of feeling, as Evan sings, "on the outside always looking in"—to see their truth reflected onstage.

This book is a look behind the scenes at what it takes to create, against the odds, that rarest, most improbable of creatures: an original, contemporary musical. But it isn't just a story of the theatrical craftsmanship and blood, sweat, and tears behind a Broadway hit. It's also the story of the extraordinary group of artists for whom *Dear Evan Hansen* almost feels like the show that they were born to create, the men and women whose particular backgrounds, temperaments, preoccupations, and talents came together to make something so deeply personal that it has become universal. It is the story of the unlikely journey that led to the creation of a musical about the quintessentially human need and desire to belong and believe who we are is enough, and our yearning to, as the English novelist E.M. Forster put it, "only connect."

Platt signs autographs ∧
at the stage door after an
April 2017 performance.

CHAPTER 1

BUDDY, YOU AND I

Benj Pasek and Justin Paul
burst onto the scene

STEPHEN SONDHEIM'S *Merrily We Roll Along*, a Broadway flop in 1981 that has gone on to become a cult classic, follows the rise to fame of a pair of musical theater songwriters and longtime best friends, except it tells their story in reverse chronological order, taking them from disillusioned middle age to idealistic youth, ending with the duo on a New York City rooftop at dawn, looking ahead to the future, as they sing:

It's our time, breathe it in:
Worlds to change and worlds to win.
Our turn coming through,
Me and you, man,
Me and you!

It seems fitting that when a pair of 18-year-old future musical theater songwriting partners, and soon-to-be friends, Benj Pasek and Justin Paul, met as college freshmen, one of the things they bonded over—along with an obsessive knowledge of show tunes, a gift for nimble, smart-alecky banter, and an unwarranted confidence in their skills as freestyle rappers and beat-boxers—was a worshipful devotion to Sondheim in general and *Merrily*

We Roll Along in particular. Paul had starred in a high school production of it, prophetically playing the composer Franklin Shepard (you can find snippets of his heartfelt performance on YouTube), and both knew the lyrics to every song from the show, though "Our Time" spoke to them with special urgency. "What kid with the completely unrealistic belief that he's going to make it on Broadway doesn't see himself in that song?" Pasek says. "It's that mixture of naiveté and arrogance and hope, that heady spirit of 'Look out world—here we come.'"

"Our Time" could serve as a kind of anthem for the moment in which Pasek and Paul, still fresh-faced and bristling with enthusiasm at 32, find themselves. With Tonys for *Dear Evan Hansen* and Oscars for their lyrics to the song "City of Stars" from *La La Land* on their mantels, the duo has a big-screen Hugh Jackman musical, *The Greatest Showman*, about to hit theaters, a live-action Snow White film in the works for Disney, and some half dozen other theater and film projects at various stages of development. Fourteen years into their partnership, the two find themselves no longer the bright, talented kids with promise, but new members of the aristocracy of success.

Theirs is a marriage of opposites. A practicing Christian married to a journalist and a father to a 1-year-old daughter, Paul is lanky and pale with a swoosh of blond hair. (Fun fact: He met his wife, Asher, when she wrote her graduate school thesis on new musical theater writers and interviewed the pair.) Jewish, single, and gay, Pasek is swarthy and compact. And they play off each other with the practiced timing of a vaudeville team—or a pair of songwriters who finish each other's sentences, riff on each other's jokes, and shoot each other glances that only they understand.

"The idea is to make the songs sound like they emerged from one mind and one voice."

Every song begins and ends with Paul at the piano, composing the music, and Pasek on his MacBook, writing the lyrics. But the key to their partnership, they say, is how they complement each other, how their individual strengths and weaknesses dovetail to create a whole that is greater than the sum of its parts: not Benj Pasek and Justin Paul, but Pasek and Paul.

Since the beginning, they have shared credit for both music and lyrics. "The idea is to make the songs sound like they emerged from one mind and speak with one voice," Paul says.

"I think if you separate things too much, you end up fighting," Pasek adds. "I mean, we fight all the time—"

"Seriously, all the time—"

"Seriously. But not over turf. Sharing song credit allows us to not fight over individual pieces and to focus on..."

Almost simultaneously, they finish the thought: "...the song as a whole."

OF ALL THEIR ACHIEVEMENTS, THERE'S no question that *Dear Evan Hansen* remains closest to their hearts. "It's the culmination," Paul says, "of everything we've done, and everything we've wanted to do, since we first started writing songs together."

Paul grew up first in St. Louis and then Westport, Connecticut, the son of a pastor, who, along with Paul's mother, instilled in him a love of music. He started singing with his father in church as a young boy, later picking up the piano as well, and the soaring emotionality of gospel embedded itself in his musical DNA. But after he was cast in a local production of *Oliver!* and got his hands on the original cast recording of *Cats*, his life became all about musical theater—performing in shows, playing in the orchestra pit, conducting, and in his spare time listening to cast albums and teaching himself songs on the piano from Broadway "fake books."

Pasek followed a parallel trajectory in Ardmore, a suburb of Philadelphia. His early musical influence was his mother, a developmental psychologist, who, he recalls, "moonlit writing children's music." "She wrote songs that chronicled my childhood," he says. "They were big hits on the synagogue circuit. So I was always tracking how moments from real life could be translated into songs." Pasek's gateway drug into musical theater, at age 11, was *Rent*. "I remember being so moved by it and feeling that I had found these incredible characters and a secret community of people that related to them," he recalls. "That opened the floodgates."

Pasek and Paul may not have based the hero of *Dear Evan Hansen* on their younger selves—neither of them was pathologically anxious or depressed—but they did mine the sense of alienation, not uncommon to kids who find their way to the performing arts, that each felt as an adolescent. "I really hate the phrase 'fit in,' and yet there's a reason that we always use it," Paul says. "I remember many of my decisions—and I was a pretty independent-minded kid—being based to a degree on wanting to fit in and feel part of some group or some clique or some bunch of people who did the same things. I found that with musical theater. When I think about Evan and think about myself, I identify because, at the end of the day, you just want to feel that you're not the only one who isn't part of something."

Pasek also found a refuge with the theater kids at his school. But, he says, "for me, it was less about fitting in and more about finding my identity. A lot of people at that age, myself included, don't know who they are. That's how I identify with Evan the most. He's given a chance to have a strong sense of self, but it's built on a fabrication, so it's sitting on very, very shaky ground. You want to feel that you are loved and heard and seen and valued when you don't feel that way behind closed doors. That's very much how I felt at 17—waiting to like myself and wondering if other people would ever think I was worth liking."

(right) Paul as F. Scott Fitzgerald in *The Pursuit of Persephone* and Pasek as Yertle the Turtle in *Seussical*, both in productions at the University of Michigan.

∨ (below) Paul, left, and Pasek
perform a concert of their songs
at Joe's Pub in New York in 2006.

BY THE TIME THEY MET AT THEIR FRESH-man orientation weekend, entering the prestigious Musical Theatre program at the University of Michigan, they had both decided to pursue careers as performers. They saw themselves as potential triple threats, but before the end of their first ballet class, Pasek says, they discovered that they were "completely inept—literally the two worst dancers in the class," so they downgraded themselves to potential "double threats." They didn't get cast in either of the big school musicals their first year, and came up empty their sophomore fall when the show was *A Chorus Line*, for obvious reasons. Finally, when *City of Angels* was announced as the spring show, they felt sure their time had come, largely because it was a musical with minimal dancing. But when the cast list was posted, they learned that Pasek would be playing Man With Camera, while Paul would be portraying Harlan Yamato, a coroner and backup dancer. "It was pretty depressing," Pasek recalls. "And we started to realize, *Hmm, I think we might be getting down to zero threats.*"

At a crossroads, Pasek and Paul had an idea. If no one would cast them in a musical, why not write one of their own and put it on themselves? They had taken a stab at a songwriting collaboration as freshmen and already had three songs ready to go. "When we got in the room, we had this perfect combination of ADD and a creative spark together," Pasek says. Those earlier collaborations, though, had been pop songs. Now, they decided to try their hand at theatrical songs that they could imagine in a musical, guided by the questions they had learned to ask in their acting classes: Who are you talking to? What do you want? What's your obstacle?

When it came time to pick a subject for their first collaboration, Pasek recalls, "We kept noticing that a trope in the musical theater canon was these songs about young people who had big dreams. So we were, like, we're going to write a song that's going to be our 'Corner of the Sky,' or whatever. And we literally wrote a song called 'Boy With Dreams.'"

"And the tag phrase," Paul adds, "was, 'I'm a boy with dreams.' Zero subtext. No angle whatsoever. Just dead on the nose. But it was a start."

Pasek and Paul had what they call their "dark night of the soul" over spring break in Florida, where they committed to writing a full show—and to each other as collaborators.

Lacking the know-how, not to mention the time, to write a full book musical (a musical with a plot), they decided to create a song cycle (a group of thematically linked songs). Back at school, they booked the ninety-nine-seat Kerrytown Concert House near the Ann Arbor campus for April 3, 2005, invited everyone from their department, enlisted four fellow *City of Angels* rejects as performers, and, spurred by the looming performance, spent the next three weeks racing against the clock to write another eleven songs and teach them to the cast. The result was *Edges*, whose title is a nod to a lyric from *Merrily We Roll*

"If no one would cast them in a musical, why not [produce it] themselves?"

Along's "Our Time" ("Edges are blurring all around/And yesterday is done"). The one-night-only concert was a smash, and their peers seemed to connect to their clever, tuneful songs about young people on the edge of adulthood, trying to maneuver the challenges of romance, friendship, responsibility, and ambition. One number, "Be My Friend" (which has come to be known as "The Facebook Song"), pokes fun at the way the then-new phenomenon turns friendships into superficial transactions.

Both Facebook, which was available only to college students at the time, and YouTube were in their early days. Though Pasek and Paul may have been prescient to identify the pitfalls of social media, they were equally savvy in recognizing its potential for promoting their work. They uploaded videos of their concert to YouTube and, through Facebook, figured out which colleges had

theater departments and pitched the show to those schools. Within a year, thirteen colleges had mounted *Edges*. After its first professional production in 2007, it has since been performed all over the world.

Pasek and Paul received many invaluable professional and mentorship opportunities early in their careers. First came a summer internship in New York with Jeff Marx, one of the co-writers of *Avenue Q*, who loaned Paul $7,000 so he could continue to write rather than take a summer job to pay for school-related expenses, with the proviso that he repay him if and when Paul's first show opened on Broadway before he turned 30. (He repaid Marx on opening night of *A Christmas Story: The Musical* in 2012.) Then, Pasek and Paul won the prestigious Jonathan Larson Award, which is open only to college graduates, a condition they satisfied by cramming their credit requirements into the fall semester of their senior year and graduating early. By the time they moved to New York in December 2006, they had a concert of their songs at Joe's Pub under their belts and had lined up a job writing songs for the Disney Channel show *Johnny and the Sprites*.

LIVING A BLOCK AND A HALF FROM EACH other on the Upper West Side, Pasek and Paul sought out mentors in the business, among them the songwriting team behind *Ragtime* and *Once on This Island*, Lynn Ahrens and Stephen Flaherty. They credit Ahrens and Flaherty with teaching them that not every song has to tell a character's entire life journey in one anthemic three-minute sitting. They also captured the attention of Stephen Schwartz, a composer who boasts among his many credits such groundbreaking musicals as *Godspell* and *Wicked*. Schwartz advised them to start using pure rhyme and introduced them to a particularly crucial songwriting concept.

"He was, like, 'You guys need to learn about subtext,'" Paul recalls. "'Sometimes characters say or sing one thing...'"

Pasek jumps in: "'...but mean another.'"

"Right. We're, like, 'Oh, interesting. Wow.'"

By the time Pasek and Paul got the chance to write their first musical, they were ready to apply what they'd learned. They met up with Paul's middle- and high-school friend, playwright Peter Duchan, to brainstorm projects to work on together. Duchan suggested an adaptation of *Dogfight*, a 1991 film about a group of marines who organize a contest to see which of them can bring the ugliest girl to a dance. The trio developed the musical *Dogfight* over the next several years, leading eventually to its critically acclaimed New York premiere at Second Stage in 2012.

Around the same time as Pasek and Paul embarked on *Dogfight*, Ahrens introduced the two to Tim McDonald at iTheatrics, who was developing a musical version of Roald Dahl's *James and the Giant Peach*. The songwriters immediately clicked with McDonald and hit the ground running with the show, which premiered in 2010 at Goodspeed Opera House and has since been produced across the country. While *James* was still in development, they heard that Jerry Goehring was looking to develop a musical adaptation of the beloved film *A Christmas Story*, and the writers convinced their agent to secure them a meeting for the job. While still in college, they had discussed the classic holiday movie as a tale that could really sing and would make a great musical. They landed the gig, which became their Broadway debut and earned them their first Tony Award nomination.

With three musicals and a Tony nomination under their belts before they'd turned 30, Pasek and Paul had established themselves among the best and the brightest of the upcoming generation of musical theater writers. By 2013, after having written a traditional Broadway score influenced by the sounds of the 1960s for *Dogfight*, another for the 1940-set *A Christmas Story: The Musical*, plus a sprightly, eclectic pastiche for *James and the Giant Peach*, they longed to return to the kind of contemporary sound and setting they had first explored in *Edges*. And, after three musicals based on existing material, they wanted to write one that was completely original.

As it happened, they already had an idea in mind, based loosely on an incident from Pasek's high school days. Pasek had first floated the idea to Paul back at the University of Michigan, and the two of them had batted it around on and off ever since. When a producer named Stacey Mindich, a longtime fan of their songs, approached them with the hope of commissioning their next musical, Pasek and Paul knew what they wanted to write. It was, as Paul put it in an email to Mindich, "a story from our lives and from our hearts."

WE START WITH STARS IN OUR EYES

Stacey Mindich asks the writers to pitch their dream project

**EING THE LEAD PRODUCER** of a Broadway musical—which is to say the person ultimately responsible for the hopes, dreams, creative labor, live-lihood, and income of many, many people—is not for the faint of heart. Some produc-ers have been known to han-dle the stress less than gracefully (throwing cell phones at assistants, chewing out press agents, sending nasty emails to critics). That's not Stacey Mindich. Elegant, articulate, and preternaturally calm, Mindich is an oasis of No Drama in a milieu that is, by definition, all about drama. And if, in the almost eight years it took *Dear Evan Hansen* to go from a not obviously commer-cial premise to a Tony-winning smash, Mindich some-times had to step into the role of den mother, it takes

nothing away from her taste, passion, perseverance, and business acumen that made the musical possible.

For Mindich, whose résumé includes producing *The Bridges of Madison County* and creating Encores! Off-Center at City Center, *Dear Evan Hansen* began with her desire to work on something—anything—with Benj Pasek and Justin Paul. "I just knew that they wrote the songs that I would listen to again and again," she says. "That was probably my only contribution to this whole thing, other than keeping it together all these years: I chose really well."

Being the lead producer of a Broadway musical ... is not for the faint of heart."

TO: "Paul, Justin"
Cc: "Mindich, Stacey"

FROM: "Pasek, Benj"
DATE: Mon, Jan 31, 2011 at 8:34 AM
SUBJECT: Re: Congratulations

Stacey,

This really is a dream come true. We have been wanting to breathe life into this idea for the last 5 years, and feel honored to have an opportunity to get it off of the ground. We cannot thank you enough for your commitment to our work, and your follow-through in making this all happen.

Here's to our exciting new collaboration!

Benj

> On Sun, Jan 30, 2011 at 11:47 PM, Justin Paul wrote:
>
> STACEY!
>
> HELLO!!! :) :) :)
>
> So many words come to mind when I think of how I feel - honored, excited, challenged, encouraged! Certainly....grateful. Thank you for believing in us.
>
> So yes, here's to this new show!
>
> See you on Tuesday...and from the bottom of our hearts...thank you.
>
> Quite fondly,
>
> Justin
>
>> On Jan 28, 2011, at 5:20 PM,
>> Stacey Mindich wrote:
>>
>> Dear Benj and Justin,
>>
>> Wherever you are tonight, I hope you are smiling.
>>
>> Here's to a new Pasek and Paul musical - one that will be nurtured and treasured and carefully guided to, as they say, the "Big White Way."
>>
>> Looking forward to a celebratory lunch on Tuesday. (And then, I guess, we'll have to get to work!)
>>
>> Fondly,
>>
>> Stacey

A SELF-DESCRIBED "MUSICAL THEATER nerd," Mindich grew up on Long Island listening to her parents' original cast recordings and regularly accompanying them into the city to see Broadway shows. While performing in the chorus of a high school production of *Carousel*, she came to the conclusion that she had neither a singing voice nor a future on the stage. Luckily, she wanted to be a reporter. "From the time I could write," she says, "I had a family newspaper with a very small circulation, because I was an only child." After graduating from Syracuse University with a degree in journalism in 1986, she went on to a long and successful career as a writer and editor at *The New York Times* and *Town and Country*, among other publications. But, by 2006, after nearly twenty years in the business—now married to hedge fund manager Eric Mindich, with whom she was raising three young sons—she was ready for her next chapter. "I could think clearly again and not feel like I was tied to writing at home at midnight to be able to do all my other mom duties," she says. "I realized that the whole world had changed in those years, and everything had gone online. I didn't feel suited to it."

Happily, Mindich had never abandoned her first love. An obsessive fan of the *Falsettos* and *25th Annual Putnam County Spelling Bee* songwriter William Finn, Mindich put up the money to jumpstart a stalled production of his Off-Broadway revue *Make Me a Song* in 2007, and though it wasn't a success, she realized that she'd found her calling. "I understood very quickly that producing and magazine editing are incredibly similar," she says. "It's the same skill set. It's finding ideas that you're passionate about and putting together the people to make those ideas happen—taking care of them and making sure they have what they need to create great things—then slowly trying to get your own things in there when needed. I think dealing with artists is the most important thing a producer does. Being a mom, and having been an editor, the whole aspect of nurturing comes easily to me."

"I think dealing with artists is the most important thing a producer does."

We wanted to create a musical that explored why people are so interested in needing to be seen...to be heard...to be noticed."

IN ADDITION TO HER WORK ON *MAKE ME A Song*, Mindich, along with her husband, sat on the board of Lincoln Center Theater, where they established a fund to commission new musicals. One of them was Pasek and Paul's *Dogfight*. As a fledgling producer looking for fresh talent, she had come across a recording of a few of their songs and fallen in love. Mindich went on to order a CD of their work from their website, and despite never receiving it—something she still teases the writers about—knew she wanted to work with them. So, in September 2010, she arranged a lunch with the young songwriters, to which she arrived armed with ideas for possible musicals.

"The minute I sat down with them at the lunch table and my ideas started running through my head, I realized that they were a 40-something woman's idea of a good musical, not a pair of 24-year-olds'," she recalls. "So I switched gears in the middle of that lunch. I just knew I couldn't tell them my ideas. I knew I wanted to leave that lunch with a relationship with them. I wanted to call their agent and make a deal and have that be the first thing that I would originate as the lead producer. I wound up doing many things in the eight years since then, but I just knew that was what I really wanted to do."

So, she asked them a simple question: What's the musical you've been longing to write?

The answer was compelling, if not fully formed, drawing on an incident from Pasek's teenage years, when a fellow high school student had died of a drug overdose over summer break. Pasek recalls, "The next year, he became this sensationalized figure, and everyone, including many people who weren't close with him, mourned the death of their newfound friend who had died, and everyone remembered his life and attached themselves to his narrative and made themselves a part of his story—trying to claim his tragedy as part of their own. And I remember doing the same thing myself."

The experience had haunted Pasek. When he recounted it years later, in college, to his songwriting partner, Paul immediately recognized the phenomenon he was describing—Paul had seen a similar kind of emotional exhibitionism in the grief that had swept through his high school following 9/11.

"When I told Justin about it, we immediately realized that this was something a lot of people had experienced," Pasek says, and the two began discussing ways of dramatizing the phenomenon, which seemed to only have intensified with the advent of social media. "We wanted to create a musical that explored why people are so interested in needing to be seen and needing to be heard and needing to be noticed—and how that's only become amplified with the advent of social media, and this sort of public grieving."

Paul adds: "We were looking at it in a pretty cynical way—how people in our generation are so narcissistic—but I think that somewhere in our brains we knew we could approach this from a genuine point of view. Because, there's an emotional and human reason that, when a celebrity passes away, people feel they need to share their connection to that celebrity and how the death affected their lives. There must be a reason that everyone wants to share in this communal experience, and its root is probably in loneliness and isolation, and how that need has been magnified with the advent of social media."

Although the show was still very conceptual, they had a basic idea for a plot, involving a high school senior in the middle of applying to colleges who gloms on to a tragedy and writes about it, claiming a nonexistent connection to a dead boy to make his application stand out. The pitch left Mindich excited, if a little confused. "I actually wasn't sure what the idea really was," she recalls, though she gave one bit of feedback upon hearing the pitch that would prove crucial to the development of *Dear Evan Hansen*. "I said, if there's a boy, there has to be a mom. They agreed early on that there was a family to be formed."

In spite of her uncertainty about the details of the idea, Mindich had no reservations about committing to the two writers. "I wanted to work with young artists and—this is so lofty—be able to contribute to the musical theater canon by choosing well and having people write things that people would want to sing. That was my dream. I thought they could do it. I just knew it."

Paul, Mindich, ∧
and Pasek at Sardi's
Restaurant in 2016.

CHAPTER 3

MAKING THIS UP AS I GO

Steven Levenson finds his place on the writing team

THERE IS NO MEMBER OF a musical's creative team more misunderstood by the general public than the book writer. Maybe it has something to do with the confusing job title: Did they write the book on which the musical is based? And if not, what's a book?

It is, in fact, the script—the story and the dialogue without which there would just be a bunch of disconnected songs. And therein lies the second popular misunderstanding: Many people view the book almost as filler, the stuff characters say while we in the audience are waiting for the next musical number to begin. Nothing, of course, could be further from the truth. The book

The book is the ground from which all else in a musical grows."

is the ground from which all else in a musical grows, giving the songs context, meaning, and emotional weight. And a book writer must be a combination of playwright-with-a-vision and self-effacing collaborator, willing to turn over his or her most stirring scenes and poetic speeches to the composer and lyricist, who will transform them into the show tunes that the audience will hopefully leave the theater humming.

Though he had never written a musical before, Steven Levenson turned out to be all that and more, winning a Tony for his book for *Dear Evan Hansen* and

> ## " I think that our naiveté and lack of experience were what led us to believe that we could do this."

the eternal gratitude of his collaborators. Looking back, he says, "I think that our naiveté and lack of experience were what led us to believe that we could do this, to be honest. Doing a contemporary musical on this subject matter—if it were to come to me today, I don't know if I would have the courage to say yes, knowing how difficult it was going to be."

Growing up in Bethesda, Maryland, Levenson had no ambition to become a playwright. But his parents were theater lovers and, from a young age, he started going with them to see plays and musicals at such Washington, D.C., venues as Arena Stage and the Kennedy Center. After playing the Ed Sullivan role in a sixth-grade production of *Bye Bye Birdie*, he caught the performing bug. He went on to perform in productions of *Pippin*, *Into the Woods*, *Hair* (minus the nude scene), and, for a change of pace, *The Crucible*.

If one looked to Levenson's childhood for the seeds that would bloom into *Dear Evan Hansen* (and his other work for the stage), one could point to the in situ grasp of family dynamics that he acquired growing up in a high-drama household filled with passionate, articulate people, where family fights could escalate into something out of Clifford Odets or Eugene O'Neill, only to be quickly forgotten. One could also point to the insecurities of a brainy adolescent, a self-described "nice Jewish boy" at an Episcopal school, which would later be writ large in the character of Evan.

"I had more than my share of anxieties, for sure, though I certainly was not where Evan is—I wasn't incapable of talking to people," he recalls. "But I don't know if my self-perception was all that different. I think I may have imagined that that's what I sounded like when I talked to people. It could feel as difficult to talk to people as it is for Evan. For Evan, a lot of what is on our minds at that age, the stuff we keep hidden, just comes out—he's incapable of holding it back. I knew kids who were that cripplingly self-conscious, and it's really hard to just constantly be battling yourself, to constantly think other people are judging you." However, Levenson is quick to point out, such anxiety is no longer relegated strictly to adolescence in an age of social media ubiquity. "The way he feels is not dissimilar to how we all feel when we

I like it I like it I like the your brain is bubbling...I want you to keep bubbling...you are the bubble boy you are like a cool spritzer to me right now

On Nov 3, 2011, at 1:47PM, Steven Lev... wrote:

I was thinking that Evan maybe has an almost crippling case of social anxiety. He freezes up around groups of people, is unable to speak in class, that sort of thing, which is why he's picked on by the bully. He never knows the right thing to say. It's not Asperger's at all, it's sort of the opposite even; he feels a tremendous amount and wants to be close to people, he's just awkward and uncomfortable in his own skin. Like Jesse Eisenberg in Adventureland rather than in Social Network. But he can, at the same time, have this really active imagination and inner life, and maybe there's a way—without being on the nose—of incorporating technology into that, so he's really into online stuff, disappearing online into other identities, etc. When he begins making up stuff, this same imaginative sense comes into play, and it's like by making up a fake person, he's able to get out of his own shell and connect.

The social anxiety makes his eventual shift, into student leader and spokesperson, all the more radical and important.

—Steven Levenson

∨ (below) Paul, Levenson, and Pasek
around the piano before the
Arena Stage production in 2015.

"

My acting bug turned out to be good for something."

open our Instagram feeds or our Facebook page: You're both desperate for people to see you and 'like' you and follow you, and then at the same time terrified that they actually will, and that you'll reveal something of yourself that you didn't mean to. Everyone's lives look so much better than our own, and even though I know it's curated and a facade, part of me is, like, 'Yeah, but their lives really *are* much better than mine.'"

LEAN AND MOPPISH, WITH A BOYISH grin—think a young, slightly nerdier Hugh Grant—Levenson continued to harbor ambitions of becoming an actor as a student at Brown University. But something shifted during an apprenticeship at the Williamstown Theatre Festival the summer after his sophomore year. "I hated it," he says. "I hated being there, and I knew that I wasn't an actor after that summer. I really knew." A tiny, non-Equity production of Sarah Ruhl's haunting play *Eurydice* showed him the way forward. "I felt like my mind had exploded," he recalls. "I just didn't know that theater

could do that. I guess I didn't know that there were contemporary plays being written—I thought David Mamet and Sam Shepard were the last people still writing plays, and so that really opened the world up for me. I loved Sarah Ruhl's lyricism, and her poetry, and the pathos. And it was a really formative moment in my life, seeing that play. It was just, like, I want to do *that*."

In his senior year at Brown, Levenson applied for and was accepted into a class called "Playwriting and Plasticity," taught by Paula Vogel, the Pulitzer Prize–winning writer of *How I Learned to Drive* and *Indecent*. (As a writing sample, he submitted the first several scenes of a play that he'd just started, which would later become the well-received *The Language of Trees*.) It was, Levenson says, "the most important thing that happened to me, maybe, ever." Just as important as the knowledge of craft that he learned from Vogel was the encouragement she gave him. "At the end of the semester, she would take everybody out for coffee and review their work," he recalls. "I was just about to graduate, and she was, like, 'What are your plans? What are you doing?' And I was, like, 'I don't know. I think I'm going to go to New York and temp.' And she told me, 'You've got to get a job in a theater.' The thing she said that stuck with me was, 'If you want to do this, I think you can.' That kept me going for years."

Out of school and living in New York, Levenson followed Vogel's advice and landed an internship in the literary department of the Off-Broadway theater Playwrights Horizons, which eventually morphed into a paying, full-time gig when the head of the department left for another job. "They just needed *somebody* to be there," says Levenson, whose duties, which included reviewing submissions and attending readings at theaters around the city, amounted to a second education. "So for six months, it was me and this other young woman named Carly Mensch, who's also a playwright—

(below) **Levenson signs copies of** ∨
the libretto for fans at the Drama
Book Shop in New York City.

we were the entire literary department. I was 22, she was 23. And Tim Sanford, the artistic director, used to walk by as if he wanted to ask somebody their opinion on something, see us, and keep walking."

Levenson got his break as a playwright almost by accident. In 2007, still semi-clinging to the last vestiges of his acting aspirations, he auditioned for the Roundabout Theatre Company's production of fellow Brown alumnus Stephen Karam's dark comedy *Speech and Debate*. Levenson had originated the role of Solomon in the play's world premiere at the Brown/Trinity Playwrights Repertory Theatre the summer after his senior year. This time around, he didn't get cast, but the theater's artistic consultant, Robyn Goodman, agreed to read one of Levenson's own plays ("out of pity, basically," he says)—a fully fleshed-out draft of the work that had won him a spot in Vogel's class.

The Language of Trees, a wrenching look at the emotional fallout of the Iraq War on a family left behind on the home front, opened at the Roundabout Underground in October 2008, establishing Levenson as a gifted young playwright to watch. ("So, in the end, my acting bug turned out to be good for something," he says with a laugh.) That play, like so many of his others, including *The Unavoidable Disappearance of Tom Durnin*, *If I Forget*, and, of course, *Dear Evan Hansen*, shows a keen insight into the fraying connections and ties that bind families in crisis. "That was something I don't think I knew at the time, but I subsequently realized has a lot to do with my feeling about this project," Levenson says. "I do really love family stories, and complicated families, and parents and children, and what we owe one another, in both directions—what parents owe their children, what children owe their parents. It's endlessly fascinating."

Levenson has also always been drawn to coming-of-age stories, as evidenced by his bittersweet 2010 comedy *Seven Minutes in Heaven*, about a group of teenagers at a party on a Friday night in 1995. Stories

∧ (above) **Mindich and Levenson out-side the Music Box Theatre before opening night on Broadway.**

about young people struggling through adolescence, Levenson says, "have these incredibly high stakes, because never in your life are the stakes higher than when you're that age. And at the same time, we in the audience know that everything's going to be okay. So it allows this irony where the characters can have those operatic emotions, but it never risks becoming melodramatic or overwrought, because there's always this knowledge we have that it's not that big a deal."

As Levenson devoted himself to writing plays, he continued to harbor a secret, long-simmering ambition: to write a musical. From the beginning, Benj Pasek and Justin Paul saw the show that would eventually become *Dear Evan Hansen* as "a play with songs," and they wanted to team up with a playwright to write the book rather than someone steeped in the musical theater tradition. Given Levenson's affinity for the themes that they wanted to explore, it's not a surprise that, when Mindich sent them the work of several young dramatists, among them Levenson, they recognized a kindred spirit.

"The first playwright we're interested in is Steven Levenson," they wrote Mindich in a February 2011 email. "We've just read three of his plays, and we think his tone and approach are REALLY right for what we're going for."

"

I do really love family stories, and complicated families, and parents and children, and what we owe one another."

CHAPTER 4

ANYBODY HAVE A MAP?

Or, how do you create a new musical from scratch?

WHEN HE TALKS ABOUT the early years of *Dear Evan Hansen*'s long and winding road to Broadway, Benj Pasek likes to invoke a quote from Ira Glass, the host of *This American Life.*

"Nobody tells this to people who are beginners, I wish someone told me. All of us who do creative work, we get into it because we have good taste. But there is this gap. For the first couple years you make stuff, it's just not that good. It's trying to be good, it has potential, but it's not. But your taste, the thing that got you into the game, is still killer.... You've just gotta fight your way through until you close that gap."

It not only captures a truth about fledgling artists finding their voice but also perfectly describes the trial-and-error journey of the show's young authors—the inspired ideas, the false starts, the dead ends, the lofty aims that fell short—as they struggled to turn a concept into an original musical that could speak to, and in the voice of, their generation.

That journey began on March 17, 2011, over lunch at Orso, a theater district hangout. Stacey Mindich had invited Steven Levenson to join them to see if the chemistry was right. They were already fans of one another's work: Pasek and Paul had read several of Levenson's plays and found in them, as Paul says, "a voice that we felt worked with ours, and one that was going to beautifully tell this story."

Levenson had listened to a CD of Pasek and Paul's songs, and, he says, "I loved that the music felt really contemporary pop–sounding, but it still was in a theatrical language, and the songs told stories." Pasek and Paul went on to tell Levenson about their concept for a show about a high school kid who fakes a connection to a dead classmate to make himself sound more interesting in his college application essay. As they recall their discussion that day:

PAUL: Basically, we had an inspiring event. And we had a bunch of themes that we wanted to write about. We didn't really have a story at that point, but we had planned for the show, in a way, to be an indictment of our generation and society.

PASEK: It was the opposite of Spring Awakening, *in the sense that* Spring Awakening *is all about how these kids are so oppressed and society is cruel to them. And our theory was society has been incredibly permissive. So, what happens when young people have unlimited power and freedom in the digital age.*

PAUL: And there was a book that we were very inspired by at the time called Generation Me. *We basically wanted to write a musical centered around that book's themes: how we're the most privileged and doted-upon generation in decades. So it was meant to be a cynical look at how the internet feeds that narcissistic beast in each of us.*

LEVENSON: And you guys told me the story and these themes and ideas, and I was super interested. The immediate question that you had was, "Is this even a musical?" And I knew nothing, but I was, like, "It's definitely a musical." Now, in hindsight, I just really wanted to do it. I had no idea.

Still, Levenson hadn't told Pasek and Paul precisely what his take on the material was, and they sent him off to come up with an outline of how he envisioned the story. Over the next several weeks, they got together to bat around ideas—but Levenson was essentially on his own. "I knew that it would be a difficult story to figure out, and I was excited about that," he says. "I like complicated characters that do morally questionable things. And it was exciting to challenge myself to figure out: How could you make a person like that understandable and likable?"

O N MAY 5, 2011, LEVENSON SUBMITTED a treatment that encompassed all that he and Pasek and Paul had talked about—a scathing satire of the Facebook generation. As a framing device, the entire story would be told as if it were actually a high school kid's college application essay, responding, as Levenson writes, "to the dreaded: 'Evaluate a significant experience, achievement, risk you have taken, or ethical dilemma you have faced and its impact on you.'" But Levenson also gave it something else: a poetic yearning and a generosity of spirit that, over time, would increasingly become the heart of the show. He wrote:

This is the story of people in pieces, of a community split apart, of a world in which we find ourselves as close to one another as the click of a button, and as remote as distant galaxies.... This is the story of a young man's noble, selfish, flawed, courageous, and utterly unforgivable actions to put all the broken pieces back together again, and it's a story about the unintended consequences of following your heart.

In more practical terms, as Levenson laid out in his proposal, it's the story of a shy, awkward high school junior—a C-plus student without a single extracurricular activity on his résumé and whose only friends are other outsiders. When a popular senior at his private high school dies suddenly at track practice, the protagonist stands up at a memorial service and pretends to have been his secret best friend. He goes on to fabricate journal entries by the dead boy, each an encomium to honesty, and in the process, achieves hero status at school and, eventually, becomes an internet celebrity. Along the way, he dates the dead boy's girlfriend, blackmails the school principal into giving him a scholarship, and publicly denounces the dead boy's mother when she threatens to expose his lie. In the end, the truth comes out and, now a senior at a public school, he emerges a humbler, more thoughtful person.

Levenson's synopsis certainly contained some of the seeds of what would become *Dear Evan Hansen*, even if its central character was not entirely sympathetic, and he and his new collaborators got right down to work.

"We had planned for the show to be an indictment of our generation and society."

But within two weeks, Levenson got called to Los Angeles to be a staff writer on a new NBC series called *The Playboy Club*. Levenson spent that summer taking the red eye to New York most Friday nights, hashing out ideas all day Saturday with Pasek and Paul, spending the night with his girlfriend, Whitney May, and heading back to the West Coast on Sunday. Pasek and Paul sometimes flew to L.A. for work sessions as well, and there was always email and Skype, but overall it was a fractured process.

I N JULY 2011, PASEK AND PAUL MET UP WITH Levenson for an intensive weekend of brainstorming at the Banff Centre in Canada, a continuing education institution that offers residencies and programs for artists of all disciplines. At this point, they only had Levenson's treatment, a few notes, and a jointly conceived name for their protagonist: Evan Hansen. "It felt right to me, because it seemed at once to be so perfectly, grimly ordinary, the very embodiment of ordinariness—for a character who feels himself to be invisible," Levenson says. "And yet it has a kind of furtive musicality to it. It reminds me of one of those classic superhero alter egos, like Clark Kent or Peter Parker. The name is meant to evoke 'Everyman,' but the very simplicity of it makes it feel almost mythical."

On their last night in Banff, as they were walking through the woods after an evening on the town, Levenson told his partners that he had bought an engagement ring earlier that week and was planning on proposing to his girlfriend. ("They were the first people I told," Levenson recalls, "these rando guys I was working on a musical with.") He also told them that they had come to a creative crossroads and had to choose definitively what kind of musical they wanted to write. "I remember saying that there were two versions of this musical," Levenson says. "One, we knew what it would be, which was sort of *Heathers*, or *Election*. And then there was something else, something more mysterious and more interesting. It had to do with not mocking the urge to personalize tragedy, but trying to figure out the human impulse beneath it and how it speaks to our need for belonging

BANFF NOTES

1. **EVAN, 17.** Desperate to be seen, noticed, to prove he's not a loser to his dad and to everyone else. Has never had a girlfriend, never spoken really to a girl. Not good at much. Afraid of life. He works at a coffee shop (or restaurant) after school to make money. He's always been in love with Becca.

2. **EVAN'S BEST FRIEND, 17.** Fellow loser. Funny. Bossy. Jonah Hill to Michael Cera.

3. **BECCA, 16.** Love interest. Junior. Younger sister of deceased. Great student, great person, destroyed by the news of her brother's death and even more destroyed by the insipid response to it by people who barely knew him. She comes to think Evan is the only one who understands her, and who truly shares her pain.

4. **EVAN'S DAD.** Checked out. Has a new young family. He's been hit hard by the recession and no longer has the money to bankroll Evan's college education.

5. **EVAN'S MOM.** Working hard to make ends meet, but a bit of a wreck. Too frazzled to notice Evan.

6. **AMERICAN HISTORY TEACHER.** The voice of reason. New to school, new to Portland. Recent college grad maybe? Believes in hard work and discipline, not interested in telling students how special they are. Unimpressed by Evan.

7. **ENGLISH TEACHER.** Terrible. Crunchy.

8. **BECCA'S MOM.**

9. **BECCA'S DAD.**

10. **BECCA'S CURRENT BOYFRIEND.**

11. **BECCA'S BEST FRIEND.**

12. **PLUS THREE ENSEMBLE STUDENTS.**

Evan's dad and English teacher are doubled, so 13 actors—8 kids, 5 adults.

and community." They left the weekend in Banff with many lingering questions, but with the certainty that it was the latter course they planned to take—even if they remained unsure exactly where it might lead.

Over the next months, Levenson continued to brainstorm ideas with Pasek and Paul. In an email dated November 7, 2011, he suggested a notion that would come to define Evan's character and the show itself. "I was thinking that Evan maybe has an almost crippling case of social anxiety," he wrote. "He freezes up around groups of people, is unable to speak in class, that sort of thing. He never knows the right thing to say. It's not Asperger's at all, it's sort of the opposite even; he feels a tremendous amount and wants to be close to people, he's just awkward and uncomfortable in his own skin. Like Jesse Eisenberg in *Adventureland* rather than in *The Social Network*."

"Steven essentially took the lead from there," Pasek recalls, "and really sort of crafted the first impulse and gesture of what would be the story of *Dear Evan Hansen*." That gesture took the form of a first act draft without songs that Levenson turned out over the early part of the winter.

DATED JANUARY 13, 2012, AND TITLED *The Dennis Project* (the doomed school loner who would eventually be named Connor Murphy was, at this point, named Dennis Morse), it opens on Evan on the eve of his 18th birthday, delivering a soliloquy in which he describes his social anxiety, his summer as an apprentice park ranger, and his crush on Zoe Morse, Dennis's sister. He has an absent dad and an overworked mom who is prodding him to submit an essay, in the form of a letter to himself, to a scholarship contest to help pay for college. That morning, at school, Dennis ends up stealing Evan's essay, along with some of his Zoloft. Later, after Dennis overdoses, perhaps accidentally, on a lethal combination of Adderall and the stolen pills, the letter is mistaken for a suicide note addressed to Evan, whom Dennis's parents assume was a close friend of their son. The act also includes his friend Jared warning him that his letter is going to go viral and ruin his life; his fellow students—led by the lonely Alana—remembering Dennis with more emotion than they felt for him while he was alive; and Dennis's parents finding solace in the fictitious, rosy picture Evan paints of his friendship with their son.

But it's the scholarship essay as a letter that will turn out to be Levenson's key plot and character breakthrough: having Evan stumble into a misunderstanding that snowballs out of control, rather than deliberately setting out to lie, and making the letter itself a mournful, self-deprecating cry of the heart went a long way toward making him a relatable, even sympathetic, figure.

As soon as Pasek and Paul read Levenson's draft, they knew that he had found the framework and voice for their musical. "We had written a couple of songs for

Stacey that were just out of nowhere, and the language was so different than what it ended up being," Pasek recalls. "Because when we read Steven's language, we were, like, *that's* the language that we want for this show."

WITH LEVENSON STILL COMMUTING from L.A. and Pasek and Paul's attention being pulled by both *Dogfight* and *A Christmas Story: The Musical*, the writing was not always smooth and swift. By May 2012, though, they had a finished draft of a first act and an outline for a second, with the working title *The Connor Project*. The first act had nine songs, some of them partially written, including an "I Want" song for Evan called "Total Reinvention" and a comic number for Jared called "Goin' Viral." Pasek and Paul had also written a gorgeously plaintive duet for Connor and Evan's mothers, "In the Bedroom Down the Hall," that reflected the impulse to make the show as much about parents as children.

In the bedroom down the hall
You had that Ninja Turtle night light for protection
You used to say it kept the bad guys far away
Remember?

In the bedroom down the hall
You had that super hero comic book collection
Each Halloween we dressed you up like Wolverine
Remember?

The soccer cleats and race car sheets
That you picked out yourself
Those dominoes and GI Joes unopened on your shelf

Anything to make you happy
Anything at all
Anything for my boy
In the bedroom down the hall

Though none of the songs in this draft would make it into the final version, many of them contained the essence of what was to come, overflowing with Pasek and Paul's trademark soaring melodies and heartfelt poetry. For the most part, the songs and the book seemed to be speaking with the same voice—though, Pasek says, "we still hadn't quite caught up to Steven." Sure, it was too long, and in spots it still seemed to be clinging to its cynical roots, but the major characters, plot points, and themes—the basic architecture—were in place. And the show now had a protagonist with a clear, specific, and universal desire—to connect with other people—and a powerful obstacle in his way, namely his own crippling anxiety.

As soon as Mindich read the script she knew that it was in good enough shape to show to a director, and she had one in mind. "We didn't go to Michael Greif until I felt we had something that was worthy of Michael Greif," she says. "It was too scary to think of losing that opportunity."

ORIGINAL
"DEAR EVAN HANSEN" LETTER:

Dear Evan Hansen,

Nobody else understands me. What's worse is, nobody else wants to try. You're the best friend I have.

Or, let's face it: the only friend I have. It's just you and me here, so let's be honest with ourselves. Because why not, right?

Mom didn't want me. Dad didn't want to stay. Mom got stuck with me. Mom had to deal with me. Dad got to start over. Why didn't we get to start over? Nobody let us start over. Why does nobody ever let you start over? Why can't I start over? I want to start over so badly, I want to be somebody new, but I look in the mirror and, big surprise, it's still the same old me.

Everybody else has a family. I just have parents. Everybody else has a home. I just have a house. A lonely little house, with a tiny little bed, and the carpets have smelled weird since the day we moved in. Everybody else has dreams. I just have setbacks. Everybody else has a network. I just have Facebook. Everybody else has connection. I just have collisions.

And then there's Zoe. Like, all my hope is pinned on Zoe. Like, everything I am is invested in Zoe. Like, my entire existence is wrapped up in Zoe. Like, everything would be ok if only there were Zoe. Who I don't even know and who doesn't know me. But I feel like if I knew her, I could love her. And I feel like if she knew me...

Who am I kidding? Let's be honest with ourselves. Let's just try to be honest with ourselves.

Never going to happen. Zoe doesn't care. Does anybody even care? If I disappear tomorrow, nobody's going to care.

They don't even know my name.

I'm giving up. I'm giving in. I'm not fighting it anymore. Nothing changes. It doesn't get better. It doesn't get easier. You don't get any wiser. You just get older. Your skin gets thinner. Your nerve gets weaker. Your feelings get hurt enough times that you'd rather not feel anymore. You give up. I give up.

I give up. Once and for all, I give up.

Sincerely, Me

CHAPTER 5

YOU ARE NOT ALONE

Michael Greif takes the helm

F A MUSICAL CAN BE SAID TO HAVE A spiritual ancestor, *Dear Evan Hansen*'s would have to be *Rent*, the Pulitzer- and Tony-winning 1996 contemporary retelling of Puccini's *La Bohème* by Jonathan Larson, who died unexpectedly at the age of 35 the night before the musical's first Off-Broadway preview. Like *Dear Evan Hansen*, *Rent* told the story of troubled young people in search of belonging and tackled subjects not usually associated with the musical stage—homelessness, drug addiction, AIDS. And the score featured songs that sounded like what East Village bohemians might be listening to on their headphones, while remaining rooted in traditional musical theater storytelling. After transferring to Broadway, the show went on to run for twelve years, generating productions around the world, spawning the anthem "Seasons of Love," opening up musical

"He has assumed the mantle of the grown-up in the room."

theater to a new generation, and attracting an army of obsessive fans who dubbed themselves "*Rent*-Heads."

Another Pulitzer- and Tony-winning musical, Brian Yorkey and Tom Kitt's 2009 *Next to Normal*, would have to be considered a forebear of *Dear Evan Hansen* as well, with its jagged rock score and its story of manic depression, suicide, and a broken suburban family in search of healing and grace. Like *Rent* before it, *Next to Normal* challenged conventional notions of what a Broadway musical can be, the kinds of stories it can tell, and the complexity of the characters who populate it.

(top right) **The cast of *Rent* at the New** >
York Theatre Workshop in March 1996.
(right) **The marquee for *A Chorus Line***
at the Shubert Theatre in 1980.

"By some miracle, he found his way to directing school musicals, which he also co-wrote."

Aside from the obvious musical and thematic connections, *Rent* and *Next to Normal* share one other thing in common: They were both directed by Michael Greif, who brought the same sharp dramaturgical eye, affinity for wounded outsiders, and largeness of heart to *Dear Evan Hansen*, completing what he sees in retrospect as a kind of trilogy. Greif was not much older than *Dear Evan Hansen*'s young creators when he started working on *Rent* almost twenty-five years ago. Now he has assumed the mantle of the grown-up in the room. It's a role that he happily took on in the first year or so of working with Benj Pasek, Justin Paul, and Steven Levenson as they were finding their way with *Dear Evan Hansen*—and one that he was just as happy to step back from as he watched them gain confidence and take ownership of the material. "The writing is just incredible," Greif says. "You know that these young gentlemen have a lot of wisdom, and they've dug very deep into their own insecurities to create these vivid characters."

HE KNOWS WHAT HE'S TALKING ABOUT: Greif was born in Brighton Beach, Brooklyn, in 1959, to an insurance auditor mother and optician father, and he remembers himself as "a fairly typical, lonely, isolated gay boy—I was a fat kid, too—in a nasty, sports-crazy, anti-intellectual, working-class environment." For years, he spent his weekend nights alone in his room in front of the TV with a bag of candy, and he took pleasure in watching old musicals on *The 4:30 Movie* after school, particularly the Gene Kelly and Judy Garland vehicle *Summer Stock*. His smart and spirited older sister was a kind of Auntie Mame figure in his eyes. She let him hang around with her and her friends, a group of sharp, funny gay guys, and introduced him to politics and the arts, showing him that there might be a life different from the one he knew.

Greif got his first real glimmer of that life as a high school student in the early '70s, when, by some miracle, he found his way to directing school musicals, which he also co-wrote. Knowing his audience, Greif never failed to put in several production numbers featuring a large chorus of girls in leotards. "That was always the most popular part," he says.

One day when he was 16, he came across a double-page ad in *The New York Times* for Michael Bennett's groundbreaking musical *A Chorus Line*, which was about to move to Broadway. He had no idea what the show was about, but at that moment, he recalls, "it was like music played—I needed to see this musical." Greif insisted that his parents buy tickets for the entire family. Mesmerized by the production, he remembers glancing over at his parents during the actor Sammy Williams's monologue about growing up in a tough neighborhood as an effeminate boy obsessed with old movies and thinking: *What did I get myself into?*

He returned to *A Chorus Line* again and again, ultimately seeing the show close to a hundred times over the next several years, until it became part of his theatrical DNA. "It was about honoring the person in the back and not the star, and that really rocked my world—and continues to—in terms of an interest in people with esteem problems," he says. "Also, its structure and its craft is so perfect. Talk about essential—in an almost empty room, to be able to create that kind of theatrical magic with lights and a few scenic effects was just my idea of how you should do a play or a musical."

In high school, he interned at the Manhattan Theatre Club and began going to shows every night. "It was my education, that six months," he says. Greif continued his formal education as a theater and performance studies major at Northwestern University, where he confirmed that he preferred directing to acting. He went on to study the craft under Arthur Wagner and Alan Schneider

as a graduate student at the University of California, San Diego, and this led to a stint as an assistant to Des McAnuff, the artistic director of the La Jolla Playhouse (years later, Greif himself would take over the job, running the theater from 1994 until 1999). During his time assisting McAnuff, Greif met artists like Robert Woodruff, Peter Sellers, and Michael Weller. In one memorable exchange with Weller, Greif remembers asking the playwright for advice on how to become a theater professional. When Weller told him, "You just have to do your own work. You have to pay for your own work," Greif recalls, "I thought that was unfair and unjust. It shouldn't work that way—someone should give me an opportunity."

As it turned out, Greif ended up doing exactly as Weller suggested. A few years after his move back to New York, in 1989, he created his own opportunity by raising the money to produce and direct a production of Sophie Treadwell's rarely seen 1920s expressionist tragedy *Machinal* at the Naked Angels Theater. Kevin Kline came to see it, as did the Public Theater's impresario Joseph Papp, who invited Greif to direct three plays at the Public starting with *Machinal*. The production opened on October 16, 1990, and in his rave review for *The New York Times*, Frank Rich wrote that, "in the hands of a young director named Michael Greif, making a sensational debut," a lost masterpiece "has been miraculously reborn." At the age of 29, Greif had arrived.

Among the many admirers of this production of *Machinal* was the young songwriter Jonathan Larson, who, along with New York Theater Workshop's artistic director Jim Nicola, brought his half-finished musical *Rent* to Greif and asked him to take the reins. While the director had no idea he would be signing on to a life-changing project, he did know that he related to the material, which summoned the still-fresh memory of seeing so many of his friends and peers die from AIDS in the 1980s. Greif gets emotional when he talks about those years, and he believes that *Rent* managed to tap

into similar feelings on a wider scale—feelings that were only compounded for Greif and the team by the author's sudden death. "It was a very accessible look at the crisis we were all living through in a most humane, simple, and accessible way," he says. "Appealing, attractive, troubled young people who questioned their worth and validity were facing their own mortality."

GREIF CLEARLY FEELS AN ARTISTIC kinship with outsiders and families in crisis, so it's no surprise that he was Stacey Mindich's first choice to direct Pasek, Paul, and Levenson's still nascent musical. In June 2012, she invited him to come up to her office and take a look at what they had. Sitting around a conference table, Mindich, her assistant, her production company's general manager, and Pasek and Paul all took parts and read the show for him (Levenson was on his honeymoon), with Paul at the piano.

Greif immediately knew that this was something that he wanted to be a part of. He also had two instincts about the show, both of which would prove crucial to shaping what it became. First, he knew that the internet needed to be presented in an innovative and visual way—he envisioned screens and projections—and he believed that a traditional onstage ensemble of singers and dancers could be replaced with a chorus of virtual voices. Second, as a father (he has a 22-year-old son and an 18-year-old daughter with a lesbian couple), Greif responded particularly strongly to the complex dynamics between parents and children presented in the musical, and he believed that the writers needed to focus the story even more sharply on the two families at its heart.

Not long after, Greif joined all three writers in Los Angeles for ten days, during which time they went through the entire script and scrutinized every scene, song, plot point, and line of dialogue, determining what was missing and what they could lose. They discussed the best use of "real estate"—which moments needed to be given time and which could be handled swiftly—and pacing. "It had three openings, and it took way too long to get to the heart of the material, which was the lie Evan tells the Murphys, 'I knew your son, we were friends,'" Greif recalls. They also worked together to identify the highest stakes in each scene. One of the

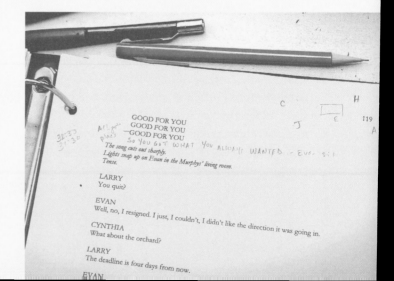

(below) Greif talks with Ben ∨
Platt at a tech rehearsal
at Second Stage.

Ben Platt. "What I think is the most important thing for this whole piece is that we all felt emotionally like we could go for it without reserving anything. I think, without him, that wouldn't have been possible."

To the amusement, and sometimes chagrin, of the actors, once performances started, Greif gave them notes that were, literally, notes—dozens and dozens of white slips of paper with handwritten comments, sometimes suggestions, sometimes compliments, which he would then discuss with them after they'd digested the feedback. (It's a practice Greif has cultivated over the years. Ask anyone in this cast or that of any of the shows he's directed, and they will produce a stack of Greif's white slips that they've saved.)

Rachel Bay Jones remembers one particular note that she received repeatedly, asking her to take a pause out of a speech that she felt belonged there. "I would argue with him and he would say, 'Okay,' and then the next day he would hand me another slip of white paper asking me to take the pause out, and I would say, 'No, and here's why,' and he'd say, 'All right.' And then the next day he'd come in with the piece of paper and he would say,

"He gave us permission to follow our impulses, and that allowed us to go to dark places."

moments that Greif homed in on was what he called "The Orchard Song"—a yet-to-be-written number that at this point existed in the script only as an I.O.U.

This will become a song in which Evan attempts to tell the story below about Connor.

Whenever Evan hesitates, Cynthia and Larry fill in the gaps, finishing his sentences, and thus inadvertently aiding the lie.

As the song goes on, Evan sheds his nervousness and acquires the confidence and ease of a master storyteller—or a skilled liar.

On balance, he turns in a tour de force performance.

"I was, like, 'You guys, this is going to be the incredible turning point of the musical,'" Greif recalls telling them. And though the writers would tease him about his unshakeable belief in—and constant reference to—"the glorious orchard song," he was validated when, months later, they wrote the soaring "For Forever," which is no less lovely and heartbreaking for being a lie, as Evan becomes caught up in the fantasy of his friendship with Connor.

The writers came away from the retreat with their marching orders, along with a detailed, scene-by-scene outline and a list of new songs to be written—a blueprint for what would become *Dear Evan Hansen*. "He gave us permission to follow our impulses, and that allowed us to go to dark places," Levenson says. "There were so many times when we said to him, 'We have two options. We want to do this, but we think the rules say this.' And he would always say to do the first thing."

Years later, when the show was starting to get on its feet, Greif took on a similar role with the actors. "What makes him superhuman is his ability to create an environment where you feel like you can go out on these emotional limbs, and you have a full net and are completely safe, and that you can leap off those cliffs," says

'Perhaps today is the day that you can see your way through to doing what I need you to do.'" One night, when the show was in previews Off Broadway, she decided to take Greif's suggestion and see what happened. "I came to a completely new level of respect for the man when I realized that, once that little thing was gone, everything that came after it, that tumbled into place afterward, was so massive and important—it changed everything," she says. "The great directors have that. They can see all of it. He's got a vision and a plan, and he's not sharing it with me, but if I do what he says, most of the time he's right." Jones pauses for a moment, as if lost in thought, and then laughs. "He's right."

"WAVING THROUGH A WINDOW"

NO SONG HAS BECOME MORE SYNONYMOUS with *Dear Evan Hansen* than its now-iconic anthem "Waving Through a Window." The first song that Evan sings, "Waving" instantly makes clear who he is and what he longs for in spare, poetic language, while firmly establishing the contemporary musical vernacular of the show. It's hard to imagine the show without it, and yet the writers took years to discover the best version of it. Their first stab was called "Total Reinvention," a more conventional "I Want" number. "It was so 'musical theater.' Like, 'I need to do this with my life' stated in the most obvious way,'" Pasek says.

The songwriters had just come off penning *Dogfight* and *A Christmas Story*, both of which Pasek describes as having more traditional musical theater structures. Once Levenson joined the team and began creating a language for the musical, the songwriters knew that they wanted to match his style and tone, and compose a score that did not hew to the standard musical theater formula, in which every major scene culminates with a song. "A lot of our struggle in writing the show was Justin and Benj really being stubborn about not writing musical theater songs, where the book could do that work instead—like not forcing things to be a song," Levenson says.

The songs also had to match the naturalism of the book. Paul says that the litmus test for whether something could be a song was reading the dialogue and making sure there was no "little jerk" into song. "When Evan started singing, it needed to feel like the same Evan that was carrying on the scene," he says. Compounding the challenge they had set themselves, the songwriters sought to employ a more pop-inspired approach to the lyrics and music. "It was finding the pop influence for each song, while remaining theatrical," Paul says. "That then could be paired with contemporary-feeling language, which sometimes takes on a quasi-heightened poetic nature, that tells a story."

This goal was a tall order, considering Top 40–sounding hits aren't exactly known for their narrative-driven emotion, and it took a while for Pasek and Paul to find the right balance of pop and pathos. Their second attempt at an "I Want" song for their main character was called "Infinite Island." In the lyrics, Pasek and Paul tried to add subtext, but ultimately, the main image of the song—the idea of being stranded on an island—didn't work with the story. "What works about 'Waving' is it uses a metaphor that also makes sense with the literal nature of the internet and glass and screens," Pasek says. Composing this tune was also the first time they realized that they could use a more repetitive refrain. "If the book, direction, choreography, etc., could take on some of the responsibility that the lyrics usually carry in pushing the story forward, we had permission to play with the words to try to have a more repetitive chorus, like what you hear in pop songs," adds Pasek. "We wanted the lyrics and melody to get stuck in your head."

However, the writers didn't initially know what they had when they wrote the refrain for "Waving Through a Window," which was at one point called "Waving Back at Me." Two hours before a meeting with Mindich and Greif, during which they were supposed to present a new version of the song, Pasek and Paul still didn't have a chorus. They were terrified, and they tried to hammer it out quickly before the meeting. When they presented what they had written over the course of two hours to the producer and the director, they were shocked by the positive reaction. Ultimately, though, the composers came to see the number as a road map of sorts for the rest of the musical. "That was the first song of the new, the real version of this show," Paul says. "It was, like, 'This is what the show will sound like, and this is the vernacular of the score.'"

This is what the show will sound like, and this is the vernacular of the score."

"TOTAL REINVENTION"
(MAY, 2012 DRAFT)

Evan continues down the hallway, painfully aware of the eyes focused on his UGGs.

EVAN

Refuel / Maybe lose the shoes / Is she smiling— / Shit, she's looking at my feet

Stay cool / And they won't confuse / Who they thought they knew / With who they're about to meet

No more kid who threw up in choir / Who once lit his own pants on fire / It's "goodbye" to that guy / 'Cause i'm ready for my

Total reinvention / A wholesale sort of change / Today they pay attention / Try to believe what you see / You'll forget what came before / This reinvention of me

Da da da da da da / Da da da da da / Da da da da da da / Da da da da da

"INFINITE ISLAND"
(JULY, 2013 DRAFT)

EVAN

I've learned to slam on the brake / Before I even turn the key / Before I make the mistake / Before I lead with the worst of me

Give them no reason to stare / No slipping up if you slip away / So I got nothing to share

Step back step back from the stove / When you keep gettin' burned / Step back step back from the stove / Because you've learned, because you've learned

And oh standing on the edge of an infinite island / Oh shouting at the wind I wave my hands / And oh hanging off the edge of an infinite island / Oh watching ev'ry word fall to the sands / But maybe across the sea / Someone on their infinite island is waving back at me

Lights shift and Zoe enters.

CHAPTER 6

YOU WILL BE FOUND:

BEN PLATT

on becoming Evan Hansen

T HAS BECOME COMMONPLACE, WHEN an actor fits seamlessly with a character, to say he was born to play the role. But when the actor is Ben Platt and the role is Evan Hansen, no other phrase will do. Platt's performance as the conflicted high school senior is a fearless, almost unbearably honest portrait of anxiety, loneliness, despair, and hunger for connection.

It's a performance that has made him a star, along the way earning him critical praise, fan adoration, and, of course, a Tony Award. "Ben has played Evan since the very first reading of the show, and at this point he literally embodies the character," says Justin Paul. "Talk about someone who takes a character that makes complicated decisions and does potentially questionable things but makes you understand why he does what he does. There is no one who pulls that off better or who brings such complicated humanity and sympathy to a character. And to do it at such a young age? He is gifted beyond gifted."

It is precisely Evan's moral complexity that makes the part so endlessly fascinating to Platt. "I love that he makes choices that aren't very easy for people to get on board with," Platt says, "but that he's pure and good and understandable enough that you feel you know him—or you feel you are him." It's a feeling that Platt clearly relates to, as well—even though the actor undergoes a complete physical transformation to play the character, he sees much of himself in the role. "The fact that he's a kid who struggles with one of the only things that I struggle with—which is anxiety—is kind of a blessing that I didn't expect and that makes this whole experience special in a way that I could never have foreseen," Platt says. "To be creating a kid who lives in the world that I live in and who deals with things that I do is incredibly rewarding."

> "It's not a character that comes along in musical theater a lot, especially for guys, somebody that's so vulnerable and has all the sides, all the colors."

Playing Evan Hansen has been a dream come true for the 23-year-old actor. "It's not a character that comes along in musical theater a lot, especially for guys, somebody that's so vulnerable and has all the sides, all the colors," he says. Though Platt had no idea what the musical would eventually become, and no inkling of how profoundly it would change his life, when he took part in the first informal reading of the still-untitled show in 2014, he knew immediately that he needed to be a part of it. "It just didn't feel like your average commercial musical, so I didn't necessarily think, *This is going to be the biggest hit in the world*, but it was exactly what I had always wanted to do."

Platt was raised around the theater, and show tunes were the lingua franca of his childhood. His father, Marc Platt, is a successful film and Broadway producer (*Wicked* numbers among his credits), and his parents met during a production of *Peter Pan* in college. Growing up in southern California, he and his four siblings (two older sisters, an older brother, and a younger brother) would listen to original cast recordings on every car ride and stage their own musicals in the backyard. His family earned the nickname the "von Platts" by performing together at special events, such as Ben's musical-themed bar mitzvah, at which waiters were costumed as ushers and tables were named after different Broadway shows. Platt entered the party to "Walk Like a Man" from *Jersey Boys*, dressed in a blue blazer just like the ones the Four Seasons wear in the show. His brothers and dad wore matching jackets, as they performed the song together to synchronized choreography devised by his sister. Later in the evening, his parents and siblings sang a medley from *Company* with rewritten lyrics like "Benny, baby, bubbie." They've kept up the tradition of

family performances—at his brother Jonah's wedding, they sang a version of "Satisfied" from *Hamilton* called "Plattisfied." (The evidence is on YouTube.)

Platt didn't stay in the backyard for long. As a young child, he starred in a Camp Ramah production of *Guys and Dolls* (in Hebrew no less), and at age 9, he went on his first audition, to play the role of Winthrop in *The Music Man* at the Hollywood Bowl, alongside Eric McCormack and Kristin Chenoweth. The casting agents for the show had come to Platt's extracurricular theater program, the Adderley School for the Performing Arts, in search of students to fill the role, and though his parents insisted he continue to make schoolwork a priority even if he got the part, they allowed him to audition. Platt booked the role, his first professional

gig, and a couple years later, he took on the part of Noah on the *Caroline, or Change* national tour.

Platt was still in high school when he traveled to New York to audition for a new Off-Broadway musical called *Dogfight*. This was no ordinary audition for him. He was obsessed with the songwriters—he even sang "Like Breathing" from the pair's first musical, *Edges*, at his high school senior showcase. "They were very much worshipped among my musical theater friends growing up," Platt says. "And so, if you had asked me, in the days of me dreaming about what would happen in the future, who would you want to write your first original musical, it would hands down have been Pasek and Paul." While the team was impressed with Platt's abilities, he was a

> **I really understood Steven's rhythm and the character's rhythm, and felt like the humor was an immediate match–the self-effacing, too-fast-for-his-own-mind kind of thing was in my wheelhouse."**

little too young for the part in *Dogfight*. But Benj Pasek reached out on Facebook to let Platt know that he might be right for another project they were working on and they would keep him updated. "I thought, that's very kind," Platt says, "but things like that never really come to fruition."

Except when they do. When Platt received a call about the first reading of *Dear Evan Hansen*, he was no longer a high schooler traveling from home for auditions. The summer after he graduated from Harvard Westlake in Los Angeles, he was preparing to begin his freshman year at Columbia University in the fall, when he landed the role of nerdy, misunderstood, magic-obsessed Benji Applebaum in a small film called *Pitch Perfect*. He decided to defer college for a year to make the movie, which turned into an unexpected box office smash, going on to become one of the highest-grossing music comedies of all time, before blowing up into a major franchise, and giving Platt his first taste of stardom. A year later, he dropped out of Columbia for good when he landed the role of Elder Cunningham in *The Book of Mormon*, first in Chicago and then on Broadway. Pasek came to see *The Book of Mormon* and asked Platt if he'd be interested in coming in to do a cold read of the lead character in a new musical he, Paul, and Steven Levenson were working on with Michael Greif. With the exception of a few demo recordings Paul sent Platt the night before the reading, Platt knew almost nothing about the role. However, it didn't take long for him to fall for the part. "The character and I clicked right away," Platt says. "I really understood Steven's rhythm and the character's rhythm, and felt like the humor was an immediate match—the self-effacing, too-fast-for-his-own-mind kind of thing was in my wheelhouse."

Platt's performance more than clicked with the creative team that day—they had found their guy. "He brought everything. He brought the germ of everything you're seeing now," Greif recalls. "He brings astonishing facility

"He brings the most extraordinary emotional transparency you can ever dream of."

with language. He brings the ability to wring humor out in the most natural way. He brings the most extraordinary emotional transparency you can ever dream of. He does it all, and he does it really instinctively and quickly."

And his reading of the role proved to the writers that it was possible for audiences to sympathize with the character of Evan, in spite of the morally questionable choices he makes. "Then we started really digging in and rolling up our sleeves and writing," Paul says. "Because we could finally see that there was definitely a world where you could get on this character's side. And Ben helped us with that."

When he was first approaching the role, Platt initially identified some classmates from high school as inspira-

tion for the character. Over time, though, he found himself bringing more and more of himself and his own insecurities to the role, allowing them to surface in both physical and emotional ways. "I had developed a lot of anxieties surrounding health and living by myself and flying and all sorts of different things, and I think that when I sat down and saw the character, a light bulb went off as a way to maybe channel some of that," he says. He thought about

how his own nervousness would manifest if he "wasn't as mature or as good at hiding it," and imagined that it might include a lot of nail-biting and knee-shaking, Platt says. Once he had built a repertoire of behavioral tics, he and Greif worked together to identify which felt essential and which felt extraneous. "Michael and I were able to edit it down to the things that were really effective."

Uncovering the nuances of the character was only one of the challenges that Platt would face as he embarked on the role. Preparing himself physically for the rigors of the part was another. When the show was at Arena Stage, Platt didn't have an understudy, and he realized quickly that he needed to implement a strict regimen to keep himself in peak health to fulfill the demands of the role. He cut out gluten and dairy to prevent mucus build-up, added daily vitamin supplements to his diet, and stuck to a firm sleep schedule. "When I saw how the show was affecting people, I felt a responsibility to deliver it consistently and honestly," he says. "That's why I doubled down on the discipline and made sure I was going to be able to always be there."

When the show moved to New York, he began attending physical therapy regularly to mitigate the damage done to his posture through inhabiting Evan's crumpled, almost doubled-over physicality, and he increased his voice lessons with teacher Liz Caplan to twice a week. Much of their time together was focused on "Words Fail," a song that called upon Platt to belt and sob simultaneously, a challenging combination to say the least. Shaping his performance of the song, Caplan assisted Platt in uncovering a way "to make the sounds in a healthy way and not sacrifice the emotionality and the physicality," Platt says. If this sounds abstract, it was anything but. "So we worked on when can I swallow so the mucus comes down my throat? Or where can I lengthen the back of my neck so that sound's not being squeezed? Where can I take a deep breath and make it look like a re-attack or a heave? Where can I lift my legs to remind myself to have my upper body strength to get notes out that I'm not squeezing from my neck?"

His physical endurance is all the more impressive considering how few moments Platt has to rest, let alone drink water, during the course of each performance.

< (left) Platt sits while a cast is put on his arm before a performance.

"Bathroom breaks are even fewer and farther between," he says. "The show for me is choreographed within an inch of its life." For instance, there's a strategically placed glass of water on the dinner table in the scene at the Murphys in which he sings "For Forever," and he's also able to rehydrate quickly during "Requiem." However, after his break at intermission, he goes through Act Two "without a gulp," as he's always either onstage or changing costumes quickly. "In some ways, it's an advantage not to have many breaks in the action, as I can ride the story through, beat to beat, without having to reset at any point," he says. "It's one long emotional roller coaster."

"Emotional" is the key word. In addition to his physical preparation, Platt had to learn how to maintain a balanced mindset while diving into the thoughts of a depressed and anxious teenager every night onstage. "At first, it was definitely scary, and I think it's going out on a limb I've never been out on before. It's revealing myself in every possible way I can—like getting naked. It took some getting used to," he says. "At the beginning, there were some days I stayed in that rut, but now I've figured out, even if I feel that way, how to get back out of it. It's been such a joyful experience that that's usually doable."

One way he keeps his routine lighthearted and joyful is by hosting and DJing a dance party with the cast before each show in his dressing room, a tradition that started when they were at Arena Stage. (He tries to keep the playlist varied, but Beyoncé is a group favorite.) "It's an excellent way for us to bond as a cast and to release some of the stress and tension," Platt says.

On the days when the demands of the role weigh more heavily, Platt's sense of responsibility to the fans is what keeps him going. His dressing room is full of fan art, and he has saved several letters that people have sent him. On his dressing room wall, next to a picture of him with his parents, Platt keeps one note in particular, an anonymous letter he received during the second week of Broadway previews, which simply reads: "You stopped me from letting go."

"That sums up the experience to me," he says. "If I ever have a day where I come in, and I'm, like, I can't do this, it's 1:45 p.m., and I don't want to cry, and sing, and scream, I just think about that."

As Platt prepares to leave the role that has become a defining pillar of his professional career, he is looking forward to the future, for himself and for the incoming Evan Hansens: Noah Galvin and Taylor Trensch. "It fills my heart with insurmountable gratitude and pride to see these singular human beings and talents will carry on the Evan legacy," Platt wrote in a Facebook post. "How lucky are we."

It's going out on a limb I've never been out on before. It's revealing myself in every possible way."

CHAPTER 7

TAP, TAP, TAPPIN'

Alex Lacamoire finds the sound of the musical

F YOU LISTEN TO JUSTIN PAUL ACCOM-pany Benj Pasek on the piano as he sings "Waving Through a Window" (there are several versions to choose from on YouTube), you'll notice that he begins by playing a vamp, consisting of a simple, bright, three-chord progression—A/C#-D-E suspended, to be precise. Simultaneously, Paul taps out a repeated single note that, even as Pasek starts to sing and the piano arrangement builds, runs through the rest of the song like a quickened pulse.

Now, listen to the song on the cast album, or in the theater, and you'll hear that same three-chord vamp, once again played on the piano. Only now, you'll notice that the pulse has an unwavering beat, as well as a distinctly computerized quality, achieved by sampling the note as a guitar harmonic layered with a Rhodes (played by a sequencer) and then running the note through a loop with a delay. And this time, an acoustic guitar chord announces the lyric "Step out, step out of the sun," which is accompanied by bass, drums, and electric guitar, kick-

ing the song into high gear. As soon as Ben Platt sings the next line, "If you keep gettin' burned," he is answered by a pizzicato fill of plucked string instruments, and almost immediately those same strings return, this time played with bows, swelling and building as he sings, "Because you've learned, because you've learned"—until, suddenly, the bottom drops out and we're back to where we started, with just the piano and the digital pulse, as Platt sings, "On the outside always looking in."

The music and lyrics and structure of the song are all Pasek and Paul's, but the instruments and what they add to our experience of the music are courtesy of the orchestrator Alex Lacamoire, who won a Tony for his work on *Dear Evan Hansen*, adding to the ones already on his shelf for *In the Heights* and *Hamilton*. An orchestrator's job, fundamentally, is to take a composer's songs and translate them into musical charts that tell the instrumentalists which notes to play and when, not to

"You try to keep your listener guessing."

The first band rehearsal for the ∧
Broadway production.

mention how fast, how loud, in what manner, and with what kind of feeling. But Lacamoire also sees himself as an interpreter of the song's intentions whose job is to add color and texture to supplement the emotional arc of the score. "You try to be varied, you try to be creative, you try to keep your listener guessing, in a way," says the buoyant and curly-haired Lacamoire, who is affectionately known as "Lac." "But you also want to do it in a way that doesn't draw attention to itself"

From the moment that *Dear Evan Hansen*'s score began to take shape, Pasek and Paul knew that they wanted Lacamoire to orchestrate it. "I really believe he's a musical genius," Paul says. "He can work in any style or genre, but I think he's particularly strong, probably the best there is, in terms of his ability to straddle the worlds of contemporary music and theatrical storytelling."

Lacamoire's essential task upon joining *Dear Evan Hansen* was to choose the instruments that would make up the band. He kept it relatively small (its musicians amounting only to the same number as cast members): a keyboard, two guitars, drums, bass, violin, viola, and cello. "I wanted to be expressive and exciting at the same time," he says. "And I wanted the strings to be as dynamic as possible, to show that they could kick ass in a pop song. So I pulled out all the stops."

As Lacamoire animatedly discusses the various stops he pulled out on "Waving," it becomes clear that every decision was driven by both what would work musically and what it would reveal about Evan's character. For instance, Lacamoire chose that pizzicato string fill that follows the line "If you keep gettin' burned" partly because he liked the percussive sound, but also because it felt like the musical equivalent of Evan's hesitant longing.

He employs other musical signatures throughout "Waving." One of his favorites involves filling the pauses between vocal lines—"'We start with stars in our eyes.' Rest. Rest. Rest," he sings/speaks. "'We start believing that we belong.' Rest." In these vocal pauses, Lacamoire inserts musical motifs played on the strings, which he sees as melodic answers to the questions posed by the lyrics. As Paul remembers listening to Lacamoire's arrangement for the first time, he says, "It was such a rush and

just so thrilling to hear someone capture the energy—that pop and that pocket—that the song needed, yet maintain the sort of tender, aching heart that was just as essential."

THE CUBAN-AMERICAN LACAMOIRE, born in Los Angeles, grew up mostly in Miami. He became "obsessed" with music at a young age, sitting transfixed in front of the stereo, and taught himself to play a simple tune called "Music Box Dancer" on his toy piano at age 4, prompting his parents to send him for piano lessons. He quickly advanced past the point where his teacher, a 17-year-old music student, had anything left to teach him. As he moved on to other instructors in his study of classical piano, his musical taste was being shaped by early-'80s MTV—think Madonna, Cyndi Lauper, and Wham!—and he started teaching himself to play pop tunes by ear while also taking up the guitar and bass.

Lacamoire found his way to musical theater at age 11, when he was asked to play keyboard bass for a summer school production of *Bye Bye Birdie*. By age 16, he was playing piano in the band for his high school's production of *West Side Story*. He was hooked. He went on to attend Berklee College of Music, and soon after graduation landed a gig as an audition pianist for *The Lion King* as it searched for talent in Boston. The show's Broadway musical director sat in one day and, impressed by the 23-year-old Lacamoire's keyboard wizardry, offered him a gig subbing on keyboards in the show's orchestra pit on Broadway. *Bat Boy* was his first big Off-Broadway gig as an orchestrator and arranger, and his first time working with producer Kevin McCollum. McCollum, one of the lead producers on *In the Heights*, introduced Lacamoire to Lin-Manuel Miranda, with whom he would go on to collaborate on *Heights*, *Bring It On!*, and *Hamilton*.

Lacamoire's musical gift is all the more astonishing given that he has suffered from hearing loss since the age of 4, when he first began wearing hearing aids. (Without them, consonants and high-pitched noises are difficult for him to decipher.) Not wanting to constantly ask classmates to repeat stories or jokes he couldn't hear, he felt alienated in social situations throughout his childhood, so it's easy to see why Lacamoire identifies so strongly with the teenager at the center of *Dear Evan Hansen*. "It gave me a feeling of unworthiness, a feeling of wanting to be included in something and feeling like you're not," he says. "So, I kept to myself a lot."

For all his creativity, Lacamoire never had any aspirations to compose his own music. "The blank canvas is really hard for me, because you could go anywhere," he says. "I need a little bit more structure in order for me to really fly." The structure of Pasek and Paul's score clearly set him free, and he cites such musical influences as Madi Diaz and Sara Bareilles—artists with a folksy and singer-songwriter quality—as inspirations for his work on *Dear Evan Hansen*. He points also to a Ben Folds homage in the distortion on the bass line of "Sincerely Me." A similar distortion is used for a leitmotif that he calls "the lying sound," a droning undercurrent that turns up in such songs as "For Forever," signaling that Evan is becoming caught up in his own fantasies—another example of Lacamoire's use of orchestration to reveal character.

Some songs, like "So Big, So Small," required very little treatment, and Lacamoire stayed true to its perfectly simplistic roots. Paul played the tune for the cast and team for the first time on guitar, and if you start the track on the album, the sole instrument you hear is guitar, not supplemented by the band until halfway through. "It's very naked. It's very exposed. It's very simple," Lacamoire says. "I thought that the song needed to be as raw, as uncluttered as the lyric."

However, for some songs, like "You Will Be Found," Lacamoire broke out the big guns. When Paul first presented the tune, he asked if the orchestrator wanted to discuss how to proceed. Lacamoire responded, "Nope, I got it. I'm going to kick this song in the nuts." "It's an anthem and just a glorious melody, great hook—I think everything about the song is perfect," he adds. Lacamoire responded to the song's gospel influence, looking to Dave Matthews Band's "Crash" and some of the pointillist musical effects in Sondheim's *Sunday in the Park With George* to lend the song what he calls the "pixely sound of the internet."

HE BROUGHT THIS SAME LEVEL OF meticulousness to his work on the cast album, which he produced with Pasek and Paul and Atlantic Records Executive Vice President and Head of A&R Pete Ganbarg. Lacamoire, who had previously worked with Ganbarg on the *Hamilton* album, invited the music executive to see *Dear Evan Hansen* at Second Stage, and it paid off. "We're in. What do we need to do?" Ganbarg said as soon as the lights came up.

Typically, Broadway cast recordings are put together in one day, with the entire company and orchestra coming in together. The *Dear Evan Hansen* team worked with most musicians and actors separately. This gave Lacamoire more control over all elements of the songs, from the quality of the vocal tracks to the acoustic nuance of each instrument. "When you try to do everything all at once, so much is going to fall by the wayside," he explains.

Before the album release, there was a so-called virtual listening party. Stacey Mindich and the team reached out to fans—from high schoolers with minimal social media followings to celebrities like Anna Kendrick—and direct messaged them an exclusive link to the album on Twitter. The listeners shared real-time reactions, and the production hosted a conversation about the album on Facebook Live. "Our goal was to create an interactive experience and establish a space where fans could connect with one another as they experienced the music for the very first time," says Damian Bazadona, president and founder of Situation Interactive, *Dear Evan Hansen*'s digital marketing agency. "People from around the world who had never met one another were connecting and speaking to each other throughout the evening to share their love and excitement for the album."

Lacamoire counts himself lucky to be involved with the project. The album would go on to debut at number eight on the *Billboard* 200 chart—the highest cast album bow since *Camelot* in 1961. "People are going to be listening to this on repeat, because every song is so strong," he says. "That's the other reason I wanted to make sure every track was perfect. There's something special about the music, and I think it's apparent to anyone who pops it on and listens to it. There's a fire to it. It breathes."

< (left) Actors in the studio for the original cast recording.

IT TAKES A
LITTLE PATIENCE

Three readings and one workshop

NCE UPON A TIME, in June 1944, *Variety* announced that "a group of youngsters have gotten together to stage a musical." Six months later, the composer Leonard Bernstein, the librettists Betty Comden and Adolph Green, and the choreographer Jerome Robbins, all in their twenties, made their Broadway debuts with *On the Town*, which opened at the Adelphi Theater after a ten-day tryout in Boston and two previews in New York City. Today, of course, such a breakneck timeline would be unthinkable, and a show's creators often spend years developing the work even before putting it on its feet in a series of readings and workshops. What the process loses in spontaneity, speed, and bravado, it gains in the opportunity for the material to find its voice and grow deeper, richer, and more unified. Such was the case with *Dear Evan Hansen*, which had its first reading more than four years after the youngsters who would go on to write its score first brought the idea to Stacey Mindich. And in the year of readings and workshops that followed, the still somewhat shaggy musical was trimmed and shaped to clarify its storyline and keep its focus where the creative team increasingly knew it belonged: on the title character.

But in the spring of 2014, Evan Hansen's name wasn't even part of the title, which was still up for grabs. (The writers had come up with an exhaustive list of possibilities, including *The Evan Project, The Orchard, Only Connect, The Lying Tree, For Forever, A Part of Me,* and *Inventing Evan Hansen*.) As for the untitled musical itself, after two years of laboring on the script and songs, they still weren't satisfied. Despite the enthusiastic encouragement of both Mindich and Michael Greif, they were convinced that they had not yet unlocked the key to allowing audiences to sympathize with Evan.

"They could have had a reading nine months earlier, in my opinion, with the material they already had," Greif says. In the end, Greif finally convinced them to go through with it by promising to keep it low-key, telling them, "Look, we just need to hear it. We'll have Ben learn a few songs, you guys will perform the rest, and everyone else will just read their parts."

A show's creators often spend years developing the work even before… a series of readings and workshops."

ALL IS NEW

FINALLY, ON MAY 19, 2014, THE
production and creative team of what was then called the *PPL Project* gathered in a rehearsal room at Pearl Studios in Manhattan, joined by a group of actors, to get their first look at what they'd created. Among them was Ben Platt, who would be reading the part of Evan, along with the gifted Broadway veterans Rachel Bay Jones as his frazzled mother, Heidi, and Jennifer Laura Thompson and Michael Park as the grief-stricken Cynthia and Larry Murphy. Even though they would be reading only dialogue this time, Greif cast these three with an eye to the future, knowing he would eventually need great actors who could really sing. Rounding out the cast that day was Will Pullen as the doomed Connor Murphy; Barrett Wilbert Weed as his sister, Zoe; Alex Wyse as jokester Jared; and Erin Wilhelmi as the nerdy Alana.

The night before, Justin Paul emailed rough iPhone recordings of three songs to Platt, including "Waving Back at Me," as "Waving Through a Window" was then known, so he could begin to learn them. "I got no information other than that I would be reading the lead, which was just terrifying but also amazing," Platt says. "I tried to glean what I could from the music, but I still had no idea what anything was." The other actors knew even less: None of them had heard a

single note or been told anything about the show, much less received a script, so they would all be reading it cold. Guided only by Greif's warning not to peek or read ahead, they began.

As Paul remembers it, barely five minutes in, Greif turned to him and whispered, "We're on our way." It was clear that Evan was a sympathetic hero, particularly as played by Platt, who seemed to inhabit Evan's skin—not to mention knock his songs out of the park. (Steven Levenson, who until then had only a hazy picture of the character in his mind, recalls, "As soon as I saw Ben do it, I was, like, 'That's him!'") It was also apparent that the outline Greif and the authors had hammered out in Los Angeles was not just inspired but structurally sound—all the tentpoles were in place. The story not only worked, it was genuinely suspenseful, a feat few musical plots accomplish. Platt says, "I remember just sitting there the whole time wanting to turn the pages to find out what happens next." By the end, it was clear to everyone in the room that something special was happening.

WE'RE NOT GIVING UP BEFORE WE'VE TRIED

A THIRD READING WAS HELD THAT FALL
in September, at the Manhattan Movement and Arts Center. In the interim, the team had recast the part of Zoe, giving it to Laura Dreyfuss, whom they felt embodied the character's combination of intelligence and vulnerability, and he brought in yet another actress—Emily Skeggs, this time—to play Alana. Despite the presence of a small audience (Mindich invited a few producers and representatives from out-of-town theaters), the atmosphere remained focused and intimate, and the relationships among the show's characters—and the actors playing them—only continued to deepen: The company of *Dear Evan Hansen* was becoming a family, on and offstage.

There were problems, of course. The show was still too long and there were still too many beginnings. The opening number, "This Is Me," a sardonic song of Facebook status updates, in which all the teenage characters brag about their exaggeratedly incredible summers, felt like

MAY 2014
First reading, Pearl Studios

JULY 2014
Second reading, Chelsea Studios

A LITTLE PERSEVERANCE

HOPING TO KEEP THE MOMENTUM
going, Mindich scheduled another reading only two months later, in July 2014, at Chelsea Studios. This time around, Greif had a chance to rehearse with the actors beforehand (Will Roland and Mike Faist had been added as, respectively, Jared and Connor, along with a new Alana, Emily Walton), and Pasek and Paul taught them some of the songs. At just under three-and-a-half hours, the show was running a tad long, but as the actors began finding their

way into the characters and the musical moments began to take real shape, everything started to feel better. The day after the reading, Pasek sent the team an email with the subject line "Thank you," that read: "For a great week! Can't wait to keep working on this show with you lovely people!"

CAN WE TRY TO HAVE AN OPTIMISTIC OUTLOOK?

SIX MONTHS AFTER THE THIRD reading, *Dear Evan Hansen*, which until then had been nurtured largely under wraps, suddenly stepped into the sun, so to speak. Mindich sent out invitations emblazoned with the show's newly minted title, inviting several hundred producers, investors, and other members of the theater industry to a staged workshop ahead of a planned run at Washington, D.C.'s Arena Stage that summer. Greif had sixteen days to rehearse the actors (including the fourth Alana, Alexis Molnar), who would be performing without scripts, and block the show, incorporating rudimentary sets, costumes, and test projections. All the while, Pasek and Paul and music supervisor and orchestrator Alex Lacamoire would put them through their paces on the songs. Greif also worked with choreographer Danny Mefford to stage some of the numbers, many of which included an ensemble of four teenagers, a sort of singing-and-dancing Greek chorus that still remained part of the show. Among the numbers that Mefford put on its feet was "Sincerely Me," which would remain virtually unchanged all the way through Broadway, and the soon-to-be-cut "Goin' Viral," whose booty-shaking choreography quoted moves from online videos and, Mefford says, "had a very Justin Bieber 'Sorry' feel to it."

The show was performed twice, on March 25 and 26, 2015, at the Gibney Dance Center, in a studio with no risers, for about a hundred audience members each time. "You could feel the buzz of excitement in the room," Mindich recalls. "It was standing room only both days, and the first time I actually had to stand because there was no seat for me."

The version of the show presented on those days had many virtues, not the least of which was seeing the actors fully embody their characters. No longer tethered to a music stand, Platt found himself increasingly free to explore and give himself over to Evan's physicality. "I started to really find the tics, and the posture, and just the way it was going to feel to actually get up and do it," he says. "It was the first time Rachel and I were on the couch, getting to really be intimate with each other, and it just started to come to life."

On the other hand, the projections at this stage were more confusing than illuminating, and the four-member teen ensemble seemed to carry a whiff of something old-fashioned that was out of place with the rest of the show. "I'd like to think that when I did *Rent*, we used the ensemble in a contemporary way and everyone had a purpose," Greif says. "We never had a purpose for those four people other than to be students at school. I think it was Steven who wisely said after the workshop, 'Why don't we get back to the purity of what we once talked about and cut the ensemble?'"

> **Arena Stage** ✔
> @arenastage
>
> *Following*
>
> Replying to @BenPlattFANCLUB
>
> @BenPlattFANCLUB @DearEvanHansen @pasekandpaul We just watched a sneak peek workshop and Ben Platt was flawless! You're in for a treat.
>
> RETWEET 1 LIKE 1

---

a leftover from an earlier incarnation of the show. And Alana, soon to be played by a fourth actress, remained hard to pin down, a perky, chirpy character that didn't seem to fit the increasingly heartfelt tone of the musical. But Greif and the writers were clear on what they needed to do, which largely meant taking plot moments away from supporting characters and giving them to Evan, allowing him to drive the crucial events of the musical. "What we realized," Levenson says, "was that the show worked when you were 100 percent following Evan's journey through the story."

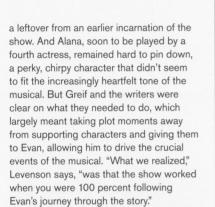

SEPTEMBER 2014
Third reading, Manhattan Movement and Arts Center

MARCH 2015
Full workshop, Gibney Dance Center

THE AUDIENCE RESPONSE WAS ENTHUsiastic, though it was clear that not everybody was convinced of the show's commercial potential. "People were intrigued," Mindich says. "They were also stunned by the topic, and dubious."

Levenson, Pasek, and Paul were stunned, too, and even more dubious. For them, seeing the show staged highlighted all its flaws, and they turned sour on everything about it. "We never thought that until after that workshop," Pasek says. "We then began to hate the piece itself, and we thought that we were really wrong in having conceived it the way we had. Up until that point, we were excited by it."

They wanted to pull the plug on the project. But, Paul, says, "We were, like, 'We can't do that to Ben Platt.'"

Levenson adds, "It was honestly, like, we have this cast. They love this show. They really believe in it. They're really good in it."

Still, with the show scheduled to head to D.C. in a few months, it started to feel like a runaway train, and the writers begged Mindich to delay the Arena Stage production. "We are insecure people," Pasek says. "When we talk about being rigorous, it's motivated out of insecurity. It comes from being scared that our flawed work will be seen by the world when it's not ready." But Mindich wouldn't let them give in to their terror. The show would go on as planned.

And so the writers got back to work, spending the weeks before Arena creating new material, making cuts, and doing rewrites in a race to get their musical in shape to be seen by a paying audience.

CHAPTER 9

SO BIG, SO SMALL:
RACHEL BAY JONES

mines her own story as Heidi Hansen

ARELY DO AN ACTOR and a character's lived experiences line up as providentially as they did in March 2015 during rehearsals for the upcoming workshop of *Dear Evan Hansen*, when Benj Pasek and Justin Paul first introduced the emotional 11 o'clock ballad, "So Big/So Small," to Rachel Bay Jones. As Paul accompanied himself on an acoustic guitar, Jones was stunned by the way the authors were able to get at the truth of an experience that all parents, and particularly single parents, know well—the need, in the most dire of circumstances, to swallow your own fears and doubts and summon a strength

> **You forget who you are, you become so completely invested in your child."**

that you aren't even sure you possess for the sake of your child. Her performance of the song that day left everyone in the room in tears, including Jones, a single mother herself, who turned to the songwriters with wet eyes and asked: "How can you possibly know that this is what I'm going through? And how do you know that this is what I'm feeling? How do you know that this is what I want to say?"

The number now leaves audiences wiping their eyes night after night, startled by the honesty, transparency, and vulnerability of Jones's breathtaking performance, which earned her a well-deserved Tony Award. And while the actress has performed the song countless times over three productions, it has yet to lose any of the immediacy or emotional acuity she felt the first time she heard Paul play it on an acoustic guitar in a tiny downtown rehearsal room two years ago.

"Survival—that's something I can totally relate to," says Jones, who was a single parent when her child was young (she now lives with her daughter and her longtime partner, actor Benim Foster). "The need for everything to be okay is so great, because there's no time for analysis. There's no time. There's just work to be done, constantly, and fighting for a future for your kid and for yourself. You forget who you are, you become so completely invested in your child. That always felt real to me."

With her blond tresses cascading down her back and an effortlessly boho-chic sense of style, Jones looks more like an ethereal grad student than a middle-aged mom. She draws on her own experiences as both a mother and a child to play Heidi, and through playing the role, she has come to understand herself and

her own parents better. Heidi loves Evan more than anything and works overtime to keep a roof over their heads. But like any parent, she makes mistakes along the way, and in her single-minded determination to do all that she can to provide for her child, she misses many of the warning signs that he is in trouble. In the end, when Evan seeks forgiveness from his mother for the lies he has told and the pain he has caused, Heidi must seek forgiveness of her own, stunned at how blind she has been to her child's suffering.

The role of Heidi has reminded Jones how difficult it can be for parents to ask forgiveness from their children, and she has come to be more forgiving of her own mom and dad as a result. "So much of what we do as parents is putting on a show for our kids in an effort to protect them from who we are," she says, noting that parents don't want to burden their children so they feel safe and protected. "We don't want them to know who we are because we don't know what we're doing, right? So we've got to pretend we've got our shit together all the time."

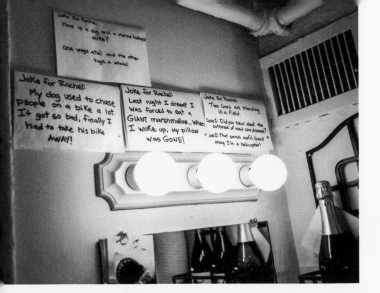

"

So much of what we do as parents is putting on a show for our kids in an effort to protect them from who we are."

Her musings call to mind the words she sings in the show's opening number:

Does anybody have a map?
Anybody maybe happen to know how the hell to do this?
I don't know if you can tell but this is me just
pretending to know.

Jones's path to *Dear Evan Hansen* and this moment has indeed been a wandering one, slowly preparing her to take on a role as emotionally rich as Heidi and imbue it with such depth, complexity, and soul. She was born in New York, where her parents were working actors. With a new child, however, they decided to give up show business for something more stable, and moved to South Florida to open a health food store. But, Jones recalls, "Even though they were no longer acting, they were *actors*—they were quintessential actors—and they came from a time when the theater was something to be passionate about, and it was important and it was life-changing and it was going to change the world." After the move south, her parents started performing with local community theaters before moving on to smaller regional companies. While these modest productions, performed at venues like the Burt Reynolds Dinner Theatre in Jupiter, Florida, may not have changed the world, Jones says that it blew her mind to suddenly see her parents in a new light. "They both became these stars of South Florida theater," she says. "To see them shine that way, it was really powerful, it was very moving."

Despite her upbringing, Jones never seemed destined for the stage. A shy, studious child—more science and literature than tap lessons and school musicals—she didn't show any inclination toward acting. One

∧ (above) After each performance, a stagehand gives Jones a "bad joke" to help her recover from the emotional demands of the role.

(right) Jones performs at a TimesTalk >
event honoring Michael Greif, with
Alex Lacamoire on piano.

day, though, she picked up a script that her mother was reading for an audition and noticed that there was a part in it for a 13-year-old girl. Much to her mother's surprise, Jones, who was 12 at the time, said, "I could do that." So what if the role called for a heavyset child, and Jones was very slight? She had her grandmother sew a padded suit for her audition. She got the part.

For Jones, the realization that she could get up on a stage and act in front of people—and enjoy it—was a pivotal moment of self-discovery, which years later would find an echo in, and provide yet another point of entry into, *Dear Evan Hansen*. "It was a really beautiful way—and it still is—for me to connect," she says, of performing. "I think we all want to be seen, so there's something about this that allows me to not hide. I have always, especially as a teenager, had to fight that impulse to hide. I somehow knew that wasn't what I needed to be doing, I think." Jones describes her teenage self as being, in style and attitude, more Connor Murphy than Evan Hansen—which is to say that she dressed in black, listened to punk and metal, started drinking and doing drugs, and felt angry at the world. "Rather than conforming and trying to get what I wanted *that* way, there was a lot of, you know, 'Well, fuck you, I'm going to show you,'" she says.

At 19, Jones found her way to New York City, where she shared an apartment with a friend in Hell's Kitchen, a now gentrified neighborhood that was "pretty intense" back then, as Jones puts it. Depriving herself of war stories about working as a waitress or as a temp while awaiting her big break, within a few weeks of her arrival she got cast as the understudy to the lead in *Meet Me in St. Louis* on Broadway, which ran for almost a year. Soon after, she went on tour with *Grand Hotel* for a year and a half.

But she hated auditioning ("I had a lot of fear about it, a lot of panic," she says), and she felt ambivalent about acting, not sure that it was what she wanted to do with her life. So she followed a boyfriend to North Carolina, where she worked at a summer theater and, during the off-season, got jobs at a veterinary clinic and a food co-op while singing bluegrass at local clubs. Although she returned to New York after a few years, her next decade was punctuated by sabbaticals—to South Florida, Austin, and Maui, where she had her child. "I sort of blew it in the normal exploratory years," she recalls. "The high school and college years for most people are where they try to figure out what it is that they want to be as adults. My early adulthood became about stepping into the pond again and then leaving and trying to find something else and not really ever being satisfied."

Eventually, Jones returned to New York for good, realizing that it had become her home, finally ready to commit herself to acting. But now she was in her mid-thirties, largely unknown after so much time away, and—her agent having died in the intervening years—without representation. She performed in industrial shows, dabbled in comedy, took small parts, and lived off her savings, all while raising her daughter. Eventually, she started to land bigger roles. One was a lead, as the protagonist's mom, in the pre-Broadway tour of *A Christmas Story: The Musical*, giving her a chance to sing Pasek and Paul's lovely "What a Mother Does," their warm-up for "So Big/So Small." The other was a plum role in the revival of *Pippin*, directed by Diane Paulus, who had cast Jones in the Broadway revival of *Hair* a few years earlier. Taking the part in *Pippin*, though, meant making the difficult decision not to go to Broadway with

"She knew that Heidi was a part she wanted to play—and one she understood intimately."

A Christmas Story. It turned out to be the right choice: Her widely lauded performance as Pippin's lover, Catherine, to which she brought comic charm and earthy sensuality, caught the attention of Michael Greif, who instantly thought of her when he was looking for someone to play Evan's mom in *Dear Evan Hansen*.

From the moment she opened the script at the show's first reading, she knew that Heidi was a part she wanted to play—and one she understood intimately. "I think the thing that hooked me then, and that has continued to keep her so close to my heart, is she's just so real," Jones says. "Many women in musical theater—and many moms in musical theater—are stereotypes, and so a large part of the work that I've had to do over the years in musicals, unfortunately, is like: Okay, how can we pack meaning into these necessarily small book scenes? How can I layer a moment that's just about advancing the plot with depth? How can I infuse this two-dimensional character with life?" *Dear Evan Hansen* was different. "Reading this script, it was all there. You didn't have to invent everything. That was the excellence of the writing and the truth that was inside of it. It's something we're all aching to explore."

Clearly, Heidi's inner life resonates for Jones, and she recognizes in Heidi's relationship with Evan aspects of her own with her daughter, which she describes as "you and me against the world, us on a life raft just trying to survive, and you're my everything." Even Heidi's look is reminiscent of Jones's own style. The wig that she wears for the show is modeled after her own hair, and Heidi's flared jeans and T-shirts are items that could be found in Jones's closet. In fact, Jones worked closely with the show's costume designer Emily Rebholz to ensure that Heidi's clothes reflected the psychological nuances of the character. "She doesn't want to grow up, and she doesn't know how to master her role as an adult, so she's still dressing like a 20-year-old in her mid-forties," Jones says. "She's single, so there's still an effort to be sexually attractive, but she doesn't have much money, and her clothes look a little trendy, a little cheap." Jones points in particular to the statement that Heidi's wardrobe

makes in a crucial scene in Act Two. "For the scene where she goes to the Murphys', these rich people's house, I wanted her to put on all her jewelry—lots of turquoise and brass rings and bracelets—and her good leather jacket, good flare jeans, and good boots. It felt really right."

That eye for the small but telling details is a large part of what makes Jones's Heidi so complex, singular, and true, and even now she remains on the lookout for new facets to add to her performance. "When you're developing a character or living with a character, things will occur to you in every aspect of your life," she says. "Dreams, interactions with your family, interactions with strangers, things you see on the street, other art that you witness—anything can be material. Sometimes I'll see a woman walking by and think, *Oh, a Heidi!* There's something about her: Is it the processed hair? Is it the look on her face? So, she's a person, and I live with her, and that's what makes this time so fruitful and alive and rich. If the whole world is my palette for painting Heidi, then there's no limit."

(above right) **Jones backstage at the 2017 Tonys after winning the award for Featured Actress in a Musical.**

CHAPTER 10

ON THE OUTSIDE ALWAYS LOOKING IN

The visual world of *Dear Evan Hansen*

FROM THE BEGINNING, THE authors of *Dear Evan Hansen* knew that the internet and social media would be at the center of the show's story and aesthetic. However, finding a compelling way to transpose Instagram thumbnails, Facebook reactions, and Snapchat filters from the scale of a smartphone screen to that of a proscenium stage was not exactly self-evident. Nor was it obvious how to capture the intimate, insular experience of scrolling through a Twitter feed for hundreds of strangers in a dark theater. So when scenic designer David Korins, projection designer Peter Nigrini, and lighting designer Japhy Weideman signed on to "depict the internet" onstage, they had their work cut out for them.

Korins was the first to join the show. He attended a reading in July 2014, and as he watched, he folded a stray piece of paper into sixteenths, onto which he jotted down drawings responding to the show. He showed the sixteen sketches to director Michael Greif, who pointed to one of a circular disk with a bed and different rectangular shapes hanging from above. "It was a little tectonic plate of life floating in this murky, inky blackness of a technological dreamscape," says Korins. "That's exactly our show."

Figuring out what those rectangles and monitors would become and what the audience and the characters would see on them was a different story. Enter Nigrini, who conceived of the projections as visual reflections of Evan's inner journey, a journey that

unfolds in three distinct stages. In the beginning, as Evan looks back at the screens in "Waving Through a Window," he sees images of happy kids and smiling families, photos of idyllic summer vacations and joy-filled parties—a world of connection and belonging, of which he isn't a part. At the end of Act One, the online conversation becomes about him, and he stares up, wide-eyed, at videos of strangers holding up signs reading "#YouWillBeFound" (crowd-sourced footage from real fans of the show), as his speech at the assembly goes viral. Evan is no longer craving to be a part of something—he is the something. Then, in the final stage of Evan's journey, when the letter is posted online, Nigrini says, "It all goes to shit." The screens are filled with vitriolic rants against the Murphy family, and the hopeful world of connection and belong-

∧ (above) The set during a technical rehearsal at Arena Stage. (right) Projections fill the Broadway stage at the end of Act One.

ing that Evan once imagined has turned to disarray and chaos. Describing Evan's journey, Nigrini says, "It belittles the point to talk about it as his relationship to social media. It's really his relationship to other human beings."

Weideman also looked to the emotions of the characters and the "diversity of the score" to conceive the lighting, and worked very closely with Nigrini to make sure lights and projections complemented each other, so "you're not really seeing where video begins and lighting ends." The two media generally work in opposition—the brighter the lights, the more difficult it is to see the projections; the darker the lights, the more legible the projections, but the more difficult it is to see anything else onstage, including, most obviously, the actors. In order for the lights and projections to work in harmony, each moment in the show needed to be meticulously planned, and the designers worked closely to ensure that neither was in the other's way. (Due to the incredible precision of the cues, the actors need to hit their marks with extraordinary exactness in order to be seen by the audience. An inch in one direction or the other can mean the difference between a brightly lit actor and an actor in complete darkness.) For Nigrini and Weideman, the communication was mostly nonverbal—they simply made adjustments based on one another's work. "That's a better choice than the choice I was making, so I'm going to move the color palette of what I'm doing in the direction you're headed or

vice versa," Nigrini says, describing the largely spontaneous, moment-to-moment collaborative process.

Weideman also created lighting tricks with seemingly ordinary objects. For instance, when Evan opens his laptop at the top of the show, bathing his face in its glow against the darkness, he's literally opening up his "window" into the world. However, the glow of the screen alone was not bright enough to illuminate Ben Platt's face in a massive theater. To achieve the effect, Weideman used strips of LED lights, and taped them along the laptop screen. "That's coming from a place of, *Okay, how do we ground this in reality, yet give it a heightened quality to pull us in?*" he says.

The last scene in the show is the only time the hanging screens disappear from view, zooming up into the theater's fly space, replaced by a vast stretch of sky—an exquisite blue scrim. "For me, it was, *What does it really feel like when you're outside like that, in a big, beautiful green field, after this whole experience of being in all these claustrophobic, mostly interior spaces?*" Weideman says. In order to fill the back wall with light, the projections need to shut down completely, a process that takes about fifteen minutes. As Evan confesses that he has lied to the Murphys and Heidi sings "So Big/So Small," the remnants of the letter slowly disappear from view, and that fifteen-minute fade to black before the orchard scene is Nigrini's favorite part of the show. "That very delicate receding of the letter and all of that story," he says, "to me, it's the most emotional and human part of it."

NO REASON TO STARE

Emily Rebholz discovers character through costume

IN THE EARLIEST DRAFT OF THE SCRIPT, the writers had envisioned Evan wearing UGG boots, the ultimate signifier that he was trying too hard. Dozens of drafts, and several years later, when Ben Platt began to imagine what Evan Hansen would wear, he immediately thought of New Balance sneakers. For Platt, the shoes represent something an unpopular teenager would think of as "hip," when really, he has no clue where to even start. In fact, Platt based

CONNOR MURPHY

"We wanted him to feel approachable—we didn't want to go so extreme. We didn't want to put him in all black or apply crazy eyeliner. I felt like he goes to the Army Navy Surplus Store. He thrifts. He does the things that his mom would really hate. He wears an old gray denim shirt that I cut the sleeves off of and then we added that hoodie. While Evan wants to blend in, Connor wears his anger on the outside. So I felt like dark colors were right, but we felt very strongly that it should be dark gray and not black."

LARRY MURPHY

"He's very buttoned-up. He's a father that was in a fraternity, made straight As, was on sports teams, and really, really fits in. He belongs to the country club, golfs on the weekends, has his jeans tailored. He's very in control and well-liked in the community. And he has a son who doesn't identify with him at all. Even when Larry's falling apart, he always looks like he has it all together. He's not a schlubby dad—that's not his thing."

ZOE MURPHY

"She's well-off, she's pretty, she's popular. She's also in jazz band. She's kind of funky. She has the means to buy new clothes whenever she wants, but she's also a typical teenager. She's not wearing outfits with a capital O. She wears lots of jeans and jean shorts. Evan sings about how she draws stars on her jeans. Most of her jeans do have stars drawn on the bottom of them, and the Converse she wears also have stars and little notes written on them. She's got an artistic side to her. She's a cool girl, but she's not trying to be a cool girl."

CYNTHIA MURPHY

"This is the woman that has her hair blown out and that seems like all her ducks are in a row, even if they're not. So she's got her silk blouses and her cardigans. There's a softness to her. She's dressed like a mom. Even in her mourning she's put together. There's a sense of cashmere and silk and expensive gold jewelry. She's got a muted color palette, what we might think of as, like, a classy color palette: neutrals, creams, and blues, and grays. I wanted the contrast between Heidi's brighter colors and Cynthia's neutrals."

much of his performance on a good friend from high school who wore the brand, so when he met with costume designer Emily Rebholz, the first thing he wanted to discuss to shape Evan's wardrobe was footwear. "They allow him to disappear, and they're not cool," Rebholz says of the shoes.

For Rebholz, disappearing is the point. As a designer, she seeks to find costumes that allow actors to vanish into their characters. On *Dear Evan Hansen*, she worked closely with each member of the cast to ensure that the clothing felt "like a second skin." Her goal was to devise outfits that felt contemporary and relatable, while also making sure the audience knew exactly who these characters were—or believed themselves to be. And for Platt, wearing the now-iconic polo and khakis is essential to immersing himself in Evan's world. "These clothes just drop me right into the guy," he says. "I want to keep them when I'm finished."

HEIDI HANSEN

"For the first part of the show, she's in scrubs. I wanted to do a pattern—butterflies or hearts, but not so over-the-top. We were particular about her accessories. I felt really strongly that Heidi should have a rainbow-colored Swatch watch. She's a little bit sexy—she was probably a boho rocker chick back in the day and dresses a little bit too young for her age. I wanted her to have all the silver jewelry that she's had forever. It's not exactly how you think a mom would dress at first."

EVAN HANSEN

"The shirt has been with us since D.C. It was, like, the first shirt that Ben put on. I knew I wanted to start him in a polo, which feels youthful and slightly vulnerable. This is someone who shops at the sale rack at Old Navy. It's blue, which is a great color but also very generic. It needed to be something that we can watch for a while—Ben doesn't leave stage for a long time. I think, partially, that polo has become so iconic because he wears it for so long. We did khakis. Jeans just didn't feel right. It feels like a good progression to get him into jeans as he loosens up."

ALANA BECK

"When we had the first production, we went a little more Tracy Flick from *Election*, and there was a little more intensity to her clothes. I thought Alana should wear a blazer. She's, like, "I'm an adult." What everybody thought was that we needed to just pull that statement back and let the character shine through. We did keep the fact that she wears her button-down done all the way to the collar. I wanted to find ways that felt like she's that type A, wants-to-be-student-class-president, honor roll girl."

JARED KLEINMAN

"Jared is a colorful guy, and Will brings so much of himself to the role. He's funny, and he's not trying to hide. He's, like, "This is me, this who I am." He has these statement T-shirts that people don't really wear, but they're all innocuously funny. They're also the shirts of a kid who spends a lot of time in front of his TV and computer. He's definitely seen the whole series of *Game of Thrones*. He wears Adidas tennis shoes, and he has a better brand backpack. He has more money than Evan, but he's a little offbeat."

N HANSEN

the libretto

ALANA @ConnorProject   5m
PLEASE SHARE: Connor's last words--YOU NEE

#youwillbefound

A quiet buzzing begins to sound just at the edge of our awareness, an indistinct murmuring of voices, as the house lights slowly fade.

The murmuring builds, growing louder and louder, voices piling on top of one another.

Millions of fragments of emails, status updates, cat videos, dessert recipes, revenge porn—the music of the spheres.

Of a sort.

Suddenly, sharply, nothing. Silence.

Then, in the darkness, a laptop snaps open.

The gauzy white glow of the screen illuminates the face of Evan Hansen, sitting at a desk with a hard cast on his left arm, alone.

He begins to type.

EVAN:

Dear Evan Hansen: [1]

Today is going to be an amazing day, and here's why. Because today, all you have to do is just be yourself.

(Beat.)

But also confident. That's important. And interesting. Easy to talk to. Approachable. But mostly be yourself. That's the big, that's number one. Be yourself. Be true to yourself.

(Beat.)

Also, though, don't worry about whether your hands are going to get sweaty for no reason and you can't make it stop no matter what you do, because they're not going to get sweaty, so I don't even know why you're bringing it up, because it's not going to happen, because you're just, all you have to do is be yourself.

(Beat.)

I'm not even going to worry about it, though, because seriously it's not like, it's not going to be like that time you had the perfect chance to introduce yourself to

Zoe Murphy at the jazz band concert last year, when you waited afterward to talk to her and tell her how good she was, and you were going to pretend to be super casual like you didn't even know her name, like she would introduce herself and you'd be like, "Wait, I'm sorry, I didn't hear you. Chloe, you said your name was Chloe?" And she'd be, like, "No, it's Zoe, I said, Zoe," and you'd be, like, "Oh, see, I thought you said Chloe because I don't even, I'm very busy with other stuff right now is the thing." But then you didn't even end up saying anything to her anyway, because you were scared your hands were sweaty which they weren't that sweaty until you started worrying that they were sweaty, which

HEIDI: This is what you're supposed to be working on, Evan. With Dr. Sherman? Talking to people. Engaging with people. Not running away from people.

EVAN: You're right. I'm going to be a lot better.

HEIDI *(Trying to put a positive spin on it)*: No, I know. I know you are. And that's why I made you an

could use something a little sooner. Have you been writing those letters he wants you to do? The letters to yourself? The pep talks? "Dear Evan Hansen. This is going to be a good day and here's why." [3] Have you been doing those?

EVAN: I started writing one. I'll finish it at school.

HEIDI: Those letters are important, honey. They're going to help you build your confidence. Seize the day.

EVAN *(Dubious)*: I guess.

HEIDI: I don't want another year of you sitting at home on your computer every Friday night, telling me you have no friends.

(Beat.)

EVAN: Neither do I.

monologue functioned, in a sense, *as* our opening number. We decided to embrace that.

2 **Steven Levenson**

Evan does this every single time Heidi enters his bedroom—a fact that she will only begin to notice in Act Two.

3 **Steven Levenson**

In our original conception of the musical, Evan's letter was actually written in response to a deliberately inane college essay contest prompt: "Write a letter from yourself to yourself ten years from now in which you tell yourself about yourself." We arrived at the idea of the letters as an assignment from his therapist a few weeks before we began rehearsals for our first production.

ANYBODY
HAVE A MAP? [4]

HEIDI:

Can we try to have an
*   optimistic outlook?*

Huh?

Can we buck up just
*   enough*
To see . . . the world won't
*   fall apart?*
Maybe this year we decide
We're not giving up before
*   we've tried*
This year, we make a
*   new start*

Hey, I know—you can go around
today and ask the other kids [5] to
sign your cast, how about that? That
would be the perfect icebreaker,
wouldn't it?

EVAN: Perfect.

HEIDI: I'm proud of you already.

EVAN: Oh. Good.

*(Heidi exits the room, stands in the
hall, realizing that this interaction
has been an utter failure, as Evan
packs up for school.)*

HEIDI:

Another stellar
*   conversation for the*
*   scrapbook*
Another stumble as I'm
*   reaching for*
The right thing to say
Well, I'm kinda comin'
*   up empty*
Can't find my way to you

Does anybody have a map? [6]
Anybody maybe happen
*   to know how the hell*
*   to do this?*
I dunno if you can tell
But this is me just
*   pretending to know*

So where's the map?
I need a clue
'Cause the scary truth is
I'm flyin' blind
And I'm making this up
*   as I go*

4 Benj Pasek

This is a classic case of rewriting
the opening number a thousand
times. The more we rewrote the
show with Steven, we realized
that the musical was ultimately
about the relationship between
these two boys (Evan and Connor)
and their mothers, and their
potential parallel tracks. We knew
we didn't want to hear Evan sing
until "Waving Through a Window"
but we realized we needed to
understand who these boys
were right away. Who better to
illuminate them than their mothers,
desperate to find a connection
with their kids?

5 Steven Levenson

Originally, I had written "other
people" here, but in rehearsal
Rachel mistakenly said "other
kids" and I immediately changed
it. I loved the idea that Heidi still
thinks of Evan and his classmates
as "kids." That word choice tells
us so much about Heidi and how
she relates, or doesn't, to her son.

6 Justin Paul

Our goal in this chorus was to
really express the inner, frantic
psychology of what Heidi is
thinking and feeling. It's intentionally
built like a run-on sentence both
musically and lyrically, with very
little rhyme aside from an end
rhyme here or there. It's less
tight or structured than a typical
musical theater song, but hopefully
its asymmetry reflects the hearts
of Heidi and Cynthia.

(Lights shift to find the Murphys at the kitchen table. Zoe Murphy sits, eating cereal, leafing through a book. Larry Murphy, on his phone, scrolls through emails.

Connor Murphy stares blankly into his cereal bowl.

Cynthia Murphy stands, fussing over everything—pouring orange juice, topping off coffee, clearing finished dishes.)

CYNTHIA: It's your senior year, Connor. You are not missing the first day.

CONNOR: I already said I'd go tomorrow. I'm trying to find a compromise here. [7]

CYNTHIA *(Turns to Larry)*: Are you going to get involved here or are you too busy on your email, Larry?

LARRY: You have to go to school, Connor.

CYNTHIA: That's all you're going to say?

LARRY: What do you want me to say? He doesn't listen. Look at him. He's not listening. He's probably high.

ZOE: He's definitely high.

CONNOR *(To Zoe)*: Fuck you.

ZOE: Fuck you.

CYNTHIA *(Admonishing Zoe)*: I don't need you picking at your brother right now. That is not constructive.

ZOE: Are you kidding?

CYNTHIA: Besides, he is not high.

(Cynthia looks to Connor to confirm this. He does not. She sighs.)

I do not want you going to school high, Connor. We have talked about this.

CONNOR: Perfect. So then I won't go. Thanks, Mom.

(Connor leaves. Cynthia begins clearing the dishes, lost in her own thoughts.)

CYNTHIA:

Another masterful attempt ends with disaster [8]

(Larry, looking at his phone, shakes his head.)

LARRY: Interstate's already jammed.

CYNTHIA:

*Pour another cup of coffee
And watch it all crash
and burn*

(Zoe goes to pour herself more milk, shakes the carton, annoyed.)

ZOE: Connor finished the milk.

CYNTHIA:

*It's a puzzle, it's a maze
I try to steer through it a
million ways
But each day's another
wrong turn*

(Larry stands, offering Cynthia a perfunctory spousal peck.)

LARRY: I better head out.

ZOE: If Connor's not ready, I'm leaving without him . . .

(She and Larry exit.)

CYNTHIA:

Does anybody	**HEIDI:**
Have a map? [9]	*Anybody have a map?*
Anybody maybe happen	*Or happen*
To know how the hell	*To know how the hell*
To do this?	*To do this?*
I dunno if you can tell	*I dunno if you can tell*
But this is me just	*But this is me just*
Pretending to know	*Pretending to know*

"Another masterful attempt ends with disaster."

– CYNTHIA

(Evan and Connor appear in separate pools of light, just outside the school doors, fiddling with shirt collars, smoothing hair, and—for Evan—checking palms for signs of dampness, as the two young men anxiously prepare to face the day.) [10]

HEIDI:

So where's the map?

CYNTHIA:

I need a clue

HEIDI/CYNTHIA:

'Cause the scary truth is

CYNTHIA:	**HEIDI:**
I'm flyin' blind	*I'm flyin' blind*
I'm flyin' blind	*I'm flyin'*
I'm flyin' blind	*I'm flyin' blind*
And I'm making this up	*And I'm making this up*
As I go	*As I go*
As I go	*As I go*

7 **Steven Levenson**

It was important to me to establish here that Connor is not just a grim, depressive figure— he's actually charming, funny, and self-deprecating. I never wanted the audience to feel that his death was inevitable.

8 **Justin Paul**

Confession: We drove Steven Levenson bonkers in this section because we were neurotic about where we wanted clips of dialogue between sung phrases to convey the continuous conversation. We would send Steven iPhone recordings of the song with built-in pauses for where we wanted dialogue— sometimes a couple of seconds and sometimes much longer. After he (deservedly) complained about it for a while, he of course came up with the most perfect and authentic breakfast table interjections.

9 **Justin Paul**

When we wrote this, Cynthia and Heidi sang in unison at the start of the second chorus. Lac [Alex Lacamoire] was like, "Hey, what if they don't come in together and it feels a little more staggered and asymmetrical" and we were like, "WHOA, minds blown..."

10 **Steven Levenson**

From the beginning, we wanted to establish that Evan and Connor were mirror images of one another—as are Heidi and Cynthia. Two boys, lost; two mothers, desperate to find them. Benj and Justin accomplish this beautifully in the music and lyrics, and the staging here is meant to support the same idea visually.

< ACT ONE SCENE ONE >

(As Cynthia and Heidi exit, the buzz of a school bell. Lights shift, finding Evan standing in a school hallway. Alana Beck enters, a certain barely concealed desperation in the eagerness with which she approaches Evan, in her almost too-wide smile.)

ALANA: Hey. How was your summer?

(Evan looks around, not sure if she's speaking to someone else.)

EVAN: My . . . ?

ALANA: Mine was productive. I did three internships and ninety hours of community service. I know: wow. [11]

EVAN: Yeah. That's, wow. / That's really impressive.

ALANA: / Even though I was so busy, I still made some great friends. Or, well, acquaintances, more like.

EVAN *(Gathering his courage)*: Do you want to maybe . . . I don't know what you're, um . . . do you want to sign my cast?

ALANA: Oh my God. What happened to your arm?

EVAN: Oh. Well. I broke it. I was climbing a tree . . .

ALANA *(Not listening at all)*: Oh really? My grandma broke her hip getting into the bathtub in July. That was the beginning of the end, the doctors said. Because then she died.

(Evan has no idea how to respond to this. Alana plasters on a glowing smile.)

Happy first day.

(Alana exits as Jared Kleinman approaches Evan with the kind of practiced swagger only the deeply insecure can truly pull off.)

JARED: Is it weird to be the first person in history to break their arm from jerking off too much or do you consider that an honor?

EVAN: Wait. What? I didn't, I wasn't . . . doing that.

JARED: Paint me the picture: You're in your bedroom, you've got Zoe Murphy's Instagram up on your weird, off-brand cell phone . . .

JARED: Why are you asking me?

EVAN: Well, just, I thought, because we're friends.

JARED: We're family friends. That's like a whole different thing and you know it.

(He punches Evan in the arm.)

Hey. Tell your mom to tell my mom I was nice to you or else my parents won't pay for my car insurance.

EVAN: I will.

(Connor crosses.)

JARED: Hey, Connor. I'm loving the new hair length. Very school shooter chic. [13]

(Connor stops, casts a withering glance at him.)

I was kidding. It was a joke.

CONNOR *(Deadpan)*: Yeah, no, it was funny. I'm laughing. Can't you tell? Am I not laughing hard enough for you?

JARED *(Laughs nervously, bravado gone)*: You're such a freak.

(Jared, laughing, nervously exits. Connor turns to Evan. Evan laughs, uncomfortable.)

CONNOR: What the fuck are you laughing at?

EVAN: What?

CONNOR: Stop fucking laughing at me.

EVAN: I'm not.

CONNOR: You think I'm a freak?

EVAN: No. I don't—

CONNOR: I'm not the freak.

EVAN: But I wasn't—

CONNOR: You're the fucking freak.

(Connor shoves him to the ground as he storms away. Slowly, Evan stands.)

EVAN: That's not what happened. Obviously. I was, um, well I was climbing a tree and I fell.

JARED: You fell out of a tree? What are you, like, an acorn? [12]

EVAN: Well, I was, I don't know if you know this, but I worked this summer as an apprentice park ranger at Ellison State Park. I'm sort of a tree expert now. Not to brag, but . . .

(Jared says nothing.)

Anyway. I tried to climb this forty-foot-tall oak tree.

JARED: And then you fell . . . ?

EVAN: Well, except it's a funny story, because there was this solid ten minutes after I fell, when I just lay there on the ground waiting for someone to come get me. Any second now, I kept saying to myself. Any second now, here they come.

JARED: Did they?

EVAN: No. Nobody came. That's the, that's what's funny.

JARED: Jesus Christ . . .

EVAN: How was, what did you do for the, you had a good summer?

JARED: Well, my bunk dominated in capture the flag and I got to second-base-below-the-bra with this girl from Israel who's going to like be in the army . . . so, yeah, hopefully that answers your question.

(Jared turns to go.)

EVAN: Do you want to sign my cast?

WAVING THROUGH A WINDOW [14]

EVAN:
I've learned to slam on
    the brake
Before I even turn the key
Before I make the mistake
Before I lead with the
    worst of me

Give them no reason
    to stare
No slippin' up if you
    slip away
So I got nothin' to share
No, I got nothin' to say

Step out, step outta the sun
If you keep gettin' burned
Step out, step outta the sun
Because you've learned,
    because you've learned

On the outside always
    lookin' in
Will I ever be more than
    I've always been?
'Cause I'm tap-tap-
    tappin' on the glass
Waving through a window

I try to speak but nobody
    can hear
So I wait around for an
    answer to appear
While I'm watch-watch-
    watchin' [15] people pass
Waving through a window
Oh
Can anybody see?
Is anybody waving back
    at me?

(Lights shift and Zoe enters.)

ZOE: Hey. I'm sorry about my brother. I saw him push you. He's a psychopath. Evan, right?

EVAN: Evan?

ZOE: That's your name . . . ?

EVAN: Oh. Yes. Evan. It's Evan. Sorry.

ZOE: Why are you sorry?

EVAN: Well, just because you said, Evan, and then I said, I repeated it, which is, that's so annoying when people do that.

ZOE: I'm Zoe.

EVAN: No, I know.

ZOE: You know?

EVAN: No, just, I've seen you play guitar in jazz band. I love jazz band. I love jazz. Not all jazz.[16] But definitely jazz band jazz. That's so weird, I'm sorry.

ZOE: You apologize a lot. [17]

EVAN: I'm sorry.

(He catches himself.)

Or. I mean. You know what I mean.

ZOE: Well, / I'll talk to you later.

EVAN: / You don't want to sign my . . . ?

ZOE: What?

EVAN (*Instantly regretting his decision*): What? What did you say?

ZOE: I didn't say anything. You said something.

EVAN: No. Me? No way. José.

ZOE: Um. Okay . . . José.

(Zoe exits.)

"Will I ever be more than I've always been?"
— EVAN

14 **Benj Pasek**

The first draft of this song was titled "Total Reinvention," which we soon realized was too on the nose. We wanted to create an "I Want" song where Evan expresses his fear of loneliness. It allowed us to give specificity to the idea.

The next draft of the song was called "Infinite Island," using the metaphor of an island to express his solitude. It ended with the question, "Is anyone waving back at me?" In the next pass, we came up with the metaphor of "waving through a window" and the song took shape.

15 **Justin Paul**

Part of what we wanted to do musically and lyrically in these sections was to mirror this conditioned, rut-like experience that Evan is having. He is mired within his own coping mechanisms. We see the same thing later with the repetition of "falling in a forest." Evan is stuck in a loop, loop, loop.

16 **Steven Levenson**

Subtext: "Not Kenny G."

17 **Steven Levenson**

One of the principal traits of people suffering from social anxiety disorder is the compulsive need to apologize.

EVAN:

We start with stars in our
    eyes
We start believin' that we
    belong
But ev'ry sun doesn't rise
And no one tells you where
    you went wrong

Step out, step outta the sun
If you keep gettin' burned
Step out, step outta the sun
Because you've learned,
    because you've learned

On the outside always
    lookin' in
Will I ever be more than
    I've always been?

'Cause I'm tap-tap-tappin'
    on the glass
Waving through a window

I try to speak but nobody
    can hear
So I wait around for an
    answer to appear
While I'm watch-watch-
    watchin' people pass
Waving through a window
Oh
Can anybody see?
Is anybody waving . . . ?

When you're fallin' in a
    forest
And there's nobody around
Do you ever really crash
Or even make a sound?

When you're fallin' in a forest
And there's nobody around
Do you ever really crash
Or even make a sound?

When you're fallin' in a forest
And there's nobody around
Do you ever really crash
Or even make a sound?

COMPANY:

When you're fallin' in a forest   Ah
And there's nobody around
Do you ever really crash   Ah
Or even make a sound?

Did I even make a sound?   Oh
Did I even make a sound?
It's like I never made a sound   Oh
Will I ever make a sound?   Oh

On the outside   Oh
Always lookin' in
Will I ever be more
Than I've always been?

'Cause I'm tap-tap-tappin'   Oh
On the glass
Waving through a window   Oh

I try to speak   Oh
But nobody can hear
So I wait around
For an answer to appear
While I'm watch-watch-watchin'   Oh
People pass
Waving through a window   Oh
Oh
Can anybody see?
Is anybody waving . . .
Back at me?
    Oh
Is anybody waving?   Oh
Waving
Waving   Oh
Oh   Oh
Oh oh oh [18]

18 Justin Paul

This song initially ended without a coda. We thought we were being "smart" because in that version, it mirrored Evan retreating back into himself, but it played fairly anticlimactically onstage. We had to rethink it, but how could we justify a big ending? Well, Evan was feeling desperate—so couldn't he be screaming on the inside? We worked with Ben Platt to craft a new ending to the song that felt right. This is the first time we stop for a "hand" [applause] in the musical. The addition of the coda finally allowed the audience the chance to fully cheer for this character and the actor's terrific performance.

"When you're fallin' in a forest And there's nobody around…

"...Do you ever
really crash
Or even make
a sound?"

— EVAN

Heidi, in her nurse's scrubs, on her cell phone, a bit harried, an eye on the clock.

Evan, at school, on his phone.

HEIDI: Shit, honey. I know I was supposed to pick you up for your appointment. I'm stuck at work. Erica called in with the flu and I'm the only other nurse's aide on today, so I volunteered to pick up her shift . . .

(Evan is used to this, almost expected it.)

EVAN: It's fine.

HEIDI: It's just, they announced more budget cuts this morning, so anything I can do to show that I'm, you know, a team player . . .

EVAN: It's fine. I'll take the bus.

HEIDI *(Relieved)*: Perfect. That's perfect. Oh and I'm going straight from here to class, so I won't be home until late, so please eat something. We've got those Trader Joe's dumplings in the freezer . . .

EVAN: Maybe.[19]

HEIDI: Did you write one of those letters yet? Dr. Sherman's expecting you to have one. "Dear Evan Hansen. This is going to be a good day and here's why"?

EVAN *(Lying)*:[20] Yeah, no, I already finished it. I'm in the computer lab right now, printing it out.

HEIDI: I hope it was a good day, sweetheart.

EVAN: It was . . . yeah, it was really great.

HEIDI: Great. That's great. I hope it's the beginning of a great year. I think we both could use one of those, huh? Shit. I have to run. Bye. I love you.

(Heidi hangs up and goes.)

EVAN: Bye.

(A long moment alone. Evan opens his laptop and begins to compose his letter.)

Dear Evan Hansen:

It turns out, this wasn't an amazing day after all. This isn't going to be an amazing week or an amazing year. Because . . . why would it be?

Oh I know. Because there's Zoe. And all my hope is pinned on Zoe. Who I don't even know and who doesn't know me. But maybe if I did. Maybe if I could just talk to her, then maybe . . . maybe nothing would be different at all.

I wish that everything was different. I wish that I was a part of . . . something. I wish that anything I said . . . mattered, to anyone. I mean, face it: Would anybody even notice if I disappeared tomorrow?

Sincerely, your best and most dearest friend,

Me.

WAVING THROUGH A WINDOW
(Reprise) [21]

EVAN:

When you're fallin' in a forest
And there's nobody around
Do you ever really crash
Or even make a sound?

When you're fallin' in a forest
And there's nobody around
Do you ever really crash
Or even make a— [22]

[19] **Steven Levenson**

Clearly Evan doesn't enjoy Trader Joe's dumplings as much as I do.

[20] **Steven Levenson**

Even this early on in the musical, Evan is already lying to his mother.

[21] **Justin Paul**

The musical underscore for this song moment actually starts when Evan begins writing his therapy letter. When we started writing the show, there was talk about musicalizing the contents of Evan's letter. Fortunately, we realized that was ultimately a terrible idea and that the emotion we wanted could be found by reprising a more somber iteration of the "Waving" music, where Evan sings after having written the letter.

[22] **Justin Paul**

Steven is a little TRICKSTER and did a really cool thing that 99% of audience members and listeners don't notice. But it's still SUPER COOL. He cuts off "sound" in the lyric "make a sound" with Connor's first word, "so," which makes you feel like you're hearing the lyric but you're not. TRICKSTER! It was Steven's way of threading song into dialogue so you feel like the line punctuates the sung moment, even though it gets cut off. Brillz!

23 Steven Levenson

I originally imagined Connor signing his name in a completely conventional, unobtrusive manner. It was Mike's inspired idea to write "Connor" in those gigantic block letters. It instantly tells us so much about this person that he would think to write his name like that.

24 Steven Levenson

One of the many ways that Connor mirrors Evan is in the speed of his thought process. Like Evan, he races from one idea to the next. Unlike Evan, whose anxiety is always directed inward, Connor projects his fear and anger externally—everyone is always out to get him. Evan's brand of anxiety tends to curdle into self-loathing; Connor's transforms into paranoia.

(Connor enters, holding a piece of paper.)

CONNOR: So. What happened to your arm?

EVAN: Oh, I um, I fell out of a tree actually.

CONNOR (*Can't help but laugh*): You fell out of a tree? That is just the saddest fucking thing I've ever heard. Oh my God.

(Evan tries to laugh along.)

EVAN: I know.

CONNOR (*noticing*): No one's signed your cast.

EVAN: No, I know.

CONNOR: I'll sign it.

EVAN: Oh. Um . . . you don't have to.

CONNOR: Do you have a Sharpie?

(Beat. Evan reluctantly pulls out a Sharpie, hands it to Connor. Evan watches in dismay as Connor signs his name in an outsized scrawl, covering an entire side of the cast.) [23]

EVAN: Oh. Great. Thanks.

CONNOR: Now we can both pretend that we have friends.

EVAN: Good point.

(Evan takes the marker, turns to go. Connor holds out the piece of paper.)

CONNOR: Is this yours? I found it on the printer. "Dear Evan Hansen." That's your name, right?

(Evan feels a surge of fear.)

EVAN: Oh that's just a stupid, it's a paper I had to write for a, um, for an assignment . . .

(Connor looks down at the paper.)

CONNOR: "Because there's Zoe." (*Realizing*) Is this about my *sister*?

(Connor's mood shifts suddenly, abruptly.)

EVAN: No. Not at all.

CONNOR: You wrote this because you knew that I would find it.

EVAN: What?

CONNOR: You saw that I was the only other person in the computer lab, so you wrote this and you printed it out, so that I would find it.

EVAN: Why / would I do that?

CONNOR: / So I would read some creepy shit you wrote about my sister, and freak out, right? And then you can tell everyone that I'm crazy, right? [24]

EVAN: No. Wait. I don't even, what?

CONNOR: Fuck you.

(He exits with the letter, as Evan calls after him.)

EVAN: But I really, I need that back. Please. Can you just, can you please give it back?

WOULD ANYONE EVEN NOTICE

if I disappeared tomorrow?

25 Steven Levenson

In earlier drafts, Jared wondered specifically whether it was "erotic fiction."

26 Steven Levenson

In high school, I worked as a counselor in a summer camp. One of my campers suffered from severe emotional issues and would have explosive outbursts over seemingly minor issues. The selection of "line leader" was a particularly fraught subject. I was 16 and completely unqualified and unequipped to handle the situation. My "solution" was simply to name him the permanent de facto line leader. It worked.

27 Benj Pasek

At first, we weren't sure who should sing this reprise. It began as a trio for Alana, Zoe, and Jared with the intention of showing that all these young people privately shared the same sense of isolation. This felt a little forced when staged, so we gave the reprise to Connor. Doing so seemed to foreshadow his suicide and felt too dark in tone, which made the rest of the act feel uneven. Eventually, we decided to have Alana sing it as a solo. This planted the seed of her desperation for acceptance, so we understand her push to promote the Connor Project throughout the rest of the show.

Evan and Jared, online.

JARED: A letter to yourself? What the crap does that even mean? It's, like, some kind of sex thing? [25]

EVAN: No, it's not a sex thing. It's . . . it was an assignment.

JARED: Why are you talking to me about this?

EVAN: I didn't know who else to talk to. You're my only . . . family friend.

JARED *(Too pathetic to even engage)*: Oh my God.

EVAN: I don't know what to do. He stole the letter from me three days ago, and then he just, he hasn't been at school since.

JARED: That does not bode well for you.

EVAN: What is he going to do with it?

JARED: Who knows? Connor Murphy is batshit out of his mind. Do you remember when he threw a printer at Mrs. G. in second grade, because he didn't get to be line leader that day? [26]

EVAN: Do you think he's going to show the letter to other people?

JARED *(Obviously)*: He's going to ruin your life with it. For sure. I mean, I would.

(Lights out on Evan and Jared as Alana appears alone, scanning her phone for emails, texts, anything, all traces of her typical studied cheeriness gone entirely.)

WAVING THROUGH A WINDOW

(Reprise #2)[27]

ALANA:
On the outside always
  lookin' in
Will I ever be more than
  I've always been?
'Cause I'm tap-tap-tappin'
  on the glass
Waving through a window

< ACT ONE SCENE THREE >

28 Steven Levenson

I wanted to create an immediate, stark visual contrast between these two characters, to illustrate the gulf that separates them.

29 Steven Levenson

It was crucial to us that the first thing that Evan does when confronted with the misunderstanding is, in fact, to tell the truth.

30 Steven Levenson

Later, Jared will accuse Evan of fabricating his friendship with Connor purely out of self-interest. I don't find that to be true. To me, Evan's motivation for lying begins here, in this moment, in witnessing Cynthia's unbearable grief, her desperation to believe that her son left something—anything—meaningful behind.

31 Steven Levenson

Evan's broken arm is the hinge for so much that happens in this story. It's always incredible to me to remember that Benj, Justin, and I had been working on the musical for over two years before we even arrived at the idea of Evan having a broken arm.

The principal's office. Evan stands, confused. Cynthia Murphy and Larry Murphy sit.

Larry is stiff and sober, coiled fury just beneath the surface. Cynthia is shattered, reeling.[28]

They both look exhausted. Evan looks petrified.

EVAN: Good morning. Is Mr. Howard . . . ?

(They look at him, uncomprehending.)

I just, sorry, they said on the loudspeaker for me to go to the principal's office . . .

(Larry suddenly realizes what he means.)

LARRY: Mr. Howard is, uh, he stepped out.

EVAN: Oh.

LARRY: We wanted to speak with you in private. If you'd like to maybe . . .

(Larry gestures to a chair, and Evan slowly sits.)

We're, uh . . . we're Connor's parents.

EVAN: Oh.

(Cynthia reaches into her purse and pulls out a folded piece of paper. She holds it lovingly, almost cradling it.)

LARRY: Why don't you go ahead, honey, and . . . ?

CYNTHIA: I'm going as fast as I can.

LARRY: That's not what I said, is it?

(A terrible pause. Cynthia holds the letter out to Evan, her voice unsteady.)

CYNTHIA: This is . . . Connor . . . he wanted you to have this.

(Evan takes it, his face darkening.)

LARRY: We didn't . . . we'd never heard your name before, Connor never . . . but then we saw . . . "Dear Evan Hansen."

EVAN: He, um, he gave this to you?

LARRY: We didn't know that you two were friends.

EVAN: Friends?

LARRY: We didn't think that Connor had any friends. And then we see this note and it's, this seems to suggest pretty clearly that you and Connor were, or at least for Connor, he thought of you as . . .

(He points to the letter.)

I mean, it's right there. "Dear Evan Hansen." It's addressed to you. He wrote it to you.

EVAN *(Realizing)*: You think this is, you think that Connor wrote this to me.

CYNTHIA: These are the words he wanted to share with you.

LARRY: His last words.

CYNTHIA: This is what he wanted you to have.

EVAN: I'm sorry. What do you mean, last words?

(Cynthia and Larry share a look. A long, freighted silence.)

LARRY: Connor, uh, Connor took his own life.

EVAN *(Stunned)*: He . . . what?

LARRY: This is all we found with him. He had it folded up in his pocket.

(Beat.)

You can see that he's . . . he wanted to explain it, why he was . . .

(Larry recites it from memory:)

"I wish that everything was different. I wish that I were part of something. I wish that what I said mattered to / anyone."

CYNTHIA: / Please stop it, Larry.

(Evan feels the familiar rush of panic, his hands starting to sweat.)

EVAN: But, that's, this isn't . . . I'm sorry. Connor, um, Connor didn't write this. [29]

CYNTHIA: What does that mean?

EVAN: Connor didn't, he didn't write this.

CYNTHIA (To Larry): What does he mean?

LARRY: He's obviously in shock.

EVAN: No, I just, he didn't . . .

CYNTHIA (Pointing to the letter): It's right here.

EVAN: I'm sorry, but I should probably just, can I please go now?

CYNTHIA: If this isn't, if Connor didn't write this, / then . . .

LARRY: / Cynthia. Please. Calm down.

EVAN: I should go now.

CYNTHIA (Desperate to keep him here): But did he say anything to you? / Did you see anything—?

EVAN: / I really should go.

LARRY: Cynthia, honey. This is not the time.

CYNTHIA: This is all we have. This is the only thing we have left. [30]

LARRY: Honey. Listen to me. Please.

(Larry puts a hand on hers. She pulls away. She begins to break down, inconsolable.)

Cynthia.

(Evan holds out the letter to them, urgently, as though he cannot get it out of his hands quickly enough.)

EVAN: You should just, you should take it. Please.

(Suddenly, Cynthia gasps.)

CYNTHIA: Larry. Look.

(She points to Evan's arm.)

His cast.

(Evan looks down. He lifts up his cast and realizes what Cynthia has seen: "Connor" in a Sharpie scrawl. Cynthia turns to Larry, her eyes welling with tears of astonishment.)

His best and most dearest friend. [31]

"Connor took his own life."
—LARRY

Evan and Jared, online.

JARED: Holy. Shit. [32]

EVAN: I didn't say anything. I just, I couldn't say anything.

JARED: Holy. Fucking. Shit. [33]

EVAN: They invited me for dinner. They want to know more stuff about Connor and me, about our "friendship."

(Elsewhere, Alana appears in a pin spot of light, online, alone.)

ALANA (*Stunned*): Still can't believe the terrible news about @ConnorMurphy.

JARED: What are you going to tell them?

EVAN: I mean, the truth.

ALANA: I wouldn't say that we were "friends" exactly. More like acquaintances.

JARED: The truth. Really. You're going to go to the Murphys' house and explain that the only thing

left they have of their son is some weird sex letter that you wrote to yourself?

ALANA: We were in Chemistry together. I'm pretty sure.

JARED: You know, you could go to jail for this. If you get caught?

EVAN: But I didn't do anything.

ALANA: He was also, he was in my English class in tenth grade. I'm almost positive.

JARED: Yeah, I hate to tell you this, Evan, but you may have already perjured yourself.

EVAN: Isn't that only when you're under oath? Like, in a court room?

JARED: Well, weren't you under oath? In a way?

EVAN: No.

ALANA: Yeah, he was definitely in my English class.

JARED: Look, do you want to listen to me or do you want to have another meltdown like last year in English when you were supposed to give that speech [34] about Daisy Buchanan, but instead you just stood there staring at your notecards and saying, "um, um, um," over and over again like you were having a brain aneurysm?

EVAN: What do you expect me to do? Just keep lying?

JARED: I didn't say, "lie." All you have to do is just nod and confirm. Whatever they say about Connor, you just nod your head and you say, "Yeah, that's true." Don't contradict and don't make shit up. It's foolproof. Literally, nothing I tell my parents is true and they have no idea.

ALANA: Three days ago, Connor Murphy was here and now . . . now he's gone.

EVAN: They were so sad. His parents? His mom was just . . . I've never seen anyone so sad before.

JARED: Well, then good thing you're about to tell her the truth about your sex letter. I'm sure that will cheer her right up.

(Evan considers this, as Alana stares out, plaintively, yearning.)

ALANA: If Connor meant something to you, please re-tweet. Or private message me if you just want to talk. At times like these, we could all use a friend.

32 Steven Levenson

As usual, Jared knows just how to capture what we in the audience are thinking...

33 Steven Levenson

And with such eloquence...

34 Steven Levenson

I added this anecdote of Jared's midway through previews at Second Stage, so that later—when we in the audience hear Cynthia introduce the idea of Evan giving a "speech" for Connor—we immediately know what that word means for Evan.

Dinner at the Murphys.

Prominently, in the center of the table, a bowl of fresh apples. Evan is afraid to move or make a sound.

Larry serves himself seconds.

LARRY: Would anyone else like some more chicken?

CYNTHIA: I think you're the only one with an appetite, Larry.

LARRY (*Defensive*): The Harrises brought it over.

CYNTHIA (*To Evan*): Did Connor tell you about the Harrises?

(*Evan nods.*)

We used to go skiing together, our families.

EVAN (*Nods*): Connor loved skiing.

ZOE: Connor hated skiing.

EVAN: Well, right. That's what I meant. Connor loved . . . talking about how much he hated skiing. [35]

(*Zoe just stares at him.*)

CYNTHIA: So you guys, you . . . you hung out a lot? [36]

EVAN: Pretty much.

ZOE: Where?

EVAN: Oh you mean, like, where did we . . . ? Well, we mostly hung out at my house. I mean, sometimes we'd come to his house if nobody else was here. We would email a lot, though, mostly. So we wouldn't have to, he didn't want to always hang out. In person, you know?

ZOE: We looked through his emails. There aren't any from you.

EVAN: Well, no, of course, yeah, I mean, that's because he had a different account. A secret account. I should have said that before. That was probably very confusing.

ZOE: Why was it secret?

EVAN: Just so that no one else could, it was more private, I guess, that way.

CYNTHIA (*To Larry*): He knew you read his emails.

LARRY: Somebody had to be the bad guy.

(*A tense pause.*)

ZOE (*To Evan*): The weird thing is, the only time I ever saw you and my brother together was when he shoved you at school last week.

CYNTHIA: He shoved you?

EVAN: I um . . . I tripped.

ZOE: I was there. I saw the whole thing. He pushed you, hard.

EVAN: *Oh.* I remember now. That was a misunderstanding. Because, the thing was, he didn't want us to talk at school, and I tried to talk to him at school. It wasn't that big a thing. It was my fault.

ZOE: Why didn't he want you to talk to him at school?

EVAN: He didn't really want people to know we were friends. I guess he was embarrassed. A little.

CYNTHIA: Why would he be embarrassed?

EVAN: Um. I guess because he thought I was sort of, you know . . .

ZOE: A nerd?

LARRY: Zoe.

ZOE: Isn't that what you meant?

EVAN: Loser, I was going to say, actually. But. Nerd works, too.

CYNTHIA: That wasn't very nice.

ZOE: Well, Connor wasn't very nice, so that makes sense.

(Cynthia takes a breath, struggles to maintain her poise.)

CYNTHIA: Connor was . . . he was a complicated person.

ZOE: No, Connor was a bad person. There's a difference.

LARRY: Zoe, please.

ZOE (To Larry): Don't pretend like you don't agree with me.

(Cynthia's distress grows more and more difficult for Evan to watch.)

CYNTHIA: You refuse to remember any of the good things. / You refuse to see anything positive.

ZOE: / Because there were no good things. What were the good things?

CYNTHIA: I don't want to have this conversation in front of our guest.

ZOE: What were the good things, Mom? / Tell me.

CYNTHIA: / There were good things.

(Before even thinking, Evan finds the words tumbling out.)

EVAN: I remember a lot of good things about Connor.

(All eyes turn to him at once, as he realizes what he's done.)

ZOE: Like what?

EVAN: Never mind. I shouldn't have, I'm sorry, never mind.

CYNTHIA: No, Evan. You were saying something.

EVAN: It doesn't matter. Really.

CYNTHIA: We want to hear what you have to say. Please. [37]

(Beat.)

EVAN: Well, I was just . . . Connor and I . . . we had a really great time together, this one day, recently.

(Evan keeps talking, unsure if he's connecting or not.)

That's something good that I remember about Connor. That's what I keep thinking about. That day.

(His eyes land on the bowl of apples in front of him.)

At the apples, um . . . the apples . . . place.

(Beat.)

Anyway. It's, I knew it was stupid. I don't know why I even brought it up.

CYNTHIA: / He took you to the orchard?

(Evan looks at Cynthia, sees the hope in her eyes. Even Zoe has turned silent.)

EVAN: Yes. He did.

CYNTHIA: When?

EVAN: Once. It was just that once.But. He said the apples there were the best.

LARRY: I thought that place closed. Years ago.

EVAN: Exactly. Which is why we were so bummed when we got there, because it was completely, it's totally closed down now.

CYNTHIA: We used to go to the orchard all the time. We'd do picnics out there. Remember that, Zoe?

ZOE: Yeah. I do.

CYNTHIA (To Larry): You and Connor had that little toy plane you would fly. Until you flew it into the creek.

LARRY (Can't help but smile): That was an emergency landing.

CYNTHIA (To Evan): I can't believe he took you there. I bet that was fun. I bet you two, I bet you had fun.

EVAN: We did. The whole day was just . . .

< ACT ONE SCENE SIX >

FOR FOREVER

EVAN:

End of May or early June [38]
This picture-perfect
afternoon we share

CYNTHIA (*To Larry*): What was the name of that ice cream place out there we loved?

LARRY: À La Mode.

CYNTHIA: That was it. À La Mode. And they had that homemade hot fudge . . .

EVAN:

Drive the
winding
country
road
Grab a scoop at "À La
Mode" and then . . .
we're there [39]

CYNTHIA: We'd sit in that meadow with all the sycamores. (*To Zoe*) And you and your brother would look for four-leaf clovers.

EVAN:

An open field that's
framed with trees
We pick a spot and
shoot the breeze like
buddies do
Quoting songs by our
fav'rite bands
Telling jokes no one
understands
except us two
And we talk and
take in the view

All we see is sky
for forever [40]
We let the world pass by
for forever
Feels like we could go on
for forever
This way
Two friends
on a
perfect
day

LARRY: I'd completely forgotten about that place.

CYNTHIA: Well, I guess Connor didn't. (*Looks to Evan*) Did he?

EVAN:

We walk a while and talk
about [41]
The things we'll do when
we get out of school
Bike the Appalachian Trail
Or write a book, or learn
to sail
Wouldn't that be cool?
There's nothing that we
can't discuss
Like, girls we wish would
notice us but never do
He looks around and says
to me,
"There's nowhere else I'd
rather be," and I say,
"Me too"
And we talk and
take in the view
We just talk
and take
in the view

All we see is sky for
forever
We let the world pass by
for forever
Feels like we could go on
for forever
This way
This way
All we see is light for
forever
'Cause the sun shines
bright for forever
We could be all right
for forever this way
Two friends on a
perfect day

And there he goes
Racin' toward the
tallest tree [42]
From far across a
yellow field
I hear him callin',
"Follow me"
There we go
Wonderin' how the world
might look from up
so high
One foot after the other
One branch, then to
another
I climb higher and higher
I climb 'til the entire sun
shines on my face
And I suddenly feel the
branch give way
I'm on the ground
My arm goes numb
I look around

And I see him come to
get me
He's come to get me
And ev'rything's okay

All we see is sky
for forever
We let the world pass by
for forever
Buddy, you and I for
forever this way
This way
All we see is light
'Cause the sun burns
bright
We could be all right for
forever this way
Two friends
True friends
On a perfect day

(Cynthia slowly crosses to Evan.
She hugs him, hard.)

CYNTHIA: Thank you, Evan.
Thank you. Thank you. Thank you.
Thank you.

---

38 Benj Pasek

We wrote this song before we did a specific sequence of events. Once we created the timeline, we figured out that this lyric wouldn't make sense. Casts usually stay on for six to eight weeks, and if the school year starts in September, the math is a little fuzzy. But we liked the lyric, and decided that Evan probably wouldn't have gotten the math straight because he was making up the story on the spot. In a way, it worked for us because the Murphys could have figured out the lie right away if they had been paying attention. Our thought was that their desire to believe in this story was as great as Evan's desire to make it true.

39 Justin Paul

We wanted to find a name for an ice cream shop that was also a helpful rhyme, so we came up with "À La Mode." And Steven, God bless him, rejected it because he didn't feel the name was consistent with a shop that would be in their town. But the funny thing about a script is that if you leave something in the lyrics long enough, it stays there until people forget they have an issue with it. Sorry, Steven!

40 Benj Pasek

As the chorus begins, we hear of Evan's imagined perfect day with Connor in the orchard. Michael Greif and the design team changed the visuals on the panels so you see less of the digital world and more of the fantasy Evan is creating. As he becomes more engrossed in his own story, the dark colors and text give way to greens, blues, clouds, and trees.

41 Benj Pasek

This is the moment where Evan begins to embrace the fantasy of what it would be like to have a friend. He forgets he is telling a story and dives into his own desires. This culminates in the bridge where Evan re-creates the story of falling from the tree—but someone is there to help him up. Here, the song isn't just about relieving Cynthia of her pain. The lines blur. Now, Evan is also singing it to heal himself.

42 Justin Paul

We toyed with not musicalizing this moment and putting it in dialogue because we thought it was so crucial that people understood this pivotal plot point—that Evan is, in the euphoria of imagining a day with an actual friend, changing the story of how he broke his arm. But the emotion required music, so it resulted in an epically long bridge that let us take the time needed to spell it all out. Props to Steven, who wrote that beautiful monologue that inspired it.

43 **Steven Levenson**

Jared's function in the show is often to puncture deep emotional moments before we run the risk of tipping into sentimentality. It's actually quite difficult for an actor to step onstage and entirely undercut the tone and feeling of the previous scene, but Will Roland makes it seem effortless.

44 **Steven Levenson**

Jared is clearly a terrific negotiator.

45 **Steven Levenson**

Heidi doesn't always have what you would call a healthy sense of boundaries...

Evan and Jared, online.

JARED: His parents think you were lovers.[43] You realize that, right?

EVAN: What? Why would they think that?

JARED: Um. You were best friends but he wouldn't let you talk to him at school? And when you did, he kicked your ass? That's like the exact formula for secret gay high school lovers.

EVAN: Oh my God.

JARED: This is why I told you—what did I tell you? You just nod and confirm.

EVAN: I tried to. I just, you don't understand. I got nervous and I started talking, and then once I started, I just . . .

JARED: You couldn't stop.

EVAN (*Realizing the truth of this as he says it*): They didn't want me to stop.

JARED: So what else did you completely fuck up?

EVAN: Nothing. Seriously.

(*Beat.*)

I mean, I told them we wrote emails.

JARED: Emails.

EVAN: Yeah. I told them that Connor and I, Connor had a secret email account . . .

JARED: Oh, right. One of those "secret" email accounts. Sure. For sending pictures of your penises to each other.

EVAN (*Ignoring this*): Yeah and so I said, he had this secret account, and we would send emails to each other.

JARED: I mean, honestly? Could you be any worse at this?

EVAN (*It suddenly occurs to him*): They're going to want to see our emails.

JARED (*Sarcastic*): You think?

EVAN: What am I going to do?

JARED: I can do emails.

EVAN: How?

JARED: It's easy. You make up an account, backdate the emails. There's a reason I was the only CIT with key card access to the computer cluster this summer: I have skills, son.

EVAN: You would do that?

JARED: For two grand.

EVAN: Two thousand dollars?

JARED: Five hundred.

EVAN: I can give you twenty.

JARED: Fine.[44] But you're a dick.

(*Lights out on Jared. Heidi enters Evan's bedroom, carrying a sheaf of papers, still in her work clothes.*)

HEIDI: Hey you. I have some very exciting news. Look what I found online today: college scholarship essay contests. Have you heard of these?

EVAN: I think so . . .

HEIDI: NPR did a whole thing about it this morning. There are a million different ones you can do. A million different topics. I spent my whole lunch break looking these up.

(She hands him the pages, summarizing each one as she does.)

The John F. Kennedy Profile in Courage Scholarship— three thousand dollars, college of your choice. Henry David Thoreau Society, five thousand dollars . . .

EVAN: Wow.

HEIDI: College is going to be so great for you, honey. How many times in life do you get the chance to just . . . start all over again?

EVAN: No, I know.

HEIDI: You've got so much, so many wonderful things ahead of you. High school isn't always . . . the only people that like high school are cheerleaders and football players and those people all end up miserable anyway. Yeah, you're going to find yourself in college. I really think so. I mean, I wish I could go with you . . . but . . .

(Sensing Evan's lack of enthusiasm, Heidi begins to feel a bit embarrassed.)

I just thought these were . . . it seemed like a neat idea.

EVAN: It is. For sure.

HEIDI: You've always been a wonderful writer. And we're going to need all the help we can get for college. Unless your stepmother has a trust fund for you I don't know about, with all those fabulous tips she made cocktail waitressing . . . [45]

(Evan pretends to laugh along, as Heidi struggles to find a transition.)

Hey. I, um, I got an email from your school today. About a boy who killed himself? Connor Murphy? I didn't, I had no idea.

EVAN: Oh. Yeah. Well . . . I didn't really know him.

HEIDI: You know that . . . if you ever, if you want to talk about anything . . . I realize that lately it must feel like, I'm always working or I'm in class . . .

EVAN: It's fine.

HEIDI: Well, I'm here. And if I'm not here here, I'm a phone call away. Or text. Email. Whatever.

EVAN: Thanks.

(Heidi, unable to ignore the obvious any longer, points to Evan's cast.)

HEIDI: All right. It says, "Connor."

EVAN: Oh. Yeah. No.

HEIDI: You said you didn't know him.

EVAN: No. I didn't. This is . . . it's a different Connor.

(Heidi sighs, relieved, as she smiles at her own anxiety.)

HEIDI: I was so worried.

EVAN: No. I'm sure.

HEIDI *(Brightening)*: Hey, you know what? How about I bag my shift next Tuesday? When's the last time we did a Taco Tuesday?

EVAN: Oh. You don't have to.

HEIDI: No, you've been back at school for a week already and I've barely seen you. Maybe we could even start brainstorming those essay questions together . . .

EVAN: That would be great.

HEIDI: Oh. That's exciting. I'm excited now. Something to look forward to.

EVAN: Me too.

(Heidi picks up the bottle of pills by his bed, asks gingerly:)

HEIDI: Are you okay on refills?

EVAN: Yes.

HEIDI: Well. Don't stay up too late.

EVAN: I won't.

HEIDI: I love you.

EVAN: I love you, too.

(She stands there in the doorway for a moment, hesitating, unsettled somehow. Finally, she shuts the door.)

SINCERELY, ME [46]

46 Justin Paul

The scene: Arena Stage—2015—the three of us writers huddle in the back of the theater holding our collective breath as this song, the biggest tonal risk in the show, begins. We have no idea if the audience will be OK with us having Connor come back into the story this way. We get to the "nipples" line, where we know we will sink or swim based on the audience response, and they laugh! They were willing to go on the ride, and regardless of whether we had a million things to fix and change...we knew in that moment that the patient—our show—still had a fighting chance.

47 Steven Levenson

This line used to be: "Lame." I changed it to "Kinky" during previews on Broadway. It may be my favorite piece of writing in the show.

48 Justin Paul

Funny enough, this was one of the last changes Steven made to the libretto on Broadway, and yes, we are obsessed with it.

A spotlight. Connor, wearing the clothes we last saw him in, steps into it.

CONNOR:

Dear Evan Hansen:
We've been way too out
of touch
Things have been crazy
And it sucks that we don't
talk that much
But I should tell you that
I think of you each night
I rub my nipples and start
moaning with delight

(Lights snap up on Jared, seated, typing on a laptop, as Evan stands, reading over his shoulder with dismay.)

EVAN: Why would you write that?

JARED: I'm just trying to tell the truth.

EVAN: You know, if you're not going to take this seriously—

JARED: Okay, you need to calm yourself.

EVAN: This needs to be perfect. These emails have to prove that we were actually friends. They have to be completely realistic.

JARED: There is nothing unrealistic about the love that one man feels for another.

EVAN: Just, let's go back.

JARED: In fact, some would say there's something quite beautiful . . .

EVAN: Let's go back, Jared.

CONNOR:

I gotta tell you, life without
you has been hard

JARED (*Laughing*): Hard?

CONNOR:

Has been bad

JARED (*Meh*): Bad?

CONNOR:

Has been rough

JARED (*Just right*): Kinky. [47, 48]

CONNOR:

And I miss talking about
life and other stuff

JARED: Very specific.

EVAN: Shut up.

CONNOR:

I like my parents—

JARED: Who says that?

CONNOR:

I love my parents
But each day's another fight
If I stop smoking drugs
Then ev'rything might be
*   all right*

JARED: "Smoking drugs"? [49]

EVAN: Just fix it.

JARED: This isn't realistic at all. It
doesn't even sound like Connor.

EVAN: I want to show that I was, like,
a good friend. That I was trying to
help him. You know?

JARED: Oh my God . . .

CONNOR:

If I stop smoking crack—

EVAN (*Aghast*): Crack?

CONNOR:

If I stop smoking pot
Then ev'rything might be
*   all right*
I'll take your advice
I'll try to be more nice
I'll turn it around
Wait and see

'Cause all that it takes is a
*   little reinvention*
It's easy to change if you
*   give it your attention*
All you gotta do
Is just believe you can be
*   who you wanna be* [50]
Sincerely, me

JARED: Are we done yet?

EVAN: I can't just show them *one*
email.

JARED: Okay. Please stop
hyperventilating.

EVAN: I'm not hyperventilating.

JARED: You're having considerable
trouble breathing.

EVAN: I'm having no trouble
breathing.

JARED: Do you need a paper bag to
breathe in?

EVAN: I am NOT
HYPERVENTILATING.

Dear Connor Murphy:
Yes, I also miss our talks
Stop doing drugs
Just try to take deep
*   breaths and go on walks*

JARED: No . . .

EVAN:

I'm sending pictures of the
*   most amazing trees*

JARED: No . . .

EVAN:
You'll be obsessed with
all my forest expertise

JARED: Absolutely not.

EVAN:
Dude, I'm proud of you
Just keep pushing through
You're turnin' around
I can see

CONNOR:
Just wait and see

EVAN/CONNOR:
'Cause all that it takes is
a little reinvention
It's easy to change if you
give it your attention
All you gotta do
Is just believe you can be
who you wanna be
Sincerely . . .

EVAN:
Me.

CONNOR:
My sister's hot.

EVAN (*To Jared*): What the hell?

JARED: My bad.

CONNOR:
Dear Evan Hansen:
Thanks for ev'ry note
you send

EVAN:
Dear Connor Murphy:
I'm just glad to be your
friend

EVAN/CONNOR:
Our friendship goes
beyond
Your av'rage kind of bond

EVAN:
But not because we're gay

CONNOR:
No, not because we're gay

EVAN/CONNOR:
We're close but not
that way
The only man
That I love
Is my dad

CONNOR:
Well, anyway

EVAN:
You're getting better
ev'ry day

CONNOR:
I'm getting better
ev'ry day

EVAN:
Keep

CONNOR:
Getting

EVAN:
Better

CONNOR:
Ev—

EVAN:
—'ry

EVAN/CONNOR/JARED:
Day
Hey! Hey! Hey! Hey!

EVAN/CONNOR/JARED (CON'T):
'Cause all that it takes is
a little reinvention
It's easy to change if you
give it

EVAN/JARED:
Your

CONNOR:
Your

EVAN/JARED:
A-

CONNOR:
A-

EVAN/CONNOR/JARED:
-ttention
All you gotta do
Is just believe you can be
who you wanna be
Sincerely,

CONNOR/EVAN:
Miss you dearly

JARED/EVAN/CONNOR:
Sincerely, me

EVAN:
Sincerely, me

EVAN/CONNOR/JARED:
Sincerely, me
Sincerely, me

Larry and Cynthia sit in the living room, reading from a stack of printed pages.

Evan stands, anxiously awaiting some kind of response.

EVAN: These were just some of the emails I found.

(Silence.)

I mean, I can print out more. I have a lot more. Connor and I emailed all the time.

CYNTHIA: It's ... difficult. To read these. It doesn't sound like Connor.

(Evan realizes that he's made a terrible mistake.)

EVAN: I'm sorry. I um ... Maybe, I shouldn't have ...

CYNTHIA: No, no. I just ... gosh, I don't remember the last time I heard him laugh.[51] But you two, you would ...?

EVAN: No, yeah, we would, we laughed all the time.

CYNTHIA: There are more of these? More emails?

EVAN: More ...? Yeah. There are a lot more.

CYNTHIA: We would love to see them. We would love to see everything.

(She looks to Larry, who has said nothing.)

Wouldn't we?

LARRY: Mmhmm.

(Zoe enters, freezing when she sees Evan.)

ZOE: Why are you here?

CYNTHIA: Oh Zoe. Wait until you see what Evan brought us—emails from your brother.

LARRY: How was your first day back?

ZOE *(Dry)*: Terrific. All of a sudden, everyone wants to be my friend. I'm the dead kid's sister, didn't you know?[52]

CYNTHIA: I'm sure they mean well.

EVAN *(Taking the hint)*: I should probably go.

CYNTHIA: You're not staying for dinner?

EVAN: Oh. Well. Just. I hadn't planned on it ...

"Connor and
I emailed
all the time."

– E V A N

CYNTHIA: Then we'll do another night. I can cook something for you . . .

EVAN: You don't have to.

CYNTHIA: It would be my pleasure. We would love to have you.

(Cynthia looks to Zoe and Larry for affirmation. Neither says anything. Larry, picking up on the tension, motions to Evan.)

LARRY: Why don't I show you out?

EVAN: Oh. Thanks.

(Evan and Larry go, as Cynthia turns to Zoe.)

CYNTHIA: So. How was band today? I bet they're happy to have you back, huh?

ZOE: You really don't have to do this, okay?

CYNTHIA: Do what?

ZOE: Just because Connor isn't here, trying to punch through my door, screaming at the top of his lungs that he's going to kill me for no reason—that doesn't mean that, all of a sudden, we're the fucking Brady Bunch.

CYNTHIA: We are all grieving in our own way. I know how much you miss your brother. We all do.

(Cynthia sets down a stack of emails on the sofa, looks at Zoe.)

You can read these when you're ready.

(Cynthia exits. Zoe halfheartedly flips through the emails. She puts them down, instantly dismissive.)

---

51 Steven Levenson

In earlier drafts, Cynthia spoke at length here about Connor's history of mental illness. It always felt overly explanatory, overly clinical—like we were getting rid of all of the complexity and mystery of Connor as a person and turning him into a generic diagnosis, an entry in the DSM. I kept making the section shorter and shorter, cutting more and more, until this single sentence was all that remained. I realized it was all we really needed.

52 Steven Levenson

In a much earlier draft, we had a scene at school in which Alana approached Zoe with her condolences, offering a hug, trying to be her friend. That scene was eventually condensed into this one sentence.

All of a sudden,

EVERYONE WANTS TO BE MY FRIEND.

I'm the
dead kid's sister...

REQUIEM [53]

ZOE:

Why should I play this
game of pretend [54]
Remembering through a
secondhand sorrow?
Such a great son and
wonderful friend
Oh, don't the tears just
pour?

I could curl up and hide in
my room
There in my bed still
sobbing tomorrow
I could give in to all of
the gloom
But tell me, tell me what for?

Why should I have a
Heavy heart?
Why should I start to
break in pieces?
Why should I go and fall
apart for you?

Why
Should I play the grieving
girl and lie?
Saying that I miss you and
that my
World has gone dark
without your light
I will sing no requiem
tonight

[53] **Benj Pasek**

There was an earlier song that existed for Zoe called "Hiding in Your Hands." In it, Zoe talked about the happy public personas of her family members before Connor's death, juxtaposed with the pain she felt privately. During readings of the piece, we realized that the song, while about Zoe, really needed to be about her relationship with Connor more than her relationship with her parents. We then crafted the song "Requiem," where she is singing directly to Connor. The initial description for the content of the song was "I refuse to cry for you."

[54] **Justin Paul**

Writing this song was all about lighting some candles and throwing on the Ingrid Michaelson-Adele-Madi Diaz-Mindy Smith playlist. Okay not exactly, but sort of? We wanted to write in a style of music that Zoe might listen to—that sweet spot of balancing indie, singer-songwriter, and pop.

< ACT ONE SCENE NINE >

(Light reveals Cynthia in Connor's bedroom, sitting on his bed, reading emails. Larry enters, stands in the doorway.)

LARRY: I'm going to bed.

CYNTHIA: Come sit with me.

LARRY (*Sighs*): Cynthia . . .

CYNTHIA: You can't stand to be in his room for five minutes.

LARRY: I'm exhausted.

CYNTHIA: You know, Larry, at some point, you're going to have to / start . . .

LARRY: / Not tonight. Please.

(She holds out one of the printed emails.)

CYNTHIA: Just read this.

(Reluctantly, Larry takes the email without even glancing at it.)

LARRY: I'll leave the light on for you.

(He goes, stepping into the hallway.)

*I gave you the world, you
threw it away*

"I will sing no requiem tonight"

– CYNTHIA

Leaving these broken
pieces behind you
Ev'rything wasted,
nothing to say

CYNTHIA:
I hear your voice and feel
you near
Within these words
I finally find you

So I can sing no requiem

And now that I know that
you are still here
I will sing no requiem
tonight

ZOE/LARRY:
Why should I have a
heavy heart?

Within
these words
**I FINALLY
FIND YOU.**

ZOE:

Why should I say

I'll keep you with me?
Why should I go and
Fall apart for you?

Why
Should I play the grieving
Girl and lie?
Saying that I miss you
And that

My world
Has gone dark

Without
Your light
I will sing no requiem
Tonight

'Cause when the villains fall
The kingdoms never weep
No one lights
A candle to remember

No, no one mourns at all
When they lay them down
To sleep

So don't tell me that I
Didn't have it right

Don't tell me that it
Wasn't black and white

After all you put me
through
Don't say it wasn't true
That you were not the
monster
That I knew

'Cause I

CYNTHIA:

I'll keep you with me

CYNTHIA/LARRY:

Ah

Ah

LARRY:

My world
Has gone dark

CYNTHIA:

I can see
Your light [55]

Ah
Ah Ah

Ah
Ah Ah

Ah

Ah

"After all you put me through, don't say it wasn't true…

Cannot play the grieving
girl and lie
Saying that I miss you
And that my world has
gone dark . . .

LARRY:

I will sing no requiem

CYNTHIA:

I will sing no requiem

ZOE:

I will sing no requiem
Tonight

CYNTHIA/LARRY:

Oh Oh

ZOE:

Oh

ZOE/CYNTHIA/LARRY:

Oh

55 **Benj Pasek**

There was another song for
Cynthia's character called "A Little
Bit of Light" that was cut. We
were sitting in Cynthia and Larry's
grief for too long, instead of
tracking Evan's story. Originally,
"Requiem" was a solo, but once
we cut "A LIttle Bit of Light,"
"Requiem" became a trio for the
entire Murphy family to explore
processing the death of Connor.
We even included Cynthia's
old lyric idea of "I can see your
light" to show her the reimagined
version of her son.

...that you were
not the monster
that I knew."

– ZOE

56 Steven Levenson

Evan feels both horrified and exhilarated by this idea that the entire school is talking about him. It's awful and intoxicating all at once.

Evan and Alana, online.

ALANA: Evan. Hey, it's Alana. How are you? How is everything?

EVAN: Um. Fine. Thanks . . .

ALANA: Oh my God. Jared has been telling everyone about you and Connor, how close you guys were, how you were like best friends . . .

EVAN (*Troubled*): Oh.

ALANA: Everyone is talking about how brave you've been this week.

EVAN: They are? 56

ALANA: I mean, anybody else in your position would be falling apart. Dana P. was crying so hard at lunch yesterday, she pulled a muscle in her face. She had to go to the hospital.

EVAN: Isn't Dana P. new this year? She didn't even know Connor.

ALANA: That's why she was crying. Because now she'll never get the chance. Connor is really bringing the school together. It's pretty incredible. People I've never talked to before, they want to talk to me now, because they know how much Connor meant to me. It's very inspiring. I actually started a blog about him, like a sort of memorial page . . .

EVAN (*Nervous for a moment*): Were you friends with Connor, too?

ALANA: Acquaintances. But close acquaintances.

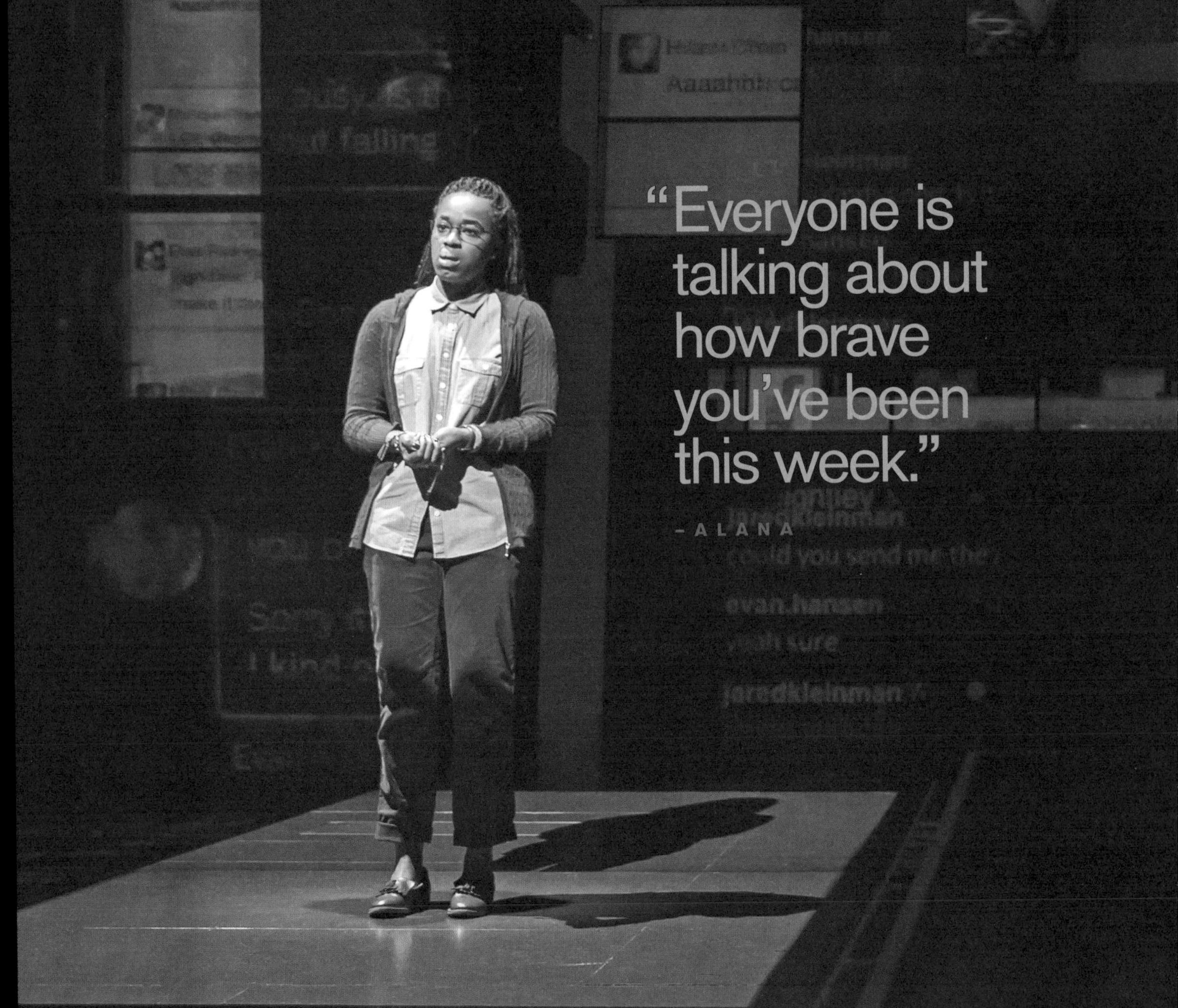

"Everyone is talking about how brave you've been this week."
— ALANA

(Evan nods, relieved.)

Can I tell you something? I think part of me always knew that you guys were friends. You did a good job of hiding it. But. I don't know.

(Heidi enters.)

I could just tell.

HEIDI: Who are you talking to on the computer?

(Evan quickly shuts the laptop and Alana disappears.)

EVAN: Oh. Um. Just Jared. It was Jared.

HEIDI *(Pleased)*: It seems like you and Jared are spending more time together. I've always said he's a great friend for you . . .

EVAN: Yeah, really great.

HEIDI: I'm proud of you. Putting yourself out there.

EVAN: Thanks.

HEIDI *(Turning to go)*: Well, I'm leaving, but I left money on the table. Order anything you want, okay?

EVAN: I thought we were doing tacos tonight. Looking at the essay questions.

HEIDI *(Suddenly remembering)*: It's Tuesday. Oh my God. Oh honey. I completely forgot. Shit.

EVAN: That's okay.

(She tries quickly to put a good face on things, spinning this as a positive development.) [57]

HEIDI: You know what? You should go ahead and take a look at the

questions without me. And then if you have any ideas, you can email me, and I can write back with any ideas that I have . . . That's better anyway, isn't it? That way you can really take your time?

EVAN *(Hiding his disappointment)*: No. Yeah. For sure.

HEIDI: We can do tacos another night, Evan. We could do tomorrow night. How about tomorrow night?

EVAN: I can't tomorrow. I have . . . I'm busy.

HEIDI *(Glancing at the time)*: Shit. I'm late.

EVAN: You should go.

HEIDI: No, let's figure this out.

EVAN: It's fine.

HEIDI: Evan . . .

EVAN: I'll make dinner for myself.

(Evan exits, leaving Heidi there in his bedroom, stricken with guilt, as lights snap up on Cynthia, calling upstairs from the Murphys' kitchen.) [58]

CYNTHIA: Dinner will be ready in ten minutes, Evan. I hope you're hungry . . .

57 Steven Levenson

Heidi is constantly doing this throughout the musical—trying to recast a disappointing development as somehow good news. It's one of my favorite things about her actually: her boundless optimism.

58 Steven Levenson

We had a lot of trouble figuring out the transition here from this scene to the next, when we landed on the idea of visually juxtaposing the two mothers. Metaphorically, we're watching as Evan begins to drift from one family to another.

Cynthia goes as lights find Evan standing in Connor's bedroom, alone, looking around, a complete stranger. [59]

A long beat. Zoe enters.

ZOE: Why are you in my brother's room?

EVAN (*Caught by surprise*): I was just waiting for—

ZOE: Don't your parents get upset that you're here all the time?

EVAN: Well, it's not like I'm, I'm not here all the time . . .

ZOE: Just two nights in a row.

EVAN: Well. It's just my mom and she works most nights. Or she's in class.

ZOE: Class for what?

EVAN: Legal stuff.

ZOE: Where's your dad?

EVAN: My dad is um . . . he lives in Colorado. He left when I was seven. So. He doesn't really mind either.

(Pause. Evan stands there, awkward.)

Your parents . . . they're really great.

ZOE (*Matter of fact*): They can't stand each other. They fight all the time.

EVAN: Everyone's parents fight.

ZOE: My dad's, like, in total denial. He didn't even cry at the funeral.

(Beat. Not knowing what to say, Evan changes the subject.)

EVAN: Your mom was saying, gluten-free lasagna for dinner. That sounds really . . .

ZOE: Inedible?

EVAN (*Laughs*): You're lucky your mom cooks. My mom and I just order pizza most nights.

ZOE: You're lucky you're allowed to eat pizza.

EVAN: You're not allowed to eat pizza?

ZOE: We can now, I guess. My mom was Buddhist last year so we weren't allowed to eat animal products.

EVAN: She was Buddhist last year but not this year?

ZOE: That's sort of what she does. She gets into different things. For a while it was Pilates, then it was The Secret, then Buddhism. Now it's free-range, Omnivore's Dilemma . . . whatever. [60]

EVAN: It's cool that she's interested in so much different stuff.

ZOE: She's not. That's just what happens when you're rich and you don't have a job. You get crazy.

EVAN: My mom always says it's better to be rich than poor.

ZOE: Well your mom's probably never been rich then.

EVAN: You've probably never been poor.

(Beat.)

Oh my God. I can't believe I just said that. I'm so sorry. That was completely rude.

ZOE (*Laughs*): Wow. I didn't realize you were actually capable of saying something that wasn't nice.

EVAN: No, I'm not. I never say things that aren't nice. I don't even *think*

sorry.

ZOE: I was impressed. You're ruining it.

EVAN: I'm sorry.

ZOE: You really don't have to keep saying that.

(Beat.)

EVAN: Okay.

(Beat.)

ZOE: You want to say it again, don't you?

EVAN: Very much so, yes.

(They smile a little.)

ZOE: You're weird.

ZOE (*Difficult to ask*): Why did he say that? In his note?

(Evan looks at her, unsure what she means. She's embarrassed to have to say it out loud.)

"Because there's Zoe. And all my hope is pinned on Zoe. Who I don't even know and who doesn't know me." [61] Why would he write that? What does that even mean?

EVAN (*Hesitates*): Oh. Um …

(Zoe looks away, realizing that he doesn't have the answer. Seeing her disappointment, [62] *Evan feels compelled to offer something.)*

I always found this an interesting and fraught moment: Evan has created this fictional persona of Connor and now he is standing in the real Connor's bedroom, surrounded by his things. He's forced, in this moment, to confront the actuality of Connor as a person—he slept in this bed, listened to music on these headphones, drank from this cup. It's a troubling moment for Evan.

[60] Steven Levenson

As we all know, Pilates is the gateway drug to the Goop lifestyle.

[61] Steven Levenson

It's telling that Zoe has memorized this section of the letter verbatim.

[62] Steven Levenson

Evan is once again compelled to lie in an effort to alleviate someone else's pain. This is a young man, you begin to suspect, who knows quite a bit about pain.

Well, I guess—I'm not sure if this is definitely it, but he was always . . . he always thought that, maybe if you guys were closer—

ZOE: We weren't close. At all.

EVAN: No, exactly. And so he used to always say that he wished that he was. He wanted to be.

ZOE: So you and Connor, you guys would talk about me?

EVAN: Sometimes. I mean, if he brought it up. I never brought it up. Obviously. Why would I have brought it up?

He thought you were . . . awesome.

ZOE (*Skeptical*): He thought I was "awesome." My brother.

EVAN: Definitely.

ZOE: How?

EVAN (*Struggling to articulate this*): Well. Like . . . whenever you have a solo. In jazz band. You close your eyes and you get this—you probably don't even know you're doing this. But you get this half smile. Like you just heard the funniest thing in the world, but it's a secret and you can't tell anybody. But then, the way you smile, it's sort of like you're letting us in on the secret, too.

(*Evan realizes he isn't getting through. He decides to start over.*)

IF I COULD TELL HER [63]

EVAN:
He said
There's nothing like
*   your smile*
Sort of subtle and perfect
*   and real*
He said
You never knew how
*   wonderful*
That smile could make
*   someone feel*

And he knew
Whenever you get bored
You scribble stars on the
*   cuffs of your jeans* [64]
And he noticed
That you still fill out the
*   quizzes*
That they put in those
*   teen magazines*

But he kept it all inside
*   his head*
What he saw he left unsaid

And though he wanted to
He couldn't talk to you
He couldn't find a way
But he would always say:

"If I could tell her
Tell her ev'rything I see
If I could tell her
How she's ev'rything to me
But we're a million
*   worlds apart*
And I don't know
How I would even start
If I could tell her
If I could tell her"

ZOE: You know the first time he ever said anything nice about me? In his note. A note he wrote to you. He couldn't even say it to me.

EVAN: He wanted to. He just . . . he couldn't.

(*Zoe hesitates, feels silly even asking.*)

ZOE: Did he say anything else?

EVAN: About you?

ZOE: Never mind. I don't even really care / anyway...

EVAN: / No no, he just, he said so many things about you. I'm trying to remember the best ones.

He thought
You looked really pretty

(He catches himself.)

Or...

It looked pretty cool
When you put indigo
streaks in your hair

ZOE (*Laughing*): He did?

EVAN:

And he wondered
How you learned to dance
Like all the rest of the
world isn't there

But he kept it all inside
his head
What he saw he left unsaid

"If I could tell her
Tell her ev'rything I see
If I could tell her
How she's ev'rything to me
But we're a million
Worlds apart
And I don't know how
I would even start
If I could tell her
If I could tell her..."

But whaddaya do
When there's this great
divide?

And whaddaya do
When the distance is too
wide?

And how do you say,
"I love you"?
I love you
I love you
I love you [65]

But we're a million worlds
apart
And I don't know how
I would even start
If I could tell her
If I could...

(Evan kisses her. It's impulsive and rash and he does it before he even thinks about it. She pulls away, stunned.)

ZOE: What are you doing?

EVAN (*Fumbling for something, anything to say*): Um... I just um...

CYNTHIA (*From off*): Dinner's ready, guys. Guys?

ZOE: Tell them to eat without me.

(She hurries out the door.)

ZOE:

But we're a million
worlds apart

He just seemed so
Far away...

It's like I don't know
Anything

63 Justin Paul

The first song we wrote for this moment was called "Obvious"—it had a very slow sort of lull-you-to-sleep feel to it. That was... problematic. There was no movement to it, no bubbling. We thought about the kind of song that Evan might want to sing, and it felt like it needed to have an intimate, awkward energy to it. To us, that meant only one thing— Plain White T's! The PWT-inspired rough guitar part slowly builds along with Evan's confidence.

64 Benj Pasek

Something we discovered that's fun about creating musicals is that if you write a lyric that requires a specific prop or costume, the other departments are sort of forced to have to include it in the show. Because we wrote this lyric, we had the extra fun of seeing stars scribbled on the cuffs of Zoe's jeans. Gotta love the attention to detail by our costume designer.

65 Justin Paul

Okay so we are probably being too cute here, but we go from "I love you" in quotes to NO quotes. See what we did there? No one watching the show in the audience would ever see that, but it's a stage direction for the actor. At some point, Evan goes from "quoting" the fictitious version of Connor to directly professing his love to Zoe. He knows it, she doesn't. #themoreyouknow

Evan and Jared, online. Jared laughs, utterly incredulous. He wears a button with Connor's face on it.

JARED: You *what*?

EVAN: I didn't mean to, it just happened.

JARED: I can't believe you tried to kiss Zoe Murphy on her brother's *bed*. After he *died*.

EVAN: Oh my God.

(Jared points to his button.)

JARED: Hey asshole, aren't you going to say anything?

EVAN (*Noticing the button for the first time*): Is that a button with Connor's face on it?

JARED: I'm selling them for a nominal fee at lunch tomorrow.

EVAN: You're making money off of this?

JARED: [66] I'm not the only one. Haven't you seen the wristbands with Connor's initials on them that Sabrina Patel started selling during free period? Or the T-shirts Matt Holtzer's mom made?

EVAN (*Not interested*): What am I going to do about Zoe?

JARED: Are you kidding? After last night? You can never walk into that house again. Besides, this whole Connor thing? In another few days, it'll be played out anyway.

EVAN: But you just said about the T-shirts and the wristbands . . .

JARED: Exactly. We are at the peak. Which is why I've got to move these buttons before the bottom drops out of the Connor Murphy memorabilia market. Because pretty soon, there will be some Third World tsunami to raise money for, and Connor will just be that dead kid whose name no one remembers.

EVAN: That's . . . that's terrible.

JARED: Hey. At least it was fun while it lasted. You got to have some quality time with your fake family, snuggle with Zoe Murphy . . .

EVAN: But that's . . . that's not why I was doing it. I was trying to help them. I just wanted to help them. [67]

JARED: Regardless, bro. It's over. A week from now? Everybody will have already forgotten about Connor. [68] You'll see.

(*Lights on Jared snap out, as they snap up on Alana.*)

ALANA: Everybody has forgotten about Connor. A week ago, the whole school was wearing those wristbands and the buttons with his

face on them. People were talking to each other that never talked to each other before. And now . . . it's all gone. Completely. You were his best friend. You can't let this happen.

EVAN: Well, I know, but . . .

ALANA (*Lightbulb*): Maybe you can ask Zoe to do something. Or maybe you guys could do something together.

EVAN: Zoe?

ALANA: Yeah, she's the perfect person to help get people interested again. You guys could write something together for the blog . . .

EVAN: Yeah, it's just . . . I don't know if that's the best way for us to get people to remember him . . .

ALANA: Well, I can guarantee you that if you don't do something, then no one will remember him. Is that what you want?

EVAN (*Struggling to respond*): But I'm just . . .

(*Alana, exasperated by his indecisiveness, exits in a huff. Evan sits there, alone.*)

What am I supposed to do?

[66] **Steven Levenson**

In one draft, Jared responded indignantly: "Yeah. It's called the free market, Comrade Hansen." As an opening-night gift, one of our guitarists, Justin, made me a card with the show's poster remade to read, "Dear Comrade Hansen," with a hammer and sickle floating just above Evan's blue polo. My wife had it professionally framed for my birthday.

[67] **Steven Levenson**

I think Evan and Jared are both right. It's not as simple as: Is Evan telling the lie for the right reasons or the wrong reasons? It's not either/or, it's both/and. Just my opinion...

[68] **Steven Levenson**

Jared inadvertently hits on one of Evan's biggest fears about himself—being forgotten.

CONNOR: Why don't you talk to Zoe?

(And suddenly Connor is there beside him.[69] *There is nothing spectral or spooky about Connor's presence, and Evan is not at all surprised to see him.)*

EVAN: I can't talk to Zoe. I already ruined everything with Zoe.

CONNOR (*Dismissive*): Says who? Jared? Why are you even talking to Jared about this?

EVAN: Who else am I supposed to talk to?

CONNOR: You can talk to me.

(Evan laughs, a ridiculous idea.)

Unless you have other options.

(Evan realizes he has none.)

EVAN: I don't know what to do.

CONNOR: Look. Zoe, my parents . . . they need you. You're the only person who can make sure everybody doesn't just forget me. [70]

(Beat.)

Oh right. They already did.

EVAN (*Empathetic*): After two whole weeks.

CONNOR: And once they've forgotten about me, what do you think happens to you? I mean, nobody cares about people like us.

EVAN: "People like us"?

CONNOR: Connor Murphy: the kid who threw a printer at Mrs. G. in second grade. Or Evan Hansen: the kid who stood outside a jazz band concert trying to talk to Zoe Murphy, but his hands were too sweaty. You know. People like that. Look:

69   **Steven Levenson**

The reason that Connor, after his death, doesn't enter or exit the stage like any of the other characters, but rather appears and disappears, is that he is nothing more or less than an extension of Evan. Because he's simply another facet of Evan, he's always already there.

70   **Steven Levenson**

If Jared is the voice of the ugly truth, then Connor is the opposite—he appears to tell Evan exactly what he wants to hear. He is always endeavoring to convince Evan to continue lying, and to continue deluding himself most of all.

"Nobody cares about people like us."
—CONNOR

DISAPPEAR

CONNOR:

Guys like you and me
We're just the losers who
*   keep waiting to be seen*

Right? I mean . . .

No one seems to care
Or stops to notice that
*   we're there*

So we get lost in the
*   in-between*

But, if you can somehow
*   keep them thinking of me*
And make me more than
*   an abandoned memory*

Well, that means we
*   matter too*
It means someone will see
*   that you are there*

No one deserves to be
*   forgotten*
No one deserves to
*   fade away*
No one should come and go
And have no one know
He was ever even here
No one deserves
To disappear, to disappear
Disappear

EVAN (*Beginning to be convinced*):
It's true.

CONNOR:

Even if you've always
*   been that*
Barely-in-the-background
*   kind of guy*

EVAN/CONNOR:

You still matter

CONNOR:

And even if you're
*   somebody who can't*
*   escape the*
Feeling that the world's
*   passed you by*

EVAN:

You still matter

CONNOR:

If you never get around to
*   doing some remarkable*
*   thing*

EVAN/CONNOR:

That doesn't mean . . .

EVAN:

That you're not worth
*   remembering*

CONNOR:

Think of the people who
Need to know

So you need
To show them

EVAN:

They need to know

I need to
*   show them*

CONNOR/EVAN:

That no one deserves to be forgotten

EVAN:

No one deserves to be forgotten

CONNOR/EVAN:

No one deserves to fade away

EVAN:

To fade away

CONNOR/EVAN:

No one should flicker out Or have any doubt

That it matters that they are here

EVAN:

No one deserves

CONNOR:

No one deserves

EVAN/CONNOR:

To disappear To disappear, disappear

CONNOR:

When you're fallin' in a forest [72]
And there's nobody around All you want is for somebody to find you You're fallin' in a forest And when you hit the ground All you need is for somebody to find you

[71] **Benj Pasek**

This was one of the more challenging songs for us to write. We were nervous to have Evan be the character to initiate the Connor Project. Would that make his actions too unlikable here? We decided we could help solve this by having Connor sing "Disappear" to Evan. This is the first time that Connor appears as an extension of Evan's subconscious. We know the sentiment is Evan's, but we see the desperation coming from "Connor." We could utilize being in Evan's head to show that his motivations aren't selfish. Evan can then believe that his motivations are not selfish; he is making the decision because he thinks he is providing relief to Connor and doing something noble.

[72] **Justin Paul**

As we wrote "Disappear," the bridge was one of those "ooh ooh ooh!" moments. When it came to the bridge of the song, it felt like the natural thing to do was to have Connor reprise the idea that Evan had instigated in "Waving Through a Window," and come back to the "when you're fallin' in a forest" motif. It also was important to us for Connor to sing something that Evan had sung before in order to reinforce that Connor isn't his own being, he's in Evan's subconscious and everything that he says is propelled and initiated by Evan.

No one
deserves to be
FORGOTTEN.

(And Connor is gone. Evan, now at school, speaks to Alana and Jared, sharing a homemade pamphlet with them.)

EVAN: I'm calling it The Connor Project.[73]

JARED *(Skeptical)*: The Connor Project.

EVAN: A student group dedicated to keeping Connor's memory alive, to showing that everybody should matter, everybody is important.

ALANA: I am so honored. I would love to be vice president of The Connor Project.

EVAN: Vice president?

ALANA: You're right. We should be co-presidents.

EVAN *(Just pleased she said yes)*: Yeah. No. Definitely. That works for me.

ALANA *(To Jared)*: You can be treasurer or secretary. Unfortunately, the co-president position has already been filled.

JARED: Well, shit. I guess I'm going to have to order new buttons. Unless you think I can squeeze the words "Connor Project" onto the old buttons... I mean, depending on the font size...

EVAN *(To Jared)*: Do you actually think we should do this?

(Alana answers for him.)

ALANA: Are you kidding, Evan? We have to do this. Not just for Connor. For... everyone.

(Evan, emboldened by the success, allows a small smile.)

EVAN:
'Cause no one deserves to be forgotten

ALANA/JARED:
No one deserves to fade away

EVAN:
No one deserves to fade away

(Jared hands each of them a button, unable to resist getting caught up in the excitement. Lights shift and Evan, Alana, and Jared are with the Murphys at their kitchen table, Cynthia and Larry eagerly perusing a pamphlet.)

We're calling it The Connor Project.

CYNTHIA *(Trying it out)*: The Connor Project.

EVAN: Imagine a major online presence.

ALANA: With links to educational materials.

JARED: A massive fundraising drive...

EVAN: ...to help people like Connor.

ALANA: And for the kickoff event, an all-school memorial assembly next week. Students, teachers, whoever wants to, they can get up and talk about Connor, talk about his legacy.

(Cynthia and Larry share a look.)

CYNTHIA: I don't know what to say.

LARRY: I didn't realize Connor meant this much to people.

ALANA: Oh my God. He was one of my closest acquaintances. He was my lab partner in Chemistry, and we presented together on *Huck Finn* in tenth grade. He was so funny. He kept calling it... well instead of *"Huck" Finn* ...[74]

(From Larry and Cynthia's faces, she thinks better of finishing the story.)

Nobody else in our class thought of that.

(Evan turns to Zoe, cautiously, testing the waters.)

EVAN: For the assembly, I was thinking maybe the jazz band could do something...

ZOE: Oh. Yeah. Maybe.

JARED: Great idea, Evan.

(Evan glares at him.)

EVAN: Thank you, Jared.

JARED: No sweat.

CYNTHIA: Oh, Evan . . . this is just, this is wonderful.

(Cynthia takes Evan's hand, unable to express her gratitude adequately in words.)

No one deserves to be forgotten

EVAN:

No one deserves to fade away

CYNTHIA/JARED/ALANA:

No one deserves to disappear

(Lights shift, as Larry, Cynthia, and Zoe exit.)

EVAN:

No one deserves to disappear

ALANA/JARED/EVAN:

No one should
Flicker out or have any doubt
That it matters that they are here

EVAN:

No one deserves

ALANA:

No one deserves

JARED:

No one deserves

EVAN/JARED/ALANA:

To disappear
To disappear

EVAN/JARED:

Disappear

ALANA:

No one deserves
To be forgotten

Disappear

JARED:

To disappear

Disappear

EVAN:

Disappear
Disappear

73 Steven Levenson

For a long time, we used *The Connor Project* as the working title for the musical.

74 Steven Levenson

This line used to continue, "...he called it the F-word Finn." In previews, we realized that the joke landed better when the audience was able to think of it themselves, rather than having it spoon-fed to them.

(Jared and Alana exit as lights shift to find Evan standing in Connor's bedroom. Cynthia holds out a nondescript necktie.)

CYNTHIA: For tomorrow. For the assembly.

EVAN (*Unsure of what she means*): Oh.

CYNTHIA: When Connor started seventh grade, all my girlfriends said, "Here comes bar mitzvah season. He's going to have a different party every Saturday." I took him to get a suit, some shirts . . . a tie.

(Beat.)

He didn't get invited to a single one.[75]

(She extends the tie to Evan.)

I thought you could wear this for your speech.

(Evan goes cold, the familiar tingling sensation returning to his palms.)

EVAN: My what?

CYNTHIA: Well, Alana said that anyone who wanted to would have a chance to say something tomorrow. I think we all assumed that you would be the first to sign up.

EVAN: I don't, um . . . the thing is just, I don't really do very well with, um, with public speaking. I'm not very good at it. You wouldn't want me to. Trust me.

CYNTHIA: Of course I would want you to. I'm sure the whole school wants to hear from you. I know Larry and I do, and Zoe . . .

(Evan says nothing. She puts the tie in his hands.)

Think about it.

(She exits. Evan sits there for a moment, staring at the tie, paralyzed. Finally, he stands. He slowly puts on the tie, a certain reverence to this.)[76]

ZOE/CYNTHIA/ALANA:
To disappear
Disappear
To disappear

Disappear

ALANA/JARED:
To disappear

Disappear

To disappear

JARED/LARRY:
Disappear

Disappear

LARRY:
Disappear

Disappear

Disappear

ZOE/CYNTHIA:
Disappear

Disappear

Disappear

(Evan takes a deep, deep breath. He reaches into his back pocket and pulls out a handful of note cards. He turns and the lights shift. The school auditorium. Evan stands there, utterly alone on an empty, endless stage, staring out into the darkness, the note cards shaking in his trembling hands. He begins slowly, tentative, terrified.)

EVAN: Good morning, students and faculty. I would, um, I would just like to say a few words to you today about . . . my best friend . . . Connor Murphy.

I'd like to tell you about the day that we went to the old Autumn Smile Apple Orchard. Connor and I, we stood under an oak tree, and Connor said, he wondered what the world would look like from all the way up there. So we decided to find out. We started climbing slowly, one branch at a time. When I finally looked back, we were already thirty feet off the ground. Connor just looked at me and smiled, that way he always did. And then . . . well, then I . . .

(His palms begin to sweat. He nervously wipes them on his shirt. It doesn't help.)

. . . I fell.

(His anxiety only builds, as he continues to wipe his hands.)

I lay there on the ground and then—

(He turns to the next card.)

Good morning, students and faculty, I would um . . .

(A shiver of panic goes down his spine as he realizes that he has lost his place in the note cards. He tries frantically to put them back in order.)

Um . . . um . . . um . . .

(Suddenly, a card drops from his hands, fluttering slowly to the ground. [77] *He crouches to pick it up. There on the ground, Evan suddenly stops. He stares out past the lights at the faces in the auditorium. A moment of pure, unadulterated terror grips him. Everything is telling him to run away. A long beat. He looks at the tie.* [78] *He makes a decision Slowly, he stands,* [79] *putting away the cards entirely. He begins once again, differently.)*

[75] **Steven Levenson**

We wanted to slowly deepen—and complicate—the audience's understanding of who Connor was as the musical goes on, by providing these little clues throughout.

[76] **Steven Levenson**

Michael Greif has staged this moment so that a single image of Connor's face—from the logo of the Connor Project—appears projected upstage of Evan as he ties the tie, as though Connor is watching somehow. It's both moving and chilling at once.

[77] **Steven Levenson**

I feel like there is nothing more difficult for an actor than to pretend to be clumsy. Dropping a note card falls into that category. Try it yourself—you will find, as I have, that it is nearly impossible to make it look convincingly real. Among his many talents, Ben Platt can fake-drop a note card like nobody's business.

[78] **Steven Levenson**

We struggled for a long time to figure out what exactly it is that gives Evan the strength to stand in this moment, before Benj came up with the obvious answer: the tie. The tie represents the friendship he never had, the person who wasn't there to catch him. By seeing the tie, he realizes that once again no one is coming to save him—this time, he has to save himself.

[79] **Steven Levenson**

The image of Evan falling recurs throughout the musical, beginning when Connor pushes him to the ground at school right before "Waving Through a Window."

YOU WILL BE FOUND [80]

EVAN:

Have you ever felt like
nobody was there? [81]
Have you ever felt
forgotten in the middle
of nowhere?
Have you ever felt like you
could disappear?
Like you could fall, and no
one would hear

(The story he has told so many times before becomes, now, suddenly, a genuine discovery.)

But see, the thing is, when I looked up . . . Connor was there. That's the gift that he gave me. To show me that I wasn't alone. To show me that I matter. That everybody does. That's the gift that he gave all of us. I just wish . . . I wish we could have given that to him.

So, let that lonely feeling
wash away
Maybe there's a reason to
believe you'll be okay

'Cause when you don't feel
strong enough to stand
You can reach, reach out
your hand
And oh, someone will
come runnin'
And I know they'll take
you home

Even when the dark comes
crashin' through
When you need a friend to
carry you
And when you're broken
on the ground
You will be found
So let the sun come
streamin' in
'Cause you'll reach up and
you'll rise again
Lift your head and look
around
You will be found [82]
You will be found
You will be found
You will be found
You will be found

(Suddenly, onstage, the screens begin to hum and buzz to life. Alana enters.)

ALANA: Have you seen this? Someone put a video of your speech online.

EVAN: My speech?

(Jared enters.)

ALANA: People started sharing it, I guess, and now . . . I mean, Connor is / everywhere.

JARED: / Your speech is everywhere. This morning, The Connor Project page, it only had fifty-six people following it.

(Cynthia enters.)

EVAN: How many does it have now?

JARED: Four thousand, / five hundred, eighty-two.

CYNTHIA: / Sixteen thousand, two hundred, and thirty-nine.

EVAN: I don't understand. What happened?

CYNTHIA: You did.

(The image of Evan's speech begins to proliferate, spreading across screens, one, two, many Evan Hansens. Evan, Cynthia, Alana, and Jared stand among the images, awash in the images, engulfed by them. The space slowly fills with people's posts, a Virtual Community. The Voices overlap and each of the individual threads becomes part of the larger stream of messages and one by one they fuse with the stream until there is no separation between them. A dreamlike feel, like we have fallen into some kind of collective hallucination. Maybe this is what life after death feels like or maybe what it would feel like to fall into the internet.) [83]

ALANA:

There's a place where
we don't have to feel
unknown [84]

(Separate Voices, one at a time, emerge to speak, to commune with one another.)

VOICES: Oh my God [85]

Everybody needs to see this

ALANA:
And ev'ry time that you call out you're a little less alone

VOICES: I can't stop watching this video

Seventeen years old

JARED:
If you only say the word

VOICES: Take five minutes, this will make your day

ALANA/JARED:
From across the silence your voice is heard

---

[80] **Benj Pasek**

The original song moment here was called "A Part of Me." We were indicting our characters. We wanted the audience to see how people glommed onto a tragedy that wasn't theirs to own. When we started the show in D.C., it was the Act One finale. We realized we weren't finding the actual humanity of this moment, and it needed to be connected to Evan, not just the community around him. That's when the note cards and speech entered the equation, and by Second Stage, "You Will Be Found" was born.

[81] **Justin Paul**

Pretty obvious, but Evan's opening verse here closely echoes much of the verbiage from "Disappear." Connor (as an extension of Evan himself) introduces these ideas to Evan, Evan internalizes and processes (or I guess it was already internal!), and then shares this with the larger group, sharing the message with students and subsequently the rest of the world.

[82] **Justin Paul**

Nothing makes me happier than Alex Lacamoire always referring to this section as "church." The sixteenth-note pattern lifts us off the ground and is meant to musically reflect the gesture of this "gospel" message spreading from the individual (Evan) out to the community and the world.

[83] **Steven Levenson**

I had no idea what I wanted this moment to look like onstage—I just knew how I wanted it to feel, so that's what I wrote. To their immense credit, our brilliant designers, Peter, Japhy, and David, understood intuitively how to capture that feeling.

[84] **Justin Paul**

Is this about finding a community? Is this about the literal internet? Both, kinda. We wanted to find a poetic way to communicate the larger meaning the internet takes on when people feel like they find a community there. Each of these lines could be referring to Twitter just as much as it could to a community of people.

[85] **Steven Levenson**

During our very early readings of the show—when it was just the creative team and Stacey reading the script around a conference table—Benj, Michael Greif, and I used to take turns reading these parts while Justin sang.

< ACT ONE SCENE TWELVE >

I know someone who really
needed to hear this today, so
thank you, Evan Hansen,
for doing what you're doing

Oh

I never met you, Connor.
But coming on here, reading
everyone's posts . . .

A/CYN/L/VV:
Oh

Z/VV/J:
Oh

It's so easy to feel alone,
but Evan is exactly right,
we're not alone

*Someone will
Come runnin'*

None of us

We're not alone

None of us

None of us

None of us is alone

Like

A/CYN/L:
Oh

Z/J:
Oh

Forward

Share.

Especially now, with everything
you hear in the news . . .

Like

Share

Re-post

Forward

*Oh
Someone will
Come runnin'*

Thank you, Evan Hansen,
for giving us a space
to remember Connor

To be together

Oh

To find each other

Share

Sending prayers
from Michigan

*Someone will
Come runnin'*

Vermont

Tampa

---

*To take
You home*

Thank you, Evan

Watch until the end

Thank you, Evan Hansen

This video is everything right now

Thank you, Evan

All the feels.

This is about community

The meaning of friendship

Thank you
Thanks to Evan

J:
*To take
You home*

Z/L:
*To take
You home*

Evan Hansen
Thank you, Evan Hansen

Oh

A/CYN:
Home

ALL:
*Even when the dark comes
    crashin' through
When you need a friend to
    carry you
When you're broken on the
    ground
You will be found
So let the sun come
    streamin' in
'Cause you'll reach up and
    you'll rise again
If you only look around
You will be found*

H/A:
You will be found

CYN/Z/VV/L:
You will be found

J:
You will be found

H/A:
You will be found

You will be found

87 Justin Paul

When we discussed this with Alex Lacamoire, Michael Greif, and the designers of the show, we always referred to this as "The Dam Bursts." We are flooded with pictures of Connor, Larry breaks down and cries for the first time, and the music and lyrics needed to take a backseat to the feeling that we wanted to create here. Everyone did their part to help make the dam burst.

88 Steven Levenson

This moment in the show never fails to move me. The rawness of Michael Park's performance here is always astonishing.

89 Justin Paul

We seriously questioned if we could do this—just repeat "you are not alone" a million times. But as we rehearsed with the cast we realized that sometimes there is an illogical power to repeating a phrase without variation. This is the one phrase we retained from the original Act One closer "A Part of Me," because we thought it communicated exactly what we wanted it to.

90 Steven Levenson

This was probably the most complicated number in the show to stage. It involves so many different elements—music, choreography, live dialogue, recorded dialogue, still photographs, video, etc. We often discussed the number like a film, in terms of close-ups, wide shots, etc., because that's exactly how we wanted it to move: cinematically. This section with Zoe is definitely a close-up—we cut from a hugely expansive moment, all of the screens fully alive, most of the company onstage, gigantic vocals, lights blaring—to Zoe, alone in Connor's bedroom, a single spot on her.

(Photographs of Connor begin to appear on the screens, mingling with the images of Evan.)

ALL (*Except for Evan and Larry*):

Out of the shadows
The morning is breaking
And all is new [87]
All is new

ALL (*With Evan*):

It's filling up the empty
And suddenly I see

That all is new
All is new

(As the darkness lifts, something inside of Larry shifts. He stares up at the screens, images of his son surrounding him. He turns to Cynthia. He can no longer hold back his emotion. In an instant, all of his defenses, all of the hurt and anger calcified over years, decades—all of it shatters at once, irrevocably. He breaks down.[88] *Cynthia holds him. They stand there, surrounded by light, holding one another.)*

A/J:

You are not alone [89]

A/J/Z/CON:

You are not alone

A/J/Z/CON/CYN/L/H/VV:

You are not alone
You are not alone

A/Z/VV/CON/L:

You are not alone

You are not alone

You are not

A/Z/CON/L:

You are
Not alone

CYN/H:

You are
Not alone

"Even when the dark comes crashin' through When you need someone to carry you..."

CYN/VV/J/H:

You are not alone

You are not alone

J:

You are not

You are
Not alone

91   Steven Levenson

For the first time, Zoe admits that her brother meant something to her. It's a huge turning point for the character.

"So let the sun come streamin in 'Cause you'll reach up and you'll rise again If you only look around…

ZOE:
Even when the dark comes crashin' through
When you need someone to carry you
When you're broken on the ground

VV/A/H/CYN/J/CON/L:
You will be found

E/Z:
So let the sun come streamin' in

ALL:
'Cause you'll reach up and you'll rise again

VV/A/CYN/J/CON/L/H:
If you only look around

A/CYN/CON/H:
You will be found

A/VV/CYN/CON/H/L:
You will be found

VV/A/H/CYN/J/L/CON:
You will be found
You will be found

(The music cuts out, sharply. Evan sits beside Zoe on Connor's bed.)

ZOE: Everything you said in your speech. Everything you've done. You don't know how much … what you've given … all of us, everyone. My family. Me.

EVAN (*Uncomfortable*): No, I … this is …

ZOE: You've given me my brother back.[91]

(Without warning, she kisses him. Stunned, he pulls away for a moment. He knows that this is the point of no return. There is no going back. He makes a decision. He kisses her. They kiss. They are reeling. The world is reeling.)

Z/E/L:
Even when the dark Comes crashin' through

When you need someone To carry you

"...YOU WILL BE FOUND"

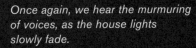

Once again, we hear the murmuring of voices, as the house lights slowly fade.

Once again, the screens buzz with text. All of it now about Connor Murphy. His absence fills the world.[1]

The murmuring grows louder and louder when suddenly everything goes black.

Lights snap up on Alana in her bedroom, speaking into her laptop screen.

ALANA: Hey everybody, it's me Alana, Connor Project co-president, associate treasurer, media consultant, chief technology officer, and assistant creative director slash public policy director for creative public policy initiatives for The Connor Project.

(Lights find Evan in his bedroom, speaking into his laptop screen, something unmistakably different about him, a newfound confidence.)

EVAN: Hi I'm Evan. I'm co-president of The Connor Project.

(Pause.)

ALANA: Wish I could see all of your amazing faces out there.

EVAN: Hope you're having an amazing day.

ALANA: Now, I know a lot of you guys have seen the inspirational videos on our website.

EVAN: Thank you for checking out the awesome new videos we put up this week with Mr. and Mrs. Murphy, Connor's sister, / Zoe . . .

ALANA: / ... and Connor's best friend, my co-president: Evan Hansen.

EVAN: As you know, Connor's favorite place in the entire world was the incredible Autumn Smile Apple Orchard.

ALANA: The stunning Autumn Smile Apple Orchard, which tragically closed seven years ago.

(Alana posts a current photo of the abandoned orchard, an empty overgrown field dotted with tree stumps, a large FOR SALE sign nailed to a rotting fence.)

EVAN: Connor loved trees.

ALANA: Connor was obsessed with trees. He and Evan used to spend hours together sitting at the orchard, looking at the trees ... *being* with the trees, sharing fun facts they knew about the trees.

EVAN: But the one thing Connor wished more than anything was that some day the orchard would be brought back to life.

ALANA: Which is where you come in ...

(Alana posts a digital architectural rendering of a blossoming orchard nestled in an idyllic park.)

EVAN: Because today we are starting a major / Kickstarter campaign.

ALANA: / One of the most ambitious Kickstarter initiatives since the internet was first created to raise— gulp—fifty thousand dollars ...

EVAN: ... fifty thousand dollars in three weeks.

ALANA: It's a lot of money, I know. But it's also a lot of amazing. So let's do it, guys, and ...

ALANA/EVAN: ... make The Connor Murphy Memorial Orchard not just a dream ...

EVAN: ... but / a rea—

ALANA (*Louder than Evan*): / But a reality.

---

1   Steven Levenson

This is a variation on a phrase that I discovered in a video work by the South African visual artist William Kentridge, "Sobriety, Obesity, and Growing Old." I find it a haunting and immensely evocative expression of the experience of loss.

A spotlight. Connor steps into it.

SINCERELY, ME

(Reprise)

CONNOR:

Dear Evan Hansen:
Life at rehab is all right I
*   like the yoga*
And the sharing circles
*   ev'ry night*
But, dude, these stories
*   sometimes scare you*
*   half to death*
So many people end up
*   sucking dick for meth*

(Lights snap up on Jared, elsewhere, typing on his computer, enjoying himself immensely. Evan, sitting at his laptop in his bedroom, shakes his head, chagrined.)

Oh, and one more thing
That's worth mentioning . . .
That guy from our school,
*   Jared Kleinman?*
Yes, the insanely cool
*   Jared Kleinman!*
I think we should start
And make him a part
Of this awesome
*   friendship we have* ²

(Jared shuts his laptop and joins Connor.)

CONNOR/JARED:

A part of this awesome
*   friendship we have*

CONNOR:

This adorably
*   heartwarming*
*   friendship we have*

JARED:

Hey!

CONNOR:

Hey!

CONNOR/JARED:

Hey hey hey hey!
'Cause all that it takes is a
*   little—*

(Unable to take any more of this, Evan stands, and the music cuts out.)

EVAN: Okay. No, Jared. Obviously not.

(Jared and Connor turn to look at Evan, confused, unsure what he finds objectionable.)

JARED: What? What's the problem?

EVAN: You weren't friends with him. That's not part of the story. I was his only friend. You know that. You can't just make things up. You need to redo it.

(Jared escorts his imagined Connor offstage.)

JARED: You're totally right. I mean, what was I thinking, just making

things up in a completely fabricated email exchange that never happened?

EVAN: Just don't change the story please, okay?

JARED: Well, if you want me to redo this email, you're going to have to wait until Monday, because I have plans all weekend with my camp friends. Or, as I like to call them: my real friends.

EVAN: Yeah, actually, I think we're good on the emails for now. We're kind of focusing on bigger stuff. The orchard. Things like that.

JARED: Oh. Well, I can definitely do more with the Kickstarter. I mean, I am the treasurer.

EVAN: I think Alana and I are pretty much set on that. I'll let you know if I think of anything, though.

JARED: Got it. Hey, I bet Zoe's happy that your cast is gone.³

EVAN: I guess.

JARED: I mean, talk about killing the mood, right? Having to see your brother's name written on your boyfriend's arm all the time?

EVAN: I'm not her . . . I don't know what we are.

JARED: Don't even worry about it, bro. The only thing you should be worrying about right now is building that orchard for Connor. Because, if there was one thing about Connor: the guy loved trees.

Or, no, wait, you love trees. That's weird. Isn't that weird?

(Evan doesn't respond. Heidi enters in scrubs.)

HEIDI: What are you up to?

(Evan shuts the computer and Jared vanishes.)

EVAN: Nothing much.

HEIDI: I feel like, every time I come into your room, you shut your computer screen.

EVAN: Not really.[4]

HEIDI: I don't know what you do on there that you don't want me to see.

EVAN: I was doing homework, Mom.

(Evan stands, begins packing up his things.)

HEIDI: Do you have a minute?

EVAN: Well, actually, I was about to go to Jared's.

HEIDI: Didn't you go to Jared's last night?

EVAN: Well, yeah, we're doing a Spanish project together. We're going to be working late again, though, so I'll probably just stay over.[5]

HEIDI: I saw the strangest thing on Facebook today.[6]

EVAN: Oh really?

HEIDI: There was a video from the, uh, something called The, uh, Connor Project? Have you heard of that?

(Evan freezes.)

Because their website, it says that you're the president.

EVAN (*Quietly*): Co-president.

HEIDI: Uh-huh. Well, this was, it was a video of you doing a speech? About that boy. Connor Murphy. How you climbed a tree together.

(Evan sits there, silent, unsure what to do, his old anxiety suddenly returning, his hands beginning to tingle.)

EVAN: I just, um . . . I don't, um . . .

HEIDI: You told me you didn't know him. That boy?

EVAN: I know. But.

HEIDI: But then in your speech, you said he was your best friend.

EVAN: Well, because it wasn't true. When I . . .

(He hesitates for just a moment. The perfect opportunity to tell the truth. He makes his choice.)

When I said I didn't know him.

2   Benj Pasek

This section was implemented during rehearsals in D.C. and was inspired by Will Roland's unique brand of off-kilter humor. We thought it would be fun to give voice to the idea that Jared's secret desire is to be a part of this forged friendship between Evan and Connor. He takes a moment to write himself into the story, especially when Evan begins to gain attention after the viral speech.

3   Steven Levenson

In earlier drafts, Jared's line here was: "I guess now that your cast is gone, you have a lot of jerking off to catch up on. That must be pretty stressful."

4   Steven Levenson

Yes, really.

5   Steven Levenson

We see here just how fluent Evan has become in lying. It's gotten easy for him.

6   Steven Levenson

I can't tell you how many debates we had as a creative team about whether or not Heidi Hansen would realistically have a Facebook account.

"You told me you didn't know him.... But then in your speech, you said he was your best friend."

— HEIDI

7 **Steven Levenson**

We just witnessed Evan come perilously close to a full-blown panic attack minutes earlier, so this claim of his that he has been cured of his anxiety is meant to ring more than a bit false.

HEIDI: So you broke your arm with him? At an orchard?

(Evan nods.)

You told me you broke your arm at work. At the park.

EVAN: Who do you think drove me to the hospital? Who do you think waited with me in the emergency room for three hours? You were at work, remember? I couldn't even, you didn't answer your phone.

HEIDI: You told me your boss took you to the hospital.

EVAN: Well, so, I lied, obviously.

HEIDI: When were you planning on telling me any of this? Or you weren't?

EVAN: When would I tell you, exactly? When are you even here?

HEIDI: I'm here right now.

EVAN: One night a week? Most people, their parents, they try to do a little bit better than that, just so you know.

HEIDI: Isn't that lucky for them.

EVAN: I have to go to Jared's.

HEIDI: I don't think I want you going out right now actually.

EVAN: I told Jared I would be at his house ten minutes ago.

HEIDI: All right, listen. I am missing class tonight so I can be here to talk to you, Evan. I would like you to please just talk to me.

EVAN: Okay. I mean, I can't just not do work for school because you decided to miss class. I can't just stop everything whenever you decide it's convenient for you.

HEIDI: I don't understand what is going on with you.

EVAN: Nothing is going on with me.

HEIDI: You're standing up in front of the school and giving *speeches*? You're president of a group? I don't know who that person is.

EVAN: You're making a big deal out of something that isn't a big deal.

HEIDI (*Increasingly desperate*): What is going on with you? / You need to talk to me. You need to communicate with me.

EVAN: / Nothing is going on with me. I told you everything.

HEIDI: I'm your mother. I'm your mother.

(The word catches in her throat. Silence. Evan says nothing. Finally, Heidi composes herself.)

I'm sorry. I was . . . I don't know why I . . . I'm happy. I'm happy you had a friend, sweetheart. I'm just so sorry he's gone. I wish I had known.

(Evan nods, suddenly ashamed.)

If you ever want to talk about it . . .

EVAN: I should go.

(Evan turns to leave. Heidi picks up a bottle of pills.)

HEIDI: You okay on refills?

EVAN: I'm not taking them anymore.

HEIDI (*Surprised*): Oh.

EVAN: I haven't needed them.

HEIDI: Really? So, no anxiety or . . . ? Even with everything that's . . . ?

EVAN: I've been fine.[7]

HEIDI: Well, great. That's great. It's . . . I'm proud of you. I guess those letters to yourself must have really helped, huh?

EVAN: I guess so.

HEIDI: Well. Don't stay up too late. It's a school night.

EVAN: I won't.

(Evan goes. Heidi stands there, utterly at sea.)

The Murphys' garage.

Larry digs through an old cardboard box, taking out a number of signed baseballs in protective plastic cases.

LARRY: Brooks Robinson. Jim Palmer.[8] Here's the entire '96 team.

Look at that.

EVAN: Wow.

LARRY: You get the right people to come to an auction like this, baseball fans, I bet you could raise a thousand bucks for the orchard, easy.

EVAN: No, it's a great idea. I'm definitely going to talk to Alana about it.

(Larry pulls out a baseball glove from the box, sets it aside, continues rummaging. Inside the baseball glove, a can of shaving cream and some rubber bands— the beginnings of a project that was never finished.)

LARRY: I swear, I have a Cal Ripken in here somewhere . . .

EVAN: This is really generous of you. To donate all this stuff.

(Zoe enters. She and Evan share a furtive smile.)

ZOE (*To Larry*): Mom says that your show is on and she doesn't want to DVR it again.

LARRY: Well, tell her we're busy.

ZOE: With what?

EVAN: Your dad had a good idea for the orchard. To do an auction.

LARRY: Evan's helping me go through my collection here.

(Beat.)

ZOE: Dad, are you torturing him?

LARRY: What?

ZOE: Evan, is he torturing you?

EVAN: No. What?

ZOE: You can tell him he's being boring and you want to leave. He won't be upset.

LARRY: He can leave whenever he wants.

EVAN: I don't want to leave.

ZOE: Evan, do you want to leave?

LARRY (*To Evan*): If you want to leave . . .

EVAN: I don't want to leave.

ZOE: Okay. Well. Don't say I didn't warn you . . .

(Zoe exits.)

LARRY (*Laughs*): Women. Right?

(Evan attempts to laugh along, one of the guys.)

EVAN: I know.

LARRY (*Gingerly*): So, you and Zoe . . . ?

EVAN (*Desperate to avoid the subject*): This glove is really cool. Wow.

(Evan picks it up.)

LARRY: You feel how stiff the leather is?

EVAN: For sure.

LARRY: Never been used.[9] You probably have your own glove at home, I'm sure.

EVAN: Oh. Uh. Somewhere. I don't know if it fits anymore. It's been a while.

LARRY: You know what? Why don't you take this one?

EVAN: Oh. No. I couldn't.

LARRY: Why not? Because, it sounds like, I mean, if you need a new glove anyway . . . This one is just going to sit here, collecting dust.

EVAN: Are you sure?

TO BREAK IN A GLOVE[10]

LARRY:

I bought this glove a
  thousand years ago
For some birthday
Or some Christmas that
  has come and gone
I thought we might play
  catch or—I don't know
But he left it in the bag
  with the tag still on

You'd have to break it in, though, first. You can't catch anything with it that stiff.

EVAN: How do you break it in?

LARRY: Your dad never taught you how to break in a baseball glove?

EVAN: I guess not.

LARRY:

It's all a process that is
  really quite precise
A sort of secret method
  known to very few
So, if you're in the market
  for . . . professional
  advice
Well, today could be a
  lucky day for you

Shaving cream.

EVAN: Shaving cream?

LARRY: Oh yeah. You rub that in for about five minutes. Then you tie it all up with rubber bands, put it under your mattress, and sleep on it. And then the next day, you

repeat. And you've got to do it for at least a week. Every day. Consistent.

And though this method
  isn't easy
Ev'ry second that you
  spend
Is gonna pay off
It'll pay off in the end

It just takes a little
  patience
It takes a little time
A little perseverance
And a little uphill climb
You might not think it's
  worth it
You might begin to doubt
But you can't take any
  shortcuts
You gotta stick it out
And it's the hard way
But it's the right way
The right way
To break in a glove

Nowadays, with your generation, I hate to say it, but it's all about instant gratification. Who wants to read a book when you can read the Facebook instead?

EVAN: Totally.

(Larry picks up the shaving cream and the rubber bands.)

LARRY: With something like this, you have to be ready to put in the work. Make the commitment.

(Beat.)

What do you think?

EVAN: I mean, definitely.

(Evan puts out a hand. Larry sprays shaving cream onto it. He sprays shaving cream onto his own hand and begins working the glove.)

LARRY:

Some people say, "Just use
  a microwave
Or try that run-it-
  through-hot-water
  technique"

(He laughs.)

Well, they can gloat about
  the time they save
'Til they gotta buy another
  glove next week

(Evan smiles. They begin to work together on the glove as their voices join.)

"You do the hard thing 'Cause that's the right thing"

—LARRY

LARRY:

It just takes a little patience

It takes a little time

A little perseverance

And
A little uphill climb
And it's the hard way
But it's the right way
The right way

'Cause there's a right way
In ev'rything you do
Keep that grit

Follow through

EVAN:

It takes a little patience [11]

It takes a little time

Perseverance

A little uphill climb

The right way

Keep that grit
Follow through

LARRY:

Even when ev'ryone
around you thinks
you're crazy
Even when ev'ryone
around you lets things go
Whether you're prepping
for some test
Or you're miles from
some goal
Or you're just trying to
do what's best
For a kid who's lost control

(Larry stops, surprised by his sudden emotion.)

You do the hard thing
'Cause that's the right thing
Yeah, that's the right thing

EVAN: Connor[12] was really lucky. To have a dad that . . . a dad who cared so much. About . . . taking care of stuff.

(Larry collects himself.)

LARRY: Your dad must feel pretty lucky to have a son like you.

(Evan lies—a reflex.)

EVAN: Yeah. He does.

LARRY: Good.

(Beat.)

Well. If you want to go catch up with Zoe . . .

(Evan nods, begins to exit. He stops, unable to let the lie stand.)

EVAN: I don't know why I said that. About my dad. It's not true. My parents got divorced when I was seven. My dad moved to Colorado. He and my stepmom, they have their own kids now. So. That's sort of his priority.

(Pause. Larry puts the glove in Evan's hands, a hand on his shoulder.)

LARRY: Shaving cream. Rubber bands. Mattress. Repeat. Got it?

EVAN: Got it.

LARRY:

It's the hard way

The right way
To break in a glove

You're good to go.[13]

EVAN:

But it's the right way
The right way
To break in a glove

[11] **Benj Pasek**

Originally, Evan didn't sing in this song. It was a solo for Larry. It was rewritten so that Evan echoes Larry's lessons. In doing so, we were able to show that both characters are getting something they've always wanted: A son gains a father and a father gains a son.

[12] **Steven Levenson**

This is the first time in the scene that anyone has said his name.

[13] **Steven Levenson**

Alex Lacamoire felt like we needed a line of dialogue here between the final lyrics of the song and the musical button, and asked me if I could come up with something. I suggested this as a temporary placeholder—it was the first thing that came to mind. It ended up sticking.

"Shaving cream. Rubber bands. Mattress. Repeat."

—LARRY

Your dad
must feel
pretty lucky
to have

**A SON LIKE
YOU.**

14 Steven Levenson

By telling Larry the truth about his father, and inviting Zoe to his house, Evan is slowly allowing himself to be seen by others. It almost seems like he's becoming comfortable with who he is, accepting himself for all of his faults. Except, as Connor will soon point out, everything in his life at this moment is premised on a lie. His transformation, in other words, is still a shallow one.

15 Justin Paul

We had this groove long before the melody came. A 6/8 acoustic guitar-driven moving ballad was, to our heads and hearts, the only way to express this moment of Evan and Zoe finally…sort of… under false pretenses…coming together. When we started writing music and lyrics it was just us singing amorphous melody shapes over chords with occasional conversational words thrown in. We were scared of interrupting the beautiful fragility and vulnerability of Steven's scene, so we definitely tip-toed our way into this song.

Evan's bedroom. Zoe slowly walks around, taking it in. Evan hovers, nervously watching. A palpable tension between them.

ZOE: So when does your mom get off work?

EVAN: She has class Sunday nights, so she won't be home for another few hours.

ZOE: We have the whole house to ourselves?

EVAN: You know it.

ZOE: We should throw a kegger.

EVAN: We should definitely throw a kegger. For sure.

ZOE: Until your mom comes home.

EVAN: In three hours.
(Pause.)

Thank you for, um, for coming.

ZOE: You realize, I've been asking to come to your house for, like, weeks, and every time you've immediately said no.

EVAN: I know. Which is why I appreciate that you're here now.[14]

(Zoe glances at papers on his desk.)

ZOE: What are all these?

EVAN (*Hurries to put them away*): Oh. Those are, my mom is obsessed with these college scholarship essay contests she found online. She keeps printing out more of them.

ZOE: There are so many.

EVAN: Yeah. I know. I mean, I'd have to win probably a hundred of them to actually pay for college. When you add it all up. Tuition, housing, books.

ZOE: Your parents, they can't . . . ?

EVAN: Not really.

ZOE: I'm sorry.
(Evan shrugs. Uncomfortable, he changes the subject.)

EVAN: Well, hey, I meant to tell you before, we had a meeting with The Connor Project a few days ago and I think we have a really great strategy for raising more money for the orchard.

ZOE: We, um . . . can we talk?

EVAN (*Crestfallen*): Oh. Shit.

ZOE: What?

EVAN: No. Just. You're breaking up with me, right? That's why you came over.

ZOE: Breaking up with you?

EVAN: God. Like, how presumptuous can I get? I don't even know if we're, like, dating officially or whatever, which isn't even . . . never mind, why am I even talking right now? It's fine. Don't worry, you can tell me, I'm not going to cry or start breaking things . . .

(Zoe just stares at him.)

ZOE: I'm not breaking up with you.

EVAN: Oh. Well. Okay. Thank you.

ZOE: Don't mention it.

EVAN: That's really great news.

(She takes a breath, struggles with how to articulate this.)

ZOE: It's just, The Connor Project . . . I mean, it's great. But maybe we don't have to talk about my brother all the time. Maybe we can talk about . . . other things.

EVAN: I just thought maybe you'd want to know.

ZOE: No, I know you did, but it's just . . . my whole life, everything has always been about Connor. And right now, I just want . . . I need something just for me. If this is going to be a . . .

(She chooses the word carefully.)

. . . relationship, I don't want it to be about my brother. Or the orchard. Or the emails. I just want . . . I want you.

ONLY US [15]

ZOE:

I don't need you to sell me
   on reasons to want you
I don't need you to search
   for the proof that
   I should
You don't have to
   convince me

You don't have to be scared
   you're not enough
'Cause what we've got
   going is good

I don't need more
   reminders of all that's
   been broken

I don't need you to fix what
   I'd rather forget
Clear the slate and
   start over
Try to quiet the noises in
   your head
We can't compete with
   all that

So, what if it's us?
What if it's us and only us?
And what came before

16 Justin Paul

Admittedly, this song doesn't go terribly far in terms of plot development—it's more about sitting and even luxuriating in a character moment. So for us, the subtle lyric progressions make all the difference. We start with a question that progresses into a statement "What if it's us?" to "It could be us" and finally "It'll be us." Nothing seismic here—slow and steady is just fine for Evan and Zoe.

17 Benj Pasek

This is the last song that Evan sings where he's able to buy into his own fantasy. It's all downhill from here!

18 Steven Levenson

Perhaps the most explicitly autobiographical moment in the musical for me.

19 Steven Levenson

A nod to *Fiddler On The Roof*, of course. I find it exceedingly easy to imagine that Jared Kleinman is a connoisseur of classic musical theater.

Won't count anymore,
or matter
Can we try that?

What if it's you?
And what if it's me?
And what if that's all that
we need it to be?
And the rest of the world
falls away
What do you say?

EVAN:
I never thought there'd be
someone like you
Who would want me

ZOE (*Laughs*): Well . . .

EVAN:
So I give you ten thousand
reasons to not let me go
But if you really see me
If you like me for me and
nothing else
Well, that's all that I've
wanted
For longer than you could
possibly know

So it can be us
It can be us and only us
And what came before
Won't count anymore
or matter
We can try that

EVAN/ZOE:
It's not so impossible

EVAN:
Nobody else but the two of
us here

EVAN/ZOE:
'Cause you're saying it's
possible

ZOE:
We can just watch the
whole world disappear

EVAN/ZOE:
'Til you're the only one I
still know how to see

EVAN:
It's just you and me

ZOE:
It'll be us [16]

It'll be us and only us
And what came before
Won't count anymore

EVAN/ZOE:
We can try that
You and me
That's all that we need it
to be
And the rest of the world
falls away
And the rest of the world
falls away
The world falls away
The world falls away
And it's only us [17]

"The world falls away And it's only us"

— E V A N & Z O E

School. Evan runs right into Alana.

ALANA: Where were you last night?

(Evan looks at her, confused.)

I waited in the senior parking lot for twenty-three minutes.

EVAN (*Remembering*): Oh, shit. I completely forgot.

ALANA: Don't worry, I went downtown and handed out the postcards without you.

EVAN: I'm really sorry. I must have put the wrong date in my phone . . .

ALANA: What is your deal, Evan? The Kickstarter deadline is a week from now and I feel like you are just like a thousand miles away. You haven't made any new videos. You haven't posted on the blog in like forever . . .

EVAN: Well, I was . . . I've been busy.

ALANA: Busy with what?

EVAN: Just . . . different stuff. How much money do we have left to raise?

ALANA: Oh. Not much. Just seventeen thousand dollars.

EVAN: I'm sure we'll get there. We just need to, you know, keep people engaged.

ALANA: Exactly. That's why I'm putting the emails between you and Connor online.

(Evan's stomach drops.)

EVAN: What do you mean?

ALANA: Mrs. Murphy sent them to me. She said, there are a ton more, too. That you, like, show her a new one every week.

EVAN: Well, but they're not, those conversations are really, they're private.

(Alana doesn't understand what he's talking about.)

"If Connor hadn't died, no one would even know who you are."

– J A R E D

ALANA: Um, not anymore. They belong to everyone now. I mean, that's the whole point. The more private they are, the better. That's what people want to see. We have a responsibility to our community to show them everything, to tell them the truth.

EVAN: Our "community"?

ALANA: I'm sending you a list of questions to answer, because some of the emails don't make sense.

EVAN: What?

ALANA: Well, like, you've been telling everyone that the first time you went to the orchard was the day you broke your arm. But then in other emails, you talk about going there together since, like, last November . . .

EVAN: Well, that's because, I mean, those are probably just typos, and it sounds like you're reading into them, like, way too much . . .

ALANA: You can explain it all when I send you the questions. You know how much the community loves hearing from you.

(Alana exits as Jared enters.)

JARED: Hey, so my parents are out of town this weekend. The last time they used the liquor cabinet was, like, Rosh Hashanah 1997,[18] so we can drink whatever we want.

EVAN: I can't this weekend. I have seventeen thousand dollars to raise. Remember The Connor Project? You're supposed to be working on this?

JARED: Uh, remember you told me you didn't need my help?

EVAN: I didn't tell you to do nothing. I know you think this is all a joke but it isn't. It's important.

JARED: For Connor.

EVAN: Yeah.

JARED: You know, when you really stop and think about it, Connor being dead, that's pretty much the best thing that's ever happened to you, isn't it?

EVAN: That's a horrible thing to say.

JARED: Well, but, no, think about it. If Connor hadn't died, no one would even know who you are. I mean, people at school actually *talk* to you now. You're almost . . . *popular*. Which is just . . . wonder of wonders, miracle of miracles.[19]

EVAN: I don't care about any of that. I don't care if people at school know who I am. All I wanted was to / help the Murphys.

JARED: / Help the Murphys. Yeah. I know. You keep saying that.

(Zoe enters.)

ZOE: Hey Jared. (*To Evan*): Hi.

(She kisses Evan and takes his hand, a public announcement of their relationship.)

JARED: Look at you, helping the Murphys.

(Jared exits.)

ZOE (*To Evan*): What was that?

EVAN (*Hiding his misgivings with a smile*): It's nothing.

...Connor being dead, that's pretty much

THE BEST THING THAT'S EVER HAPPENED TO YOU,

isn't it?

20 **Steven Levenson**

A textbook example of "Dad humor," an art form that Larry Murphy has perfected.

21 **Steven Levenson**

I love the expression on Ben's face in this moment. In a fraction of a second, you see him put together what's happening and realize all at once just how much trouble he's in.

The Murphys' living room. Larry pours wine for himself, Cynthia, and Heidi.

CYNTHIA (*To Heidi*): Evan tells us you're studying to be a lawyer?

HEIDI: Paralegal.

CYNTHIA (*Looking to Larry*): You're kidding.

LARRY: I had no idea.

CYNTHIA: Aren't you / —they're always looking for paralegals.

LARRY: / We're always, my firm, we're literally always trying to find new paralegals.

HEIDI: I have another year to go before I even . . .

LARRY: Well, why don't I give you my card at least . . .

(He reaches into his wallet.)

. . . and when you graduate, / you should absolutely . . .

CYNTHIA: / That is a great idea. Kismet.

HEIDI: Oh. No. You don't have to do that.

CYNTHIA: It's kismet.

(Uncomfortable, Heidi has no choice but to accept the card.)

HEIDI: Well. Thank you.

LARRY: Is red okay, Heidi?

HEIDI: Red would be great.

CYNTHIA: It's from a vineyard outside of Portland—completely one hundred percent sustainable, the entire production process. They had a whole feature on them in the *New York Times*. Incredible.

LARRY: Not to mention, it tastes good, too.[20] *(Larry passes out the wine glasses.)* Cheers.

(They drink.)

HEIDI: I'm so glad that you called this morning. I was, I've been agonizing over whether I should, if it was appropriate for me to reach out . . .

CYNTHIA: Oh, Heidi. We have, too. Evan says you're so busy, I didn't know if I should bother you . . .

HEIDI: I'm not that busy.

CYNTHIA: Well, I asked Evan if you minded him spending so much time here and he said it wasn't a problem because of your schedule. With classes and work . . .

HEIDI: He . . . spends so much time here?

LARRY: Evan's been a real . . . he's been a great source of comfort for us these past few months.

CYNTHIA: Well, he and Connor, they were very close.

HEIDI: I have to admit, I didn't . . . I really had no idea that he and Connor were even . . .

LARRY: We were the same.

CYNTHIA: Boys love to keep secrets.

LARRY: We'd never heard about Evan, we'd never met him . . .

HEIDI: Evan didn't tell me anything.

CYNTHIA: Secret handshakes, secret tree houses . . .

(The front door opens and Zoe and Evan enter.)

ZOE: Sorry we're late. Band went long again.

CYNTHIA: We're just in here having a glass of wine, getting to know each other.

(Evan stops cold when he sees his mother.) [21]

LARRY: We invited your mom to come join us for dinner tonight.

EVAN: Oh.

HEIDI: I didn't realize that Evan was, that you were joining us, too.

CYNTHIA: I'm sorry, I didn't think to tell you.

ZOE *(Shaking hands)*: Hi, I'm Zoe. It's so nice to meet you. Finally.

HEIDI *(Puzzled)*: Oh. Good.

EVAN *(To Zoe)*: Did you know about this?

ZOE: It was my idea.

LARRY: Why don't you guys come sit down?

(Evan and Zoe do.)

EVAN *(To Heidi)*: I thought you had work tonight.

HEIDI: Well, this seemed more important. So. I'm playing hooky.

CYNTHIA: We were just talking about how sneaky you and Connor were. Top secret.

EVAN *(Changing the subject)*: Something smells good.

CYNTHIA: Chicken Milanese . . .

HEIDI: I didn't realize you were spending so much time here.

EVAN: You've been working a lot.

HEIDI: Why did I think you were at Jared's?

EVAN: I don't know.

CYNTHIA: Oh but Evan, you call and tell your mother when you're staying the night, right?

EVAN (*Looking away from Heidi*): Of course.

LARRY: You can rest assured we take very good care of him. We've got, he has a toothbrush, so we're not sending him to bed with cavities.

HEIDI: How nice.

ZOE (*To Heidi*): Evan was showing me all of those scholarship contests that you found. That was really impressive. There are, like, a million.

HEIDI: Well, Evan is a great writer.

LARRY: I don't find that hard to believe at all.

HEIDI: His teacher last year for English said he wrote one of the best papers she'd ever read about *Sulu*.

CYNTHIA: How about that.

EVAN (*Quietly*): It's *Sula*.

HEIDI: What did I say?

EVAN: Sulu.

HEIDI: Okay.

LARRY: Sulu is a character on *Star Trek*, I believe . . . [22]

(*Everyone laughs, except for Heidi and Evan.*)

HEIDI: My mistake.

(*Zoe looks at her parents.*)

ZOE: Speaking of scholarships . . .

(*Evan looks at Zoe, confused.*)

LARRY: I guess now is as good a time as any. Cynthia, do you want to . . . ?

CYNTHIA: Well. Zoe happened to mention to us the other day that Evan was having some difficulty in

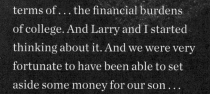

terms of . . . the financial burdens of college. And Larry and I started thinking about it. And we were very fortunate to have been able to set aside some money for our son . . .

(*Cynthia begins to falter, emotion creeping into her voice. Larry takes her hand. She waves him away, smiling stoically.*)

I'm okay. I'm okay.

(*She takes a breath.*)

I called you this morning to invite you to come join us for dinner tonight, Heidi, because . . . well, first of all, because we want to thank you for allowing your son to have come into our lives. He was a dear, dear friend to our Connor, and we have come to just love him to pieces.

(*Larry and Zoe laugh.*)

And with your blessing, we would like to give Evan the money we put away for our son so that he can use it to fulfill his dreams, just like he helped Connor . . .

(*She struggles to finish the thought.*)

. . . fulfill his.

(*A terrible silence. Heidi is stunned. Evan feels like puking. Larry, Cynthia, and Zoe look at them expectantly, hopefully.*)

LARRY: What do you think?

(*Beat. Heidi manages to plaster on a stiff smile.*)

HEIDI: Wow. I'm, that is . . . I don't know what to say. I'm . . .

LARRY: It would be such a gift to us if we could do this for Evan.

CYNTHIA: It would be a tremendous gift, Heidi.

HEIDI: Well, thank you so much, but . . . we're going to be fine. I don't have a lot of money, but I do have some.

CYNTHIA: Oh we didn't mean / at all—

HEIDI: / No, no, I understand, I'm just, we do have money. So I'm sorry that you were under the impression that we didn't. And, whatever money we don't have, Evan will either get a scholarship or he'll go to a community college and that's . . . I think that's the best thing for us to do. I don't want Evan to get the idea that it's okay to rely on other people for favors.

LARRY: It's not a favor.

HEIDI: Well, but, as his mother, I need to set that example for him. That you can't expect things from strangers.

CYNTHIA: We are not strangers.

HEIDI: No. Of course not.

(Heidi stands.)

Thank you for the wine. It was delicious.

CYNTHIA: You're not staying for dinner?

HEIDI: I think I'd better go to work after all.

CYNTHIA: Oh no.

HEIDI: If I'd known Evan was so concerned about our finances, I would never have taken the night off in the first place.

(Heidi goes, leaving the Murphys and Evan sitting there, silent.)

22 **Steven Levenson**

The incomparable George Takei, who played Sulu in the original series, came to see the show Off-Broadway and Tweeted: "@DearEvanHansen, Congrats on a groundbreaking and moving theatrical experience. And a Sulu reference? Oh Myyy." In other news: Dreams do come true.

23 Steven Levenson

I originally had a much gentler exit line here, but Michael Greif encouraged me to allow Evan to really go for the jugular. I still cringe whenever I hear Evan say this—in a good way. He is trying deliberately to wound his mother with this line, and it works.

24 Justin Paul

For some reason, the intro music to this song became the absolute bane of our collective existence. Per usual, we were trying not to ruin Steven's play by making these characters start singing at the wrong time. There was a rehearsal during Broadway previews where we probably made Rachel Bay Jones walk across the room and then start singing 17 different times using 17 different trigger lines and musical intros. We finally landed somewhere. For now...for now!

The Hansens' house. Living room.

HEIDI: Do you have any idea how mortifying it is? To find out that your son has been spending every night in somebody else's home and you didn't even know it? You told me you were at Jared's.

EVAN: If you're not here, then why does it matter where I am?

HEIDI: They think you're their son. These people.

EVAN: They're not "these people." They're my . . .

HEIDI: What? / What are they?

EVAN: / I don't know.

HEIDI: Because they act like you're their, like they've adopted you, like I'm just, like I don't even exist.

EVAN: They take care of me.

HEIDI: They're not your parents. That is not your family, Evan.

EVAN: They're nice to me.

HEIDI: Oh they're lovely, lovely people.

EVAN: Yep.

HEIDI: They don't know you.

EVAN: And you do?

HEIDI: I thought I did.

EVAN: What do you know about me? You don't know anything about me. You never even see me.

HEIDI: I am trying my best.

EVAN: They like me. I know how hard that is to believe. They don't think that I'm, that there's something wrong with me, that I need to be fixed, like you do.

HEIDI: When have I *ever* said that?

EVAN: I have to go to therapy, I have to take drugs.

HEIDI: I'm your mother. My job is to take care of you.

EVAN: I know. I'm such a burden. I'm the worst thing that ever happened to you. I ruined your life.

HEIDI: You are the only . . . the one good thing that has *ever* happened to me, Evan.

(Beat.)

I'm sorry I can't give you anything more than that. Shit.

EVAN: Well, it's not my fault that other people can. [23]

(He leaves. Heidi stands there, stunned.) [24]

GOOD FOR YOU

HEIDI:

So you found a place where
*   the grass is greener*
And you jumped the fence
*   to the other side*
Is it good?
Are they giving you a world
*   I could never provide?*

Well I hope you're proud
*   of your big decision*
Yeah I hope it's all that
*   you want and more*
Now you're free
From the agonizing life
*   you were living before*

And you say what you
*   need to say*

So that you get to walk away
It would kill you to have
*   to stay*
Trapped when you've got
*   somethin' new*
Well I'm sorry you
*   had it rough*
And I'm sorry I'm
*   not enough*
Thank God they rescued you

So you got what you
*   always wanted*
So you got your
*   dream-come-true*
Well, good for you
Good for you you
You got a taste of a life
*   so perfect*
So you did what you
*   had to do*
Good for you
Good for you

< ACT TWO SCENE SEVEN >

Are they
**GIVING YOU
A WORLD**
I could never
provide?

(School. Alana storms up to Evan.)

ALANA: Why did Connor kill himself?

EVAN (*Taken aback*): Wait what?

ALANA: He was doing better. That's what he told you. In every single email. And then a month later, he kills himself? Why do so many things in these emails just not make sense?

EVAN: Because sometimes things *don't* make sense, okay? Things are messy and complicated . . .

ALANA: Like you dating Zoe?

(Lowering her voice.)

Do you know what people are saying about you?

EVAN: Why are you so obsessed with this? I mean, you didn't even know him.

ALANA: Because it's important.

EVAN: Because you were lab partners? Or because, I don't know, maybe because you want another extracurricular for your college applications? [25]

ALANA: Because I know what it's like to feel invisible. Just like Connor. To feel invisible and alone and like nobody would even notice if you vanished into thin air. I bet you used to know what that felt like, too.

"I know what it's like to feel invisible. Just like Connor."

– ALANA

(As Alana goes, Jared enters.) [26]

EVAN (*To Jared*): We need more emails. Emails showing that he was getting worse.

(Jared scoffs.)

This isn't funny.

JARED: Oh I think it's hilarious. I think everyone would probably think it's hilarious.

EVAN: What is that supposed to mean?

JARED: It means, you should remember who your friends are.

EVAN: I thought the only reason you even talk to me is because of your car insurance.

JARED: So?

EVAN: So maybe the only reason you talk to me, Jared, is because you don't have any other friends.

JARED: I could tell everyone everything.

EVAN: Go ahead. Do it. Tell everyone how you helped write emails pretending to be a kid who killed himself.

JARED (*Like a helpless, heartbroken little kid*): Fuck you, Evan. Asshole.

(He turns and goes. Evan stands there, assaulted from all directions, unable to escape.)

25 **Steven Levenson**

I like the fact that, for all of his sensitivity and empathy, Evan manages to get Alana so wrong.

26 **Steven Levenson**

I wanted this sequence to have the feeling of a nightmare—wherever Evan turns, he's under attack. There's nowhere for him to hide.

Does it cross
your mind to be
SLIGHTLY
SORRY?

ALANA:

Does it cross your mind to
*   be slightly sorry?*
Do you even care that you
*   might be wrong?*
Was it fun?
Well I hope you had a blast
While you dragged
*   me along*

JARED:

And you say what you
*   need to say*
And you play who you
*   need to play*
And if somebody's in
*   your way*
Crush them and leave
*   them behind* [27]

JARED/ALANA:

Well, I guess if I'm
*   not of use*
Go ahead, you can cut
*   me loose*
Go ahead now, I won't mind

HEIDI:

I'll shut my mouth and
I'll let you go
Is that good for you?
Would that be good for
*   you, you, you?*

ALANA/HEIDI:

I'll just sit back while you
*   run the show*
Is that good for you?
Would that be good for
*   you, you, you?*

ALANA/HEIDI/JARED:

I'll shut my mouth
And I'll let you go
Is that good for you?
Would that be
Good for you, you, you?

I'll just sit back
While you run the show
Is that good for you?
Good for you?

So you got what you
*   always wanted*
So you got your dream
*   come true*

EVAN/ALANA/JARED/HEIDI:

Good for you
Good for you you
You got a taste of a life so
*   perfect*
Now you say that you're
*   someone new*
Good for you
Good for you
Good for you
Good for you

ALANA/JARED/HEIDI:

So you got what you
*   always wanted*

EVAN:

All I need is some time
To think
But the boat
Is about to sink
Can't erase
What I wrote in ink
Tell me how can I change
The story?

All the words that I
Can't take back
Like a train comin'
Off the track [28]
As the rails and the bolts
All crack
I gotta find a way to
Stop it stop it
Just let me out [29]

27 **Justin Paul**

7/8 in a rock song = mounting anger! Jared is pissed and he wants the world to know! We weren't sure how well the 7/8 time signature would translate within the feel of a pop/rock song, but leave it to Alex Lacamoire to find the right drum groove to make it tasty and right.

28 **Benj Pasek**

Talk about mixed metaphors! This was a way to show Evan scrambling to express what he's feeling, grasping at whatever he can think of in the moment. These phrases are also very intentionally pop-leaning; using mixed metaphors instead of one consistent image to illustrate the idea.

29 **Benj Pasek**

In the original score, Evan was supposed to cut off quickly after the word "out," but in rehearsals in D.C., Ben Platt kept holding the note longer and longer. The first time he did it we told him he couldn't keep it in the show, but of course he kept doing it anyway. We eventually stopped giving the note and ended up loving it, so we kept it in the score.

30 **Steven Levenson**

Connor again appears when Evan is at his lowest, in order to convince him to continue the lie.

31 **Steven Levenson**

I love Mike Faist's performance in this scene, because he plays against what you would expect—rather than sinister and conniving, Mike plays Connor as the kind, caring, gentle friend that we all long to have. All he wants is to help Evan to do the right thing.

Evan, alone.

EVAN: I'm not doing this. I'm done.

CONNOR: You can't just stop now. [30]

(And Connor is there.)

EVAN: I don't think I can live with this anymore.

CONNOR: What about my parents?

EVAN: No more emails.

CONNOR: How can you do this to them?

EVAN: No more Connor Project. No more orchard.

CONNOR: After everything they've done for you? They need you.

EVAN: Need me for what? To keep lying to them?

CONNOR: That lie is the only thing that's keeping them together.

EVAN: That's not true.

CONNOR: Oh really? They seemed like a pretty happy family when you met them?

EVAN: I don't want to lie anymore.

CONNOR: And what about Zoe?

EVAN: Zoe said, she just . . . she wants me.

CONNOR: Right.

EVAN: She likes me for who I am.

CONNOR: Except you didn't happen to mention that everything you've told her, it's all been one big fucking lie, did you?

(Evan says nothing.)

Oh. You left that part out.

EVAN: So then, what if . . . what if I did tell her the truth?

CONNOR: She'll hate you.

EVAN: Maybe she would understand. Maybe everyone would understand.

"Did you fall?
Or did you let go?"

—CONNOR

CONNOR: Everyone will hate you.

EVAN: Not if I can just, if I can explain it, you know?

CONNOR: You'll go right back to where you started. No friends.

EVAN: I want to be done / with this.

CONNOR: / Nobody. Nothing. Alone.

EVAN: I'm ready to be done with it.

CONNOR: If you really believe that, then why are you standing here, talking to yourself? Again?

(Pause.)

You think you're going to turn around all of a sudden and start telling everyone the truth? You can't even tell yourself the truth.

EVAN: What are you talking about?

CONNOR: How did you break your arm?

(A pall comes over Evan.)

How did you break your arm, Evan?

EVAN: I fell.

CONNOR: Really? Is that what happened?

EVAN (*Less and less confident*): I was, I lost my grip and I . . . I fell.

CONNOR: Did you fall? Or did you let go?

(Silence.)

You can get rid of me whenever you want. You can get rid of all of it. The Connor Project. The orchard. But then all that you're going to be left with is . . . you. [31]

< ACT TWO SCENE EIGHT >

FOR FOREVER

(Reprise) [32]

32 Benj Pasek

In D.C., we made the decision that Connor wasn't a ghost-like figure, but really an extension of Evan's subconscious. He could only be on stage when Evan was alone. This reprise is Evan's fantasy coming back to haunt him, where we use Connor to show that Evan is ultimately trapped in the lie that he has perpetuated.

33 Steven Levenson

This is the first time in the musical that Evan does something that I think is truly wrong—and that's because it's the only time that he does something purely out of his own self-interest, in order to protect himself. It feels right, for that reason, that this is the action that will ultimately unravel everything.

CONNOR:

End of May or early June
This picture-perfect
afternoon we share
Drive the winding
country road
Grab a scoop at
"À La Mode"
And then
we're there…

Think about it.

(Evan stands there for a moment, lost. He makes a decision. Lights shift and Evan and Alana are in their bedrooms, online. Connor is gone.)

EVAN: I've been a bad co-president. I know that. And I'm sorry. But I'm, you were right, you were absolutely right, and I'm back and I'm re-dedicating myself to doing everything I can do to make this work.

ALANA: Too late. I've moved on.

EVAN: You've "moved on"?

ALANA: You've made it abundantly clear to me that you're not very interested in being a part of The Connor Project.

EVAN: I can make more videos. I can write more stuff for the blog.

ALANA: I can do all of that myself.

EVAN: It's not the same. You know it's not the same. People want to hear what I have to say. I was his best friend.

ALANA: You know, frankly, Evan? I'm starting to wonder if that's even true.

(Evan freezes. He tries laughing it off.)

EVAN: What does that mean?

ALANA: You keep saying you were best friends. You're like a broken freaking record about it. But nobody ever saw you together. Nobody knew that you were friends.

EVAN: It was a secret. He didn't want us to talk at / school.

ALANA: / I know the story, Evan. We all know the story. We've all heard it a bazillion times.

EVAN: You've seen the emails.

ALANA: Do you know how easy it is to create a fake email account? Backdate emails? Because I do.

(Evan begins to feel desperate.)

You know what? I don't have time for this. I have to raise seventeen thousand dollars.

EVAN: I can prove it.

ALANA: How?

(Long pause.)

EVAN: Here.

(Evan sends Alana an email. Alana opens it. Her eyes widen. The letter.)

If we weren't friends, then why did he write his suicide note to me? [33]

ALANA: Oh my God.

EVAN: Do you believe me now?

ALANA (Reading): "Dear Evan Hansen:"

EVAN: Nobody else has seen this.

ALANA: "It turns out, this wasn't an amazing day after all. This isn't going to be an amazing week or an amazing year."

EVAN: You can't show it to anyone, okay? Nobody else needs to see it.

ALANA: This is exactly what people need to see. We need something to create new interest.

EVAN: Can you just please delete it now?

ALANA: Don't you care about building the orchard? This is the best way to make Connor's dream come true.

EVAN: No, it isn't.

(And the letter is suddenly everywhere, Evan's words filling the screens. Alana turns away from Evan, speaking now to the world.)

ALANA: Dear Connor Project Community:

(The blood drains from Evan's face, as he realizes what's happened.)

EVAN: You put it online.

(Alana continues to speak to the online community, ignoring Evan entirely.)

ALANA: Connor's note is a message to all of us. Share it with as many people as you can. Post it everywhere.

EVAN (*Begging*)**:** You need to take it down. Please.

ALANA: If you've ever felt alone like Connor, then please consider making a donation to The Connor Murphy Memorial Orchard. No amount is too small.

(Voices from the virtual world begin to pile up on top of each other, stacking and accumulating, accreting. Unlike before, the Voices do not fuse—they congeal. This is not a community, but a hydra-headed herd-thing, primal and ravenous and cruel.) [34]

VOICES:

Have people seen this?

Connor Murphy's suicide note

This is the actual, authentic

Forward

The whole world needs to see this.

Share it with everyone you know

This is why the orchard is so important, guys

I just gave fifty dollars for the orchard and I think everyone else should give as much as they can

Re-post

His parents present themselves

He wrote his suicide note to Evan Hansen, because he knew his family didn't give a shit

His parents, by the way, are insanely rich

YOU WILL BE FOUND

(R e p r i s e) [35]

VOICES:	A/J/VIRTUAL VOICES:
Forward	*Oh*
Share	
Like	
Maybe they should have spent their money on helping their son instead of	*Oh*
Please re-tweet	
Evan Hansen was the only one who was paying any attention	*Oh*
Favorite	
Share	
Forward	
	Oh

(Elsewhere, Zoe appears, reading her own screen, horrified.)

VOICES:

"Like all my hope is pinned on Zoe"

Zoe's a stuck-up bitch,
I go to school with her, trust me

Share

Forward

Larry Murphy is a corporate
lawyer who only cares about

Cynthia Murphy is one of
these disgusting women

ZOE: Mom? You need to see this.

(Cynthia enters.)

VOICES:

A hundred and sixty more dollars
and the orchard will be fully funded

Fuck the Murphys

Make them feel what
Connor felt

I love you guys

Oh my God, we are two hundred
dollars over our goal

Their house is at the end of the
cul-de-sac with the red door

(Cynthia reads over Zoe's shoulder.)

Zoe's bedroom window is on the right

The gate to the back is completely
unlocked

CYNTHIA: How did they . . . ?

(Larry enters.)

VOICES:

Zoe's cell phone number,
if my sources are correct

I gave twenty

CYNTHIA: It's everywhere.

VOICES:

I'm not saying to do anything illegal

All hours, day and night

A thousand

Ring the doorbell

Keep calling until they answer

A/J/VV:

Oh

VV:

Oh

*Someone will
Come runnin'*

Oh

Oh

*Someone will
Come runnin'*

A:

Oh

J:

Oh

A/J:

You are not alone [36]

A/VV/J:

You are not alone

A/VV:

You are not alone

You are not alone

J/VV:

You are not alone

You are not alone

A/J/VV:

You are not

You are not alone

34 Steven Levenson

We wanted to explore here the
dark side of social media, how
quickly it can be transformed
from a beacon of community and
connection to a tool of hatred,
exclusion, and harassment.

35 Justin Paul

The song proper of "You Will
Be Found" was written with
swirling sixteenth notes—a sort
of crazy, percolating motion
throughout. We knew that we
would repurpose it here, and the
"church" section that Lac talks
about becomes twisted, darker.
It's the opposite of the uplifted
feeling that's created in "YWBF."
Now, Evan is swallowed up by
the very thing he created and
the supportive community is
overtaken by a mob mentality.

36 Benj Pasek

We kept this lyric from the original
song, "A Part of Me," and always
knew we wanted to reprise it here
to be a nightmarish echo. This
reprise highlights that no one
can really hide from the mob of
the internet. The Murphy family
and Evan are constantly being
watched and tormented by an
online frenzy.

Lights snap up on the Murphys' living room. Larry stares at his cell phone. Zoe sits, looking at the laptop. Cynthia paces behind her. Evan stands, nauseous.

CYNTHIA: Where did they get Connor's note?

LARRY: I don't know.

EVAN: I tried to call Alana, but she's / not answering.

CYNTHIA (*To Larry*): / Some of these are adults. Do you see their pictures? These are adults.

(A cell phone rings. Zoe reaches for it.)

LARRY: Maybe let it ring, Zoe.

ZOE (*Into phone*): Hello?

(Beat. Her face remains impassive.)

LARRY: Who is it? Who is it, / Zoe?

ZOE (*Into phone*): / Have fun with your miserable life. Bye.

(Zoe hangs up.)

LARRY: What's the number?

ZOE: It's blocked. Who cares?

CYNTHIA: What did they say to you?

ZOE: It doesn't matter.

LARRY: Did they threaten you?

ZOE: It doesn't matter, Dad.

CYNTHIA: I'm calling the police. That's it.

(Cynthia digs through her purse for her cell phone.)

LARRY: Right now, maybe the best thing to do is to just wait and see if this blows over.

CYNTHIA: That's always your solution, isn't it? Do nothing.

LARRY: Is that what I said?

ZOE: Can you guys just stop?

CYNTHIA: Wait and see. Let's wait and see, right, Larry?

LARRY: What are the police going to do? It's the internet. They're going to arrest the internet?

CYNTHIA: I had to beg you, every step / of the way.

LARRY: / Okay. Hold on.

EVAN (*Quietly*): I really think they're going to stop . . .

CYNTHIA: I had to *plead* with you. For therapy, rehab . . .

LARRY: You went lurching from one miracle cure to the next.

CYNTHIA (*Laughs*): "Miracle cure." / Really. Is that what you call it?

LARRY: / Because all he needed was another twenty-thousand-dollar weekend yoga retreat.

EVAN: Maybe I should try calling Alana again . . .

CYNTHIA: And what was your alternative? Other than picking apart everything I did?

LARRY: Putting him on a program and *sticking* to it.

ZOE: No, you wanted to punish him.

CYNTHIA: Listen to your daughter, Larry.

ZOE: You treated him like a criminal.

CYNTHIA (*To Larry*): Are you listening?

ZOE (*To Cynthia*): You think you were any better? You let him do whatever he wanted.

LARRY: Thank you.

CYNTHIA (*To Larry*): When he threatened to kill himself the first time, do you remember what you said?

LARRY: Oh for Christ's sake.

CYNTHIA: "He just wants attention."

LARRY: I'm not going to sit here and defend myself.

CYNTHIA: He was *getting better*. Ask Evan. Tell him, Evan.

(Evan freezes, the unmistakable sensation of his hands clamming up.)

EVAN: I shouldn't, um . . .

CYNTHIA: Evan did everything he could.

LARRY: Evan was in denial of what was happening / right in front of him.

ZOE: / Don't put him in the middle of this.

CYNTHIA (*Going to the computer*): Read the note, Larry. Read what he said. "I wish that everything was different." / He wanted to be different. He wanted to be better.

LARRY: / I did the best I could, I tried to help him the only way

I knew how, and if that's not good enough ...

EVAN (*Overlapping them*): No ... no ... no ...

CYNTHIA: He was trying to be better. He was trying.

LARRY: And he was *failing*.

CYNTHIA: *We* failed *him*.

(*Evan can bear it no longer.*) [37]

EVAN: No you didn't.

(*They turn to look at him.*)

You didn't fail him.

CYNTHIA: Look at what he wrote ...

EVAN: He didn't write it.

(*Long pause.*)

I wrote it.

(*Silence.*)

CYNTHIA (*A ludicrous notion*): You didn't write Connor's suicide note, Evan.

EVAN: It wasn't a ... it was an assignment from my therapist. Write a letter to yourself. A pep talk. "Dear Evan Hansen: Today is going to be an amazing day and here's why."

LARRY (*Unable to make sense of this*): I don't think ...

EVAN: I was supposed to bring it to my appointment. Connor took it from me and I guess he must have had it with him when you ... found him.

ZOE: What are you talking about?

EVAN: We weren't friends.

CYNTHIA: No. No no no.

> [37] **Steven Levenson**
>
> What finally drives Evan to tell the truth is precisely what drove him to lie in the first place—he cannot bear to see the Murphys suffer.

WORDS FAIL

EVAN:

I never meant to make it
*   such a mess*
I never thought that it
*   would go this far*

CYNTHIA: There were emails. You showed us the emails.

EVAN:

So I just stand here
Sorry, searching
For something to say
Something to say [38]

LARRY: But you knew about the orchard. He took you to the orchard.

CYNTHIA: That's where you broke your arm.

EVAN: I broke my arm at Ellison Park. By myself.

CYNTHIA: No, that day at the orchard, you and Connor at the orchard . . .

EVAN:

Words fail
Words fail
There's nothing
*   I can say*

CYNTHIA (*The truth finally beginning to sink in*): Oh God.

ZOE (*Not easy to say*): But you told me that he . . . that you would talk about me and that he would . . .

(*Beat.*)

How could you do this?

EVAN:

I guess . . . I thought I
*   could be part of this*

I never had this kind of
*   thing before*
I never had that perfect
*   girl who*
Somehow could see
The good part of me [39]

I never had the dad who
*   stuck it out*

No corny jokes or baseball
   gloves
No mom who just was there
'Cause mom was all that
   she had to be

That's not a worthy
   explanation
I know there is none
Nothing can make sense
   of all these things
   I've done [40]

Words fail
Words fail
There's nothing I can say

Except sometimes you see
   ev'rything you've wanted
And sometimes you see
   ev'rything you wish
   you had
And it's right there,
   right there
Right there in front of you

And you want to believe
   it's true
So you make it true
And you think
Maybe ev'rybody wants it,
   needs it a little bit too [41]

(Zoe stands. She looks at Evan.
She goes. Cynthia goes after her.
Larry stands there for a moment.
Finally, he, too, goes. Evan turns
to see Connor there. The light
slowly, very slowly goes out on
Connor. And Evan is alone.)

This was just a sad
   invention
It wasn't real, I know
But we were happy
I guess I couldn't let that go [42]
I guess I couldn't give
   that up

I guess I wanted to believe
'Cause if I just believe
Then I don't have to see
   what's really there

No, I'd rather
Pretend I'm something
   better than these
   broken parts
Pretend I'm something
   other than this mess
   that I am
'Cause then I don't have
   to look at it
And no one gets to look at it
No, no one can really see
'Cause I've learned to
   slam on the brake [43]
Before I even turn the key
Before I make the mistake
Before I lead with the
   worst of me
I never let them see the
   worst of me

'Cause what if ev'ryone
   saw?
What if ev'ryone knew?
Would they like what
   they saw?
Or would they hate it too?
Will I just keep on running
   away from what's true?

All I ever do is run

So how do I step in
Step into the sun?
Step into the sun

38 Benj Pasek

This beginning verse used to be much longer with many more rhymes. While watching Ben perform it, the less Evan could spit out and articulate, the more impact it had on stage, so we cut a lot. It's not a traditional song structure since so much of it was excised.

39 Benj Pasek

This is the first rhyme in the song. Putting a rhyme before this would seem too perfect or pre-planned. It needed to feel like Evan was vomiting out this horrible truth, and the rhyme here is very simple and tries not to draw attention to itself.

40 Justin Paul

Call us crazy, but this moment was always so crucial to us because we need to see that Evan isn't trying to justify what he's done or ask the Murphys to forgive him—he simply must tell them the truth and explain his actions. But he cannot attempt to excuse himself because that would, in our minds, be unforgivable.

41 Benj Pasek

While we never wanted to cast blame on the Murphys, we did want to have a small section of this song show that Evan thought each of the Murphys needed and wanted his lie in some way. They were complicit to a degree by wanting to believe something so badly that they too bought into this fantasy.

42 Justin Paul

This song used to end here, but we were encouraged to make a bigger moment of this. Evan's just confessed to the family—but can he tell himself the truth? So right before the show went to D.C., we sat down at the piano and wrote one line at a time and then musicalized it. None of it rhymed and there was no logical structure. We just wrote each line until it felt right, and then went back and forth with Ben Platt as a litmus test for what really felt truthful for the character. We're so grateful for that collaboration.

43 Benj Pasek

We realized the most natural place for Evan to go was right back to the beginning with "Waving Through a Window" and then he has to make a decision. Will he overcome who he is by facing the truth, or will he continue to hide from himself?

Nothing can
make sense of
**ALL THESE
THINGS I'VE
DONE.**

(The Hansen living room. Evan enters to find Heidi sitting on the sofa, on her laptop. She looks up at him.)

HEIDI: Have you seen this? The note that Connor Murphy . . .

(Evan nods.)

It's all over everyone's Facebook.

(Beat.)

"Dear Evan Hansen."

(She looks at him, the words familiar. Evan says nothing.)

Did you . . . you wrote this? This note?

(Beat. Evan nods.)

I didn't know.

EVAN: No one did.

HEIDI: No, that's not what I . . . I didn't know that you . . . that you were . . . hurting. Like that. That you felt so . . . I didn't know. How did I not know?

EVAN: Because I never told you.

HEIDI: You shouldn't have had to.

EVAN: I lied. About . . . so many things. Not just Connor. Last summer, I just . . . I felt so alone . . .

(He can't go any further than this.)

HEIDI: You can tell me.

EVAN (*Shakes his head*): You'll hate me.

HEIDI: Oh, Evan.

EVAN: You should. If you knew what I tried to do. If you knew who I am, how . . . broken I am.

HEIDI: I already know you. And I love you.

(Beat.)

EVAN: I'm so sorry.

HEIDI: I can promise you, some day all of this . . . this will all feel like a very long time ago.

(Evan shrugs, not believing her.)

EVAN: I don't know.

HEIDI: Your dad . . . do you remember the day he drove by to get his things?

(Evan shakes his head.)

It was a few weeks after he moved out. "Temporarily," we said . . .

SO BIG/SO SMALL [44, 45]

HEIDI:
It was a February day
When your dad came by
    before goin' away
A U-Haul truck in the
    driveway
The day it was suddenly real

I told you not to come
    outside
But you saw that truck
    and you smiled so wide

A real live truck in your
    driveway
We let you sit behind
    the wheel

Goodbye, goodbye
Now it's just me and my
    little guy

And the house felt so big
And I felt so small
The house felt so big
And I felt so small

That night I tucked you
    into bed
I will never forget how
    you sat up and said:

"Is there another truck
    comin' to our driveway
A truck that will take
    Mommy away?"

And the house felt so big
And I felt so small
The house felt so big
And I . . .

And I knew there would be
    moments that I'd miss
And I knew there would be
    space I couldn't fill
And I knew I'd come up
    short a million
    diff'rent ways
And I did, and I do,
    and I will [46]

But like that February day
I will take your hand,
    squeeze it tightly and say:
"There's not another truck
    in the driveway
Your mom isn't goin'
    anywhere
Your mom is stayin'
    right here"
Your mom isn't goin'
    anywhere
Your mom is stayin'
    right here
No matter what
I'll be here . . .

When it all feels so big
'Til it all feels so small
When it all feels so big
'Til it all feels so small
'Til it all feels so small

(Evan goes. His mother lets him go.)

You'll see. I promise.

< ACT TWO SCENE NINE >

(Heidi exits. Life goes on. Hearts break and mend and break once more. Time does its work. Slowly, the sky begins to open. It is enormous.[47] *A vast green field. As far as the eye can see: rows and columns of wooden stakes planted in the grass. Tied to each stake, a small, spindly tree. An orchard. Zoe, sitting on a wrought iron bench, waits, nervous. After a moment, Evan enters.)*

EVAN: Hey.

ZOE: Hi.

(They smile, a bit awkward. Beat.)

EVAN: How are you?

ZOE: Good. Pretty good.

EVAN: You graduate soon, right?

ZOE: In two weeks.

EVAN: Wow. How's being a senior?

ZOE: Busy.

EVAN: I remember that.

ZOE: How's being a freshman?

EVAN: Oh. Well. I actually decided to take a year off . . .

ZOE: Oh.

EVAN: Yeah. Try to save some money. Get a job. I've been taking classes at the community college. So I'll have some credits to transfer in the fall.

ZOE: That's smart.

EVAN: Yeah. We'll see.

(Beat.)

In the meantime, though, I can get you a friends and family discount at Pottery Barn. If you're looking for . . . overpriced home decor.

ZOE: You know, not at the moment . . .

EVAN: Well, if you change your mind . . . I'm only working there for a few more months, though, so the window of opportunity is closing fast.

(They smile.)

ZOE: I always imagine you and Connor here. Even though, obviously . . .

EVAN: This is my first time. I mean, I've probably driven by it a thousand times. I just, every time I think about getting out of the car, I feel like . . . I don't know. I just . . . like I don't deserve to, I guess.

(Beat.)

It's nice. Peaceful.

ZOE: My parents, they're here all the time. We do picnics, like, every weekend. It's helped them. A lot, actually. Having this.

(Beat.)

EVAN: They never told anyone. About Connor's, about the note. About . . . who really wrote it.

(Zoe nods.)

They didn't have to do that. They could have told everyone. What I did.

ZOE: Everybody needed it for something.

EVAN: That doesn't mean it was okay.

ZOE: It saved my parents.

(Pause.)

EVAN: It's weird. I um . . . over the fall, I found this, um, yearbook thing my class made in eighth grade. Most people did, like, collages of their friends. Connor's was a list of his ten favorite books. I've been trying to read all of them.[48]

(Beat.)

I know it's not the same thing as knowing him—it's not, at all, but, I don't know, it's . . .

ZOE: Something.

(Pause.)

It's been . . . hard. It's been a hard year.

EVAN *(For him, as well)*: I know.

(Beat.)

I've been wanting to call you for a long time. I didn't really know what I would say, but then I just . . . I decided to call anyway.

ZOE: I'm happy you did.

(Pause.)

EVAN: I wish we could have met now. Today. For the first time.

ZOE: Me too.

(They look at one another for a long time.)

I should probably . . .

EVAN: Of course.

ZOE: It's just, exams are this week . . .

EVAN: No, totally.

(Zoe begins to go.)

Can I ask you, though? Why did, um, why did you want to meet here?

(A long pause. Zoe looks around.)

ZOE: I wanted to be sure you saw this.

(A beat, and Zoe goes. Evan takes in the immensity of all that is around him. Music begins slowly, softly underneath, as one by one the company begins to enter around him.)

EVAN:

Dear Evan Hansen:

Today is going to be a good day and here's why. Because today, no matter what else, today at least . . . you're you. No hiding, no lying. Just . . . you.
And that's . . . that's enough.

47 **Steven Levenson**

Our set designer David Korins achieves this effect by opening the back wall of the stage and revealing a giant blue scrim. It sounds simple, but the effect of seeing that tremendous burst of color after spending so much time in literal and figurative darkness is breathtaking.

48 **Steven Levenson**

This was added for the Broadway production. I wanted Evan to acknowledge the fact of Connor's life in a concrete way. Connor was not simply a prop for Evan to use as a means of self-discovery. He was a person with dreams and desires and hopes, a person whom Evan will never have the chance to truly know.

FINALE

HEIDI/ALANA/JARED:

All we see is sky
For forever
We let the world
Pass by for forever

HEIDI/ALANA/JARED/LARRY/ CYNTHIA:

Feels like we could
Go on for forever

EVAN:

Maybe some day,
everything that happened . . .
maybe it will all feel like
a distant memory.

Maybe some day no one will even
remember about The Connor
Project. Or me. Maybe some day,

HEIDI/ALANA/JARED/LARRY/ CYNTHIA:

This way

This way

some other kid is going to be standing here, staring out at the trees, feeling so . . . alone, wondering if maybe the world might look different from all the way up there. Better. Maybe he'll start climbing, one branch at a time, and he'll keep going, even when it seems like he can't find another foothold. Even when it feels . . . hopeless. Like everything is telling him to let go. This time, maybe this time, he won't let go. He'll just . . . hold on and he'll keep going.

He'll keep going until he sees the sun.

(People slowly begin to look around, to see one another, to find one another.)

ALL (*Except Evan*):

All we see is light [49]
Watch the sun burn bright
We could be all right for
  forever this way
All we see is sky for
  forever

(Evan steps forward.)

EVAN:

All I see is sky for forever. [50]

(A moment. A suspension. Black.)

— *END*

---

[49] **Benj Pasek**

We debated whether we should end the show with a "You Will Be Found" reprise instead of "For Forever." Then we saw the concept for the design elements for the end of the show: a big open blue sky, saplings, the sound of birds. Evan's fantasy from "For Forever" became real, and we were out of a digital world and into a physical one. We wanted the musical moment to work in the same way, and ended the show with this.

[50] **Benj Pasek**

The show used to end with "let the world pass by for forever" until we saw it in front of an audience in D.C. and decided we wanted the show to conclude on a more hopeful note. We wanted to indicate to the audience that Evan is going to be okay, that there is redemption, forgiveness, and a reason for hope.

CHAPTER 11

STEP INTO THE SUN

The world premiere at Arena Stage in Washington, D.C.

WHEN THE LATE WRITER Larry Gelbart was suffering through the agonizing Washington, D.C., tryout of a 1961 musical adaptation of the Preston Sturges film *Hail the Conquering Hero*, he famously remarked, "If Hitler is alive, I hope he's out of town with a musical." The authors of *Dear Evan Hansen* would no doubt second Gelbart's sentiment, given that they spent much of the time while their own show was in D.C. gripped by panic, pacing the back of the theater, and generally questioning/loathing everything that they'd conceived and written up until that point. "It was one of the more miserable experiences of my life until the first preview," says Benj Pasek.

Putting up a new musical for the first time is difficult under any circumstances, but there were several factors compounding the writers' fear in this case. They were already feeling uncertain about the material after the March workshop, which Steven Levenson refers to as "a really sobering experience." Ahead of the start of rehearsals for Arena Stage, the team axed the ensemble, slimming the cast to just the eight principals; the mothers' duet, "In the Bedroom Down the Hall," left the score; "This Is Me" was out as the opening; and Jared's "Goin' Viral" didn't make the cut. There were many more changes they wanted to implement going into D.C., but there simply wasn't enough room in the tight schedule at Arena to input all of them. Compounding the pressure, Levenson technically also had a full-time

job in Los Angeles, working on *Masters of Sex*. (Not to mention his wife was pregnant at the time.) "I was literally leaving rehearsals at night and going back to my hotel room to write and rewrite episodes in between writing and rewriting the musical," he says. "I was losing my mind. I felt so schizophrenic, and I didn't have a free moment in the day."

"Seemingly minor changes could have major implications."

NEARLY ALL OF THE CHANGES THAT THE writers made served the overarching goal of keeping the spotlight relentlessly trained on Evan, focusing the plot on his choices and their consequences. The most significant of these changes involved the stolen "Dear Evan Hansen" letter that sets the plot in motion when the Murphys mistake it for Connor's suicide note. From the very first draft through the final workshop, that letter was one that Evan had written as a response to an essay question for a college scholarship contest. But between the workshop and the start of rehearsals for Arena Stage, Levenson turned the letter into a confidence-boosting assignment from Evan's therapist. "I had always enjoyed the fact that all of these people's lives are upended by such a random, ultimately insignificant thing," Levenson says. "But it just began to feel willfully, perversely out of left field. An assignment from a therapist seemed so much more personal, so that when the letter becomes the central hinge of our story, it makes a certain emotional sense—this assignment, which is meant to act as a form of healing for Evan, actually does end up doing just that, in a very different way than his therapist had intended, obviously."

The writers also discovered that seemingly minor changes could have major implications. Ben Platt remembers huddling with Pasek, Levenson, and Justin Paul after rehearsal one evening to try to figure out a character moment for Evan between his wrenching confession to the Murphys in "Words Fail" and his returning home to Heidi to receive the tender solace of "So Big/So Small."

"I think we all felt that Evan had to come to some sort of conclusion on his own without just running home to be saved by his mother," Platt says. "I wanted it to be very clear that he was aware that the primary reason for his continuing the lie was that he liked this fake version of himself better than his real self. And then they went away for the night and came back with that beautiful soliloquy and reprise of 'Waving.'" The addition of this relatively short new section of music completely transformed Evan's arc, the writers found to their surprise, forcing the character to confront the darkest parts of his own psyche before he can receive the solace that his mother provides in "So Big/So Small."

While the writers may speak about Washington, D.C., in terms more often associated with the inner circles of Hell, the cast members refer to the experience with such phrases as "like a vacation" and "summer camp." Arena Stage housed the entire company in a new condo complex near the theater with a rooftop pool, around which the actors lounged away many an hour. Michael Park took to manning the grill like the dad he is in real life and onstage—hosting barbecues, and even a huge crab cookout on his birthday. ("I never went to a barbecue," Levenson says.) "The nice thing was there was nobody we didn't love," Platt says. "It was just a really cohesive family."

And that family-like atmosphere proved helpful as they headed into intense and stressful rehearsals. As the writers continued tinkering with the material, Michael Greif, for whom this was nothing new, was calmly putting the show on its feet. "Michael is incredibly wise about knowing when not to get involved," Levenson says. "A lot of that time, he was, like, 'I'm going to stage the show while you guys hyperventilate over there.'"

Pasek and Paul introduced a new opening, "This Will Be the Year," which made it to the stage in D.C. Much like "Anybody Have a Map," which was added Off Broadway, the song spanned both the Hansen and Murphy household, but instead of lamenting their woes, the characters sang about what was going to change in the weeks ahead with a desperate optimism. "It was a little too generic—it didn't feel like the rest of the play," Greif says of the song.

The Act One finale at Arena Stage was called "A Part of Me." It was one of the earliest songs Pasek and Paul wrote for the show and still contained fragments of their original, more cynical and satirical take on the Facebook generation. "As writers, we were judging our characters as opposed to investing in them," Pasek says. "It was us saying, 'Look at what happens when people go online and claim deaths and make them about themselves, and look at people reacting to the selfishness of needing to be seen.' We were wagging our finger at that phenomenon."

Some of the changes were difficult. Greif still regrets cutting Cynthia's solo "A Little Bit of Light" during previews in D.C., wishing that they'd realized the song didn't belong in the show sooner, before Jennifer Laura Thompson had put in the work on it. Pasek notes that the writing team was initially worried the audience wouldn't go on Evan's journey, so they overcompensated by having Cynthia tell Evan how much joy he's given her in allowing the family to remember Connor fondly. But they made the change when they saw that Cynthia's embrace of Evan after "For Forever" achieved the same emotional effect in a single gesture.

< Michael Park, Ben Platt, and Laura Dreyfuss visit the White House.

In cutting "A Little Bit of Light," the writers also decided to add Larry and Cynthia to "Requiem," which initially began as a solo for Zoe. Since Cynthia no longer had a song expressing her feelings about Connor's death, "Requiem" expanded to create a triptych of familial grief and illustrate each person's mourning mechanisms. Also, since the song is one of the only times Evan is offstage, expanding it in this way allowed the writers to economize storylines. "When we do take time away from Evan, we needed to pack in as much as we could because we have to mostly stay with him," Paul says.

Another way the writers kept the focus on Evan involved the suicide note. In previous drafts, Jared had been the one to put the suicide note online, in Act Two, to get back at Evan, but again, the writers felt the need to give their title character more agency and ultimately more moral responsibility.

Perhaps the most pressing dramaturgical question to solve at Arena was what to do with Connor, particularly now that there was no singing and dancing ensemble for Mike Faist to join after Connor's death. Pasek and Paul wrote the song "Disappear," and the writers and Greif started playing with what it would look like for the character to have scenes after his death. In D.C., Connor appeared spectrally to his family during "A Part of Me," which proved emotionally powerful, but logically problematic, as it seemed to imply that Connor had returned as a ghost. This seemed confusing to the authors, who realized that they were "trying to have our cake and eat it, too," as Levenson says now, employing the dead Connor in too many different, contradictory ways. Either Connor was a ghost who could appear at will to whomever he wished, or he was the voice inside Evan's head—he couldn't be both. After Arena, the writers would settle on the concept of three Connors in the course of the musical: Connor the living person before his death, Connor the figment that Evan and Jared create in "Sincerely Me," and Connor the inner voice of Evan. "And we realized that we had to be incredibly precise about what exactly he was," Levenson says.

In D.C., the writers and Greif also started to make more explicit connections between Connor and Evan. This led to Levenson drafting a scene in which Evan revealed that his fall from the tree was in fact a failed suicide attempt. The revelation came near the end of the musical after what is now called, in the score, "Words Fail (Part 1)," where Evan confesses his lie to the Murphys. In Levenson's new scene, as Evan left the Murphys, Connor came back to taunt him, insisting that in spite of his revelation to the Murphys, he was still lying to himself. Connor then forced Evan to admit that he hadn't fallen from the tree—he had let go. Although Greif and the cast rehearsed the scene extensively, the writers ultimately decided to cut it before previews in D.C. "There were two interrelated problems with what we were trying to do," Levenson says. "One: The information had no dramatic purpose. It did not forward the story at all. It was just a piece of information. It just sort of sat there. Two: It helped add to the confusion of who/what Connor was. *Why is he forcing Evan to admit this? To what end?*"

AS THEIR TIME IN THE REHEARSAL room wound down, the writers continued to meticulously refine every detail, anxious about bringing in an audience. "Before that first preview, we were, like, 'Steven's done his job, and we haven't taken on enough of the dramatic work in these songs,'" Pasek says. However, to the writers' shock, audiences in early previews proved more than willing to go on the journey with Evan and accept the dark and morally complicated story. Once the authors saw that people were open to embracing the thorny premise of the show, and the moral ambiguity of its central character, they were able to shift their attention and make more focused changes in response to audience reactions.

And their reactions were electric. Levenson remembers arriving at the theater during previews one day to find a line of teenagers waiting for the box office to open and thinking, *What is going on here?* "We had no idea if we would sell *any* tickets. We had a weird name.

(right) **The show's key art for** the poster and program at Arena Stage.

People had never heard of it," he says. "People started coming back multiple times and started to become, like, fans of the show." The run eventually sold out and was extended. "Word of mouth is the most authentic thing ever," Stacey Mindich says. "You leave a show, and if you didn't like it, you don't talk about it, and if you loved it, you want to talk about it all the time."

But word of mouth was only one part of the strategy in launching the show. Mindich used the Arena Stage run as what she calls an "out-of-town tryout for marketing," quickly realizing that she needed to bring on New York–based advertising, digital, and press teams to make the journey with the show. She hired Serino/Coyne for advertising, Situation Interactive to handle digital marketing, and O+M as the press representatives.

One of Serino/Coyne's first contributions was the idea of pixelating the image of Platt on the program and poster at Arena Stage. Mindich and the creative team had been unhappy with how it looked on its own, as a picture of the show's star at a laptop felt too "on the nose" and expected. Distorting the photo made the key art feel "interesting and strange in the right way," Levenson says, subtly emphasizing the role of technology in the musical, as well as themes of identity and disguise.

Notable locals took notice of the musical as well, like Supreme Court Justice Ruth Bader Ginsburg, who attended opening night on July 30, 2015. (The star-struck writers couldn't keep themselves from requesting a photo with the legendary jurist, who gamely complied.) "I believe we really took D.C. by storm," says Mindich. "We were born in D.C." She also notes that they began an important relationship with the *Washington Post*'s Peter Marks, who would go on to become one of the show's earliest and most ardent champions. He hosted a panel with the authors and director during previews,

discussing the process of creating a new musical, before he had seen the show himself. When he finally did see it, he was emotionally bowled over, partly because his own daughter suffers from anxiety. "I remember choking up—I had never seen this on the stage before," Marks says. In his review, he praised the show as "a heart-piercingly lovely new musical."

Charles Isherwood also made the trip to D.C. to review the show for *The New York Times* on opening night. "It was scary to see this piece of New York come to the theater," Levenson says. Happily, Isherwood gave them another reason to celebrate, calling the show a "a sweet, sad and quite moving new musical." He did criticize the integration of Connor after his death, an aspect the team would continue to work on in the months ahead. Following the trail of good word of mouth and positive reviews, members of the New York theater cognoscenti started hopping on the Acela to see what was going on in Washington, and two weeks after opening night at Arena, an Off-Broadway run at Second Stage Theater was announced for spring 2016. But despite the groundswell of enthusiasm for the show, the writers still weren't entirely satisfied.

At the final Arena performance, Pasek and Paul were standing at the back of the theater, cataloguing all the changes that needed to be made, and Levenson made a list of things to address before Off-Broadway rehearsals began. "Not one scene didn't get changed in some way between D.C. and Second Stage," he says. "Musicals are so precise in terms of placement—where things go, when things go, how things happen, the order of events—that tiny little tweaks have gigantic effects that you have no way of knowing before you make them."

Greif, of course, had ideas of his own. "It was very clear that the first act was overly long and spun its own wheels," he says. "And it was too mournful." But he could also give the writers perspective as they were fretting through the process. "I had had some experience with that kind of response," Greif says of the striking audience reaction in D.C. "I could try to encourage them to trust it at some point and recognize that while we're all worried about reviews and things like that, the audience was telling us something very real that they could trust in and could continue to trust in." However, he adds: "It's also good to take nothing for granted."

CHAPTER 12

IF I COULD TELL HER:
LAURA DREYFUSS

on the resilience of Zoe Murphy

F THERE'S ONE THING LAURA DREYFUSS admires about the character of Zoe Murphy, it's her resilience. The sweet, sensitive teenager is just trying to make it through her junior year of high school, which can be a challenging time for any young person, but particularly for a girl who has faded into the background her entire life as her parents' attention has largely been given to her troubled older brother, Connor. But when he kills himself, her life turns upside down, and she is forced to reckon with her ambivalent feelings toward her distant, and oftentimes aggressive, sibling. Then she meets Evan, who convinces her that Connor—in spite of all appearances—cared deeply for her, and as she buys into his version of history, she finds herself falling for her brother's "best friend." Just as she's getting close to her new boyfriend, her world flips again when he reveals everything was a lie, leaving her and her family devastated—yet again. "She doesn't allow herself to be a victim," Dreyfuss says, "and she easily could be."

Auditioning for the role tested Dreyfuss's own inner strength: When she tried out for an early reading, she thought she completely bombed. She was looking forward to going in for the show, as she was a fan of the authors and director Michael Greif, and she thought the writing felt natural and easy. So, when Greif stopped her mid-scene at the audition, she was certain she hadn't got the part. "I interpreted that as him saying, 'We don't want to see you anymore.' I thought I must have been terrible," Dreyfuss recalls. "I went home and was, like, 'Gosh, I'm so bummed. I don't know what happened.'"

Luckily, she read the director's reaction incorrectly and landed the role, but after she was cast, another

> ## [Zoe] doesn't allow herself to be a victim...and she easily could be."

opportunity presented itself that almost lost her the part. Dreyfuss had put herself on tape for *Glee*, and the weekend before the reading, she received a call that she needed to fly out to Los Angeles immediately to screentest for the series and potentially miss the reading. While Dreyfuss recognizes that actors can be easily replaced during developmental stages and there's no guarantee of a production contract, she had faith in the musical and didn't want to let anyone down.

"I was, like, that can't happen. I care about this project too much," Dreyfuss recalls. She went out to L.A., booked the role on *Glee*, and took the red-eye back to New York on Monday night, getting in at 6 a.m. on Tuesday for the reading that day. "It was one of those moments when your intuition and instincts are really strong about something, and you know that you just have to see it through."

Dreyfuss looks just like the girl next door whom every boy had a crush on in high school, and as you watch her onstage, it's not hard to see why. She radiates such authenticity and honesty that the slightest look or smirk can pluck an emotional chord in anyone's heart. As Evan's bestower of forgiveness, Zoe represents the "golden rule" (do unto others as you would have them do unto you) through her graciousness toward him at the end of the musical. Dreyfuss herself admits that when she was younger, she more resembled Zoe in the first act, clinging to grievances as her character does with Connor. "I would definitely hold grudges," she says. At this stage in her life, Dreyfuss hopes she would react as Zoe does in the final scene in the orchard. "She's able to forgive him because she's able to recognize the part that she played in all of it," Dreyfuss says. "It's hard for her to accept at first, but I think with a year's time, she is able to see it for what it is—also that she loves him for it. She loves him because it did fix her family in a weird way. It was a horrible thing, but the intentions weren't malicious."

Forming a close bond with Ben Platt onstage and off has been a joy for Dreyfuss, and the two became fast friends, carving out small rituals for themselves, like watching *The Bachelor/Bachelorette* on Monday nights. "From day one, Ben and I have always had a very deep understanding of each other and these characters," she says. "There was never a need to even talk

Laura Dreyfuss ✓
@lauradreyfuss   Following

Caught snuggling 🎭 #DearEvanHansen
#evanandzoeforever @BenSPLATT

about it. It felt so incredibly seamless. We spoke the same language, which was really exciting and fun."

Of course, onstage, Evan and Zoe's relationship is much more complicated than Platt and Dreyfuss's easy offstage one. Initially, Zoe struggles to believe Evan's lie about Connor, and she feels like she's the only one in her family who remembers her brother as he really was: a "monster." She sings to this sentiment in "Requiem," which Dreyfuss says is the "most difficult part of the show" for her. "She's wishing that he was someone she could grieve," Dreyfuss explains.

After all you put me through
Don't say it wasn't true
That you were not the monster
That I knew

As Evan takes her on an emotional ride to reconnect with her family and mourn her brother's death, she starts to fall for him, particularly when he speaks about Connor and being remembered in "You Will Be Found." "When you experience a loss, it's so therapeutic when people speak out and when people say things about that person that are kind and wonderful, and they can help you come to peace with it. He did that for her. That end of the Act Two moment is kind of her realizing how much he's healed her," she says. "I don't think it's a surprise, for example, when two people die and then their opposite spouses end up together because they were able to connect over this grief, which in a weird way brings you together."

Dreyfuss grew up about forty-five minutes outside of Manhattan, in Morristown, New Jersey. She would frequently come into the city to see Broadway shows with her mother, and was drawn to the theater at an early age. She started performing in elementary school when her mom put her in local community theater acting classes, believing Dreyfuss needed an outlet for her creative energy. "It was the first time I ever felt like I belonged somewhere," she says, calling herself a "weirdo" and adding that she was a theater dork "before drama was cool." "I felt like I was just around like-minded people. I was a really shy kid, so it felt really great to come out of my shell a bit and be comfortable doing so."

Her older sister was an understudy in *Mamma Mia!* on Broadway when Dreyfuss was 13, and seeing her sister go onstage made Dreyfuss believe she could pursue this career path as well. She calls her sister her "biggest inspiration" and her "best friend," and credits her with training her at a young age—directing her in talent shows, introducing her to scenes from her Acting 101 class at New York University, and advising Dreyfuss to attend Boston Conservatory over a college in New York because of the many respected colleagues in the industry who she knew had attended the school.

"I wish I had seen a show like this when I was in high school."

After graduating from the conservatory, where she appeared in roles such as Audrey in *Little Shop of Horrors* and Corie in *Barefoot in the Park*, she moved to New York and, two weeks later, booked the tour of the revival of *Hair* as an understudy for Crissy and Sheila. She went on to be the standby for Cristin Milioti in *Once*, taking over the role for a stint, before joining *Once* choreographer Steven Hoggett on *What's It All About?* at New York Theatre Workshop. A few months after the Burt Bacharach tuner closed, she landed the reading of *Dear Evan Hansen*.

Growing up, Dreyfuss faced many of the same struggles with self-esteem and social acceptance as the characters in the show. She recalls an especially painful memory when she dressed up in a clown-like outfit on "Freak Day" for her school's Spirit Week. Entering her classroom in full costume, she was surprised to find every one of her fellow classmates in street clothes, before suddenly realizing that she had remembered the day incorrectly. Other students would taunt Dreyfuss about this incident for years. "Kids are mean, kids are insecure, and bullies are real," she says. "It's hard, and you have to figure out how to be resilient through all of it."

Dreyfuss thinks audiences can learn something from Zoe's tenacity—as she herself certainly has. "No one is going to give you happiness—you have to find that yourself and you have to figure that out for yourself," she says. "I wish I had seen a show like this when I was in high school. We really need to celebrate what makes people unique and what makes people different. What's so great about this show is that it does that, and it teaches people that it's okay to be who you are. That's what gives you strength."

< 12 >

A LITTLE REINVENTION

Danny Mefford creates a physical vocabulary

THERE ARE MANY REASONS WHY CHARAC-ters in a musical would break into dance, but the lonely, anxious, misunderstood characters in *Dear Evan Hansen* hardly have a reason to look beyond their screens, let alone step-touch to the music. Choreographer Danny Mefford's challenge was to figure out where dance fit in, and truth be told, he says, "actual dance doesn't belong in very much." For Mefford, every impulse had to propel the plot forward, and he rarely gave the actors specific steps or told them how he wanted them to move. "What I felt like I needed to do was tell them what the story was," he says, "and let them have whatever feelings they have about that and let that inform their body."

There's really only one stop-and-dance song in *Dear Evan Hansen*: "Sincerely, Me." The number could accommodate higher-energy choreography, Mefford felt, as it's happening in the characters' imaginations—

a fictional Connor, as imagined by Jared and Evan, acting out the emails the two are fabricating. The layered motions also work on a deeper level, as the small gestures that Evan makes (a handshake, a chest bump) start to reflect in Connor's actions, subtly illustrating the idea that the Connor who returns is a concoction of Evan's psyche.

In each of the numbers, Mefford sought to use movement to reflect the characters' emotions, and he soon realized that different storytelling moments could speak to each other through choreography. Since Benj Pasek and Justin Paul wrote "Waving Through a Window" and "You Will Be Found" to be complementary numbers (the latter fulfills the "I Want" motive of the first: to be seen and heard and "found"), Mefford chose to have the movement in the two songs echo one another. In "Waving," when Platt starts to sing "On the outside always looking in," the cast, who are circled around him, turn their backs, leaving him, quite literally, on the outside. But in "You Will Be Found," as the company stands in the same ring around Platt, they sing toward him, showing that they acknowledge and celebrate his presence.

There may not be time-stepping and pirouettes, but these subtle, precise movements illustrate the inner depths of the characters' longings and insecurities in a way no fouetté ever could. "If I wanted to see people dancing impressively, I'd go to the American Ballet Theater," he says. "I feel like we go to the musical theater for something different than that. We go there to escape, but also to see ourselves in those people and to feel something true."

CHAPTER 13

WHAT WE'VE GOT GOING IS GOOD

The New York debut at Second Stage

W**HEN STACEY MINDICH** left breakfast with Justin Paul, Benj Pasek, Steven Levenson, and Michael Greif at the Mandarin Oriental in D.C. the day after *Dear Evan Hansen*'s out-of-town opening night, her first call was to Carole Rothman, artistic director of Second Stage. "I said, 'I know your season is probably overstuffed but I'm hoping you might have room for us,'" Mindich says. Rothman responded without a moment's hesitation: "If you need a home, you have one with us."

Second Stage was a natural fit for many reasons, not least of which were the strong relationships that many members of the creative team already had with the theater. Pasek and Paul's *Dogfight* had premiered there; Greif directed *Next to Normal* at the theater; and Mindich had worked with the company on shows like Quiara Alegría Hudes's *Water by the Spoonful* and Jason Robert Brown's *The Last Five Years*.

While almost every industry member who saw the show at Arena Stage—from producers to agents to managers—told Mindich she could take the show directly to Broadway, she didn't think the material was ready and neither did the writers. Even though the team was coming off a wave of positive buzz and promising reviews in D.C., the authors were scrutinizing their work more closely than ever and were eager to dive back into rehearsals and continue refining the musical. "It wasn't

like, 'This is going to be a Broadway hit.' It was like, 'Peter Marks gave us a good review,'" Pasek says. And Pasek was also coming to the material with a deeper personal connection, having lost two friends to suicide in the time since the musical has closed at Arena.

"It made me really start to think about the show from the perspective of: What does a grieving family need? As opposed to: What does a lost kid need?" says Pasek, who spent time at the funerals observing his friends' families searching for meaning and reason in the deaths. During one of the memorials, the boy's father appealed to the friends and family in attendance to share with him any anecdotes about his son after the service. Pasek saw how desperately the father wanted to hear something, anything positive about his child—a dynamic that felt eerily similar to that between Evan and the Murphys in the show. "That instinct of wanting to feel like you can provide relief for someone who is grieving, I think that that's really real," Pasek adds. "I understood Evan deeply in that moment."

A**S SUMMER TURNED TO FALL AND THE** first day of Second Stage rehearsals began to loom ever closer, the writing team got back to work. By this point in the process, the three knew how to collaborate well. Their cardinal rule from the beginning was to make sure they were all on the same page before bringing a change or an idea to another department. Pasek and Paul note that having a third person on the team proved especially useful when it came to creative disagreements, in which Levenson would often act as the tiebreaker. "Three is a good number," Paul notes. "We can take out our initial burst of frustration with one another, and that takes a little bit of the edge off," Pasek adds.

One of the times they shared a concern with the larger team was during tech rehearsals at Second Stage, when they began to hear a steady hum of white noise in the theater. The sound persisted through the first weekend of previews, and while the musical numbers would temporarily mask the low-level buzzing, the creative team noticed that audiences weren't paying attention during the book scenes with the same intensity and focus they had at Arena Stage. Greif and his designers noticed the noise as well, but with a long list of notes to address in the precious little rehearsal time left before opening, there was pressure to push the issue until later in previews. The authors, however, were indefatigable, raising the topic again and again, until finally the wider team agreed to gather in the theater and pinpoint the cause of the noise.

At midnight on a Tuesday, after a full day of rehearsals through the morning and afternoon and a performance in the evening, the entire staff of the show—from the general manager to Mindich—sat in the theater and listened. The designers turned on every lighting instrument, speaker, and projector one by one to try to determine the source of the sound. Finally, they discovered that it was a combination of moving lights, projectors, and fans—one of these would have to go. With the irreplaceable role that projections play in the musical, and the necessity of fans to cool the projectors, all eyes turned to lighting designer Japhy Weideman. "Basically, Second Stage is a concrete room, and the ceiling that's above the lights is concrete, and so it just bounced any sound down," Weideman explains. "They were right—we really did need to change the technology, because it was loud."

He and his team stayed up for the next thirty-six hours replacing a good chunk of the existing equipment and relighting most of the show. "That's the only time in my career that's ever happened," he says. "We did what we had to do." And sure enough, with the white noise gone, the book scenes began to play with the electricity and interest they had at Arena.

The incident is indicative of the holistic view the writers have of storytelling and their detail-oriented, bordering on obsessive devotion to perfecting the show on every level. "We were at the point where we knew when things weren't working and felt that we couldn't be quiet about it," says Paul, who had another factor adding to his stress. His wife was due to give birth to their daughter on the night of the first preview. Fortunately, the baby came a couple days later, but after they left the hospital, he had to duck out to go to rehearsals and watch the show on some of the first few nights his new baby was at home.

Often the writers had to fight to get rid of their own work. Toward the end of previews, Levenson cut his "favorite piece of writing in the entire show," a short scene between Evan and Zoe right before Evan puts on Connor's tie and gives his assembly speech. The scene is a touching moment in which the characters discuss the nature of grief and the urge to remember the best in people, but cutting it was necessary, Levenson concluded, to improve the flow at the end of Act One.

ZOE: I think grief can make you do weird things. Things you wouldn't do normally.
EVAN: I think that's probably true.
Pause.
ZOE: Why did he push you that day?
EVAN: Oh. I mean. I think, didn't I tell you before?
ZOE: I don't believe you.
Beat.
EVAN: I sometimes...I get scared talking to people, I guess, sort of. He was always trying to get me to be more outgoing. And he'd get annoyed sometimes. If he thought I wasn't trying hard enough. That sort of thing.
ZOE: So I guess that means you're probably pretty nervous about your speech tomorrow?
EVAN: How did you guess?
They smile.
ZOE: Well, my mom is in love with you. This whole Connor Project thing, too, she's obsessed.
EVAN: She's really awesome.
ZOE: She likes you being here. You make her feel like Connor is still here, I think, in a way. Like you bring him with you somehow. But not like how she remembers him. Different. Better than she remembers him.
EVAN: That's what happens when people leave, I think. When they're gone, you don't have to be reminded of all the bad things. They can just stay the way you want them forever. Perfect.

The music of the show went through an evolution alongside the scene changes. Deciding how to launch the musical had proven to be a challenge throughout the development of the show, and the writers were not satisfied with the solution they had reached in D.C. They knew they wanted to open the show with Evan,

"How do we get Evan to be the decision-maker without us hating him for doing so?"

New songs are brewing at #dearevanhansen rehearsals at @2STNYC w/ @rachelbayjones and @JLTsayswhat! #whoisevanhansen

but they didn't want him to sing until "Waving Through a Window." They debated not having an opening number, but "just from a practical standpoint, it's helpful to establish at the onset that song will be used to tell story," Pasek says. Realizing that the other person who could sing with expertise about Evan was his mother, and already knowing that Evan's story ended with Heidi, mother and son together on the sofa in "So Big/ So Small," Pasek explains, they "reverse engineered" the opening to act as a bookend to that number.

The composers struggled with the Act One finale as well. "A Part of Me," the number at Arena Stage, was more social commentary than character-driven—Connor's death went viral online, but it didn't seem motivated by Evan. The writers also wanted to look at the situation with more empathy, exploring the deeper human impulse behind the ostensibly superficial exhibitionism of public grieving. "So many people feel invisible and alone. While some could initially view mourning a stranger online as a selfish act, it comes from a real place of loneliness and a desperate need to connect with a community," Pasek says. "Who better to exemplify that than Evan? Evan is offering hope to those people but really ultimately to himself." From these concerns and questions, Pasek and Paul ultimately arrived at "You Will Be Found," a song that traces the viral explosion of Connor directly to Evan's speech at the assembly.

As the team developed and refined the structure of "You Will Be Found" through the preview process, they began to envision a crucial change to Evan's speech. In early versions of the speech at Second Stage, Evan actively chose at a certain point to put away his note cards and speak off the cuff, leading into the song. Pasek, Paul, and Levenson now imagined raising the stakes considerably by having Evan drop his note cards in the middle of the speech. The accident forces him in the moment to decide whether to run away in fear, as he always has in similar situations, or take the opportunity to speak from his heart.

Platt was initially anxious about how dropping the note cards would play onstage. "That was a really scary thing for me, and I had a lot of trouble with it at first because I

was so afraid of it feeling fake or feeling forced," Platt says. "Eventually, it was so meaningful and just felt exactly like what should happen, and it forces him to be courageous in a way he hasn't been. It makes the honesty of 'You Will Be Found' and that first verse way more weighted, because his other option was to crawl off the stage."

The major element that the team finessed at Second Stage was the one that had bedeviled them in D.C.—Connor. It was imperative to the writers that the audience understand that, in each of his appearances after his death, Connor is acting as an inner voice of Evan's, rather than as a ghost or a flashback. In this new iteration, Connor took on a consistency of character and intention he had lacked at Arena. In all of his scenes, Connor serves the same function, as the voice always urging Evan to continue the lie. Using Connor in this way also allowed them to solve a separate dilemma: how to have Evan make bad choices without losing the sympathy of the audience. "Being able to use Connor to convince Evan to take action was very helpful," Pasek explains, noting that it is Connor who encourages Evan to not only continue, but to expand the lie in Act One in the song "Disappear." "We were trying to figure out: How do we get Evan to be the decision-maker without us hating him for doing so?"

While driving in L.A., mid-conversation with his wife, Levenson had a realization about how to make it crystal clear to audiences that Connor was not a ghost, but a reflection of Evan's own insecurities. He added one phrase at the end of Connor and Evan's interaction in Act Two:

EVAN: I'm ready to be done with it.
CONNOR: If you really believe that, then why are you standing here, talking to yourself? Again?

That scene was also the one in which Levenson finally managed to incorporate the idea of Evan's attempted suicide into the musical. By adding it here—instead of closer to the end of the show, as he had tried in D.C.—the idea serves to activate Evan in a crucial moment of the story. "Just as Evan starts to believe that he can tell the Murphys the truth, tell the world the truth about what he has done, because maybe they will still accept him, Connor reminds him of this secret as a way of reminding him of how deeply unlovable he really is," Levenson explains. As a result, Evan doubles down on his lie and the Connor Project, choosing ultimately to share the letter with Alana. "Connor fulfills the role he has held throughout the show—as the voice pushing Evan to keep lying," Levenson continues. "Connor is really a voice of self-preservation—Evan cannot face the truth, and Connor reminds him of that. So even though Connor forces him to admit the truth to himself, it's in the service of maintaining the lie."

Other changes at Second Stage were unnoticeable to the audience, but equally labor-intensive for the creative team. Designer David Korins built the show at Arena Stage with the intention of transferring it directly to Broadway, but the space at Second Stage was significantly smaller than Arena's Kreeger Theater. "We had a real come-to-Jesus moment where it was like, are we going to try to maintain this design, or are we going to reconceive it for what would be our New York production?" Korins says. "Everyone felt very committed that we had cracked the code to the show and really wanted to make this thing happen." So they found a way to keep the basic aesthetic of the set the same. (While the smaller space was less than ideal for Korins, the decrease from 510 seats in the Kreeger Theater at Arena to only 299 at Second Stage meant that each ticket became more coveted night after night.)

The move to Second Stage also marked a new era in terms of the way in which fans could interact with the

show. Projection designer Peter Nigrini and Situation Interactive vice president Jeremy Kraus created a social media campaign asking fans to submit a video of themselves holding a piece of paper with "#YouWillBe-Found" on it, representing the millions of people in the fictional world of the show that see and are inspired by Evan's speech. Nigrini and actor Will Roland appeared in the video soliciting submissions to appear in the musical's Act One finale every night.

"We were so excited to see the videos coming in from our fans, and now, in the show, we have videos from people ages 18 to 87," Mindich says. "One of my favorites is my associate producer's grandfather. It all feels very authentic to the way real-life social media works. And it becomes very moving, when paired with the song 'You Will Be Found.'"

THE COMPANY CELEBRATED TWO OPEN-ing nights, first for the Second Stage family (staff, board members, friends of the theater) on April 24, 2016, at which the ovation for the show went on for so long that the actors had to be called back from their dressing rooms to take another bow. For the official press opening on May 1, the company, stars, and friends—such as Anna Kendrick, Darren Criss, and Leslie Odom Jr.—made their way to John's Pizzeria for an aftershow celebration.

One of the opening night guests was Michael Park, who was performing in *Tuck Everlasting* on Broadway while *Dear Evan Hansen* was at Second Stage. When Park saw John Dossett perform the role of Larry Murphy that night, he "couldn't wait to get back." And Dossett wasn't the only newcomer Off Broadway; Kristolyn Lloyd completed the cast as Alana. "Everyone was really sweet and really warm and reached out a lot," Lloyd says of joining the show at Second Stage. "Alana was a difficult part. She had gone through a lot of rewrites to solidify her as a character. So coming in, I was trying to figure out how she fits inside of me as a person, and also how she fits in the story."

From the moment the reviews came out on opening night, it was clear that *Dear Evan Hansen* was the newest hit in town. "It's the finest, most emotionally resonant score yet from this promising young songwriting team," Charles Isherwood wrote in the *New York Times*.

"Book writer Steven Levenson has found a way to dramatize the plot in ways that are inevitable within the story's logic while always remaining surprising," Jesse Green wrote in *New York Magazine*. "It belongs in that pantheon of musicals that lovers of the form seek to experience over and over," Peter Marks wrote in the *Washington Post*.

The run sold out and extended through the end of May, going on to earn Obie Awards for Pasek, Paul, Levenson, and Platt, in addition to Outer Critics Awards for book and new Off-Broadway musical, as well as the Drama Desk Award for outstanding lyrics. Before the production concluded, Mindich announced what many had already assumed: The musical would be making its way to Broadway in the upcoming season.

"After Second Stage, we felt satisfied just in knowing, 'Okay, there's an audience here in New York that connects to the show and that is excited about it,'" Paul says. "We felt like we had gotten to do a lot of the work that we wanted to do and the Second Stage audience and the New York audience, just like the D.C. audience, was extraordinarily helpful to us, and we were able to start refining things. And we came away from that with a laundry list—but a smaller laundry list than before—of the next set of things that we wanted to work on."

< (left) **The cast and creative team celebrate opening night Off Broadway.**

CHAPTER 14

IT'S THE HARD WAY, BUT IT'S THE RIGHT WAY

Mike Faist, Michael Park, and Jennifer Laura Thompson on creating a complicated family

MEET THE MURPHYS. From the outside, everything looks picture-perfect: the perky mom in yoga pants running from PTA meetings to volunteer gigs, the handsome, buttoned-up lawyer dad, and the two attractive teenage kids. But inside, the fractures run deep—the mom is searching for an identity; the dad lives behind an emotional wall; the son is troubled, seemingly beyond help; and his sensitive sister has gotten lost in the shuffle. They are clearly living in a house of cards about to fall. The suicide of the son, Connor, seems certain to break this family, when a boy named Evan appears and through a bit of revisionist history provides temporary solace and hope. It's a respite and an escape, until he reveals the truth, and the family is forced to question why they were so willing to believe a lie in the first place. These are dark places to go for an actor every night, forcing oneself into a mental place of someone who would attempt suicide or imagining what it would be like to lose a child, but somehow, Mike Faist, Michael Park, and Jennifer Laura Thompson find a way to make their performances look effortless while portraying these broken human beings.

MIKE FAIST

A KID FROM OHIO WHO GREW UP watching classic MGM musicals, dreaming of growing up to be just like Gene Kelly, isn't exactly the type of performer you might immediately think of to portray a brooding, misunderstood teenager who hides his insecurities with acts of aggression and ultimately takes his own life. Nor would you think that an actor playing a character who dies after the musical's second scene and has no song of his own would attract the attention of awards nominators. But Mike Faist earned an unexpected—and well-deserved—Tony nomination for his chilling, almost James Dean–like portrayal of Connor Murphy, the boy whose suicide becomes a rallying cry for connection by the show's hero, his schoolmates, and ultimately, a multitude of strangers on the internet searching for meaning in tragedy.

It's the type of role that Faist, who made his Broadway debut as a twirling, leaping, turn-of-the-century newsboy in *Newsies*, had been yearning to play. "I wanted to

> **"I think Connor is a person who feels too much. And he doesn't know how to express it."**

tell complicated stories," he says. "I wanted to grow in my craft as an actor. I wanted to get better."

Long and lithe, with a crookedly handsome face and hair that brushes the top of his shoulders, Faist was in the show's second reading and has been with it ever since. He didn't, however, realize that his character died so early in Act One until after the first day of rehearsal for the reading, when he went home, cracked open the script, and read it over a bottle of wine. In early drafts, Connor didn't reappear after his death. Instead, Faist would switch gears, put on a different backpack, and pretend to be another student at the school as part of a singing and dancing ensemble, which existed through the workshop until just before the first production in D.C. However, in all of the readings, Faist would always pop back into character for the rousing "Sincerely, Me," the one moment in which he's able to show off his impressive dancing skills.

As rehearsals went on, the authors began developing Connor's role in the show after his death, as the inner voice of Evan's most furtive desires and fears. They also planted more clues throughout the musical establishing that Connor and Evan may not have been so different after all. Faist found himself taking on some of Platt's physical traits, such as his hunched-over posture, as he increasingly saw the continuity between his character

In order to get into character, Faist initially devised a pre-show ritual that would take him to the dark place he needed to go."

and Evan. "The suicide is what brings it home—Connor kills himself and Evan attempted to kill himself," Faist says. "There's an instant bond because of that. It's interesting he's having these conversations with the kid, obviously, because throughout the play, it's this fabrication of this friendship. I think on a deeper level, we were a lot closer than I think we could've ever imagined."

When Faist first read the role of Connor, the part was more of a two-dimensional bully: "Connor was taunting Evan for the sake of taunting him. He was not nearly as complex as he is now." However, as the role became more complicated, doubt began to creep into Faist's mind that he had the right stuff to bring Connor to life. "For the longest time, I just felt like I was not good enough to take on this role," he says, adding that he didn't feel that he had mastered his performance until about sixty performances into the Broadway run.

Now, the character's complexity is what Faist appreciates most about the role. Audience members might feel like they know who Connor is based on his look, which his classmate Jared describes as "very school shooter chic," but when he reaches out and does the unexpected—signs Evan's cast—it's almost as if a glimmer of goodness briefly shines through from behind the mask he's created for himself. Then suddenly he's gone, and there's no time for anyone, audience or actor, to get to know who he really was and what might have been. For Faist, that's part of the tragedy—that you never really know what happened. "That's life," he says. "You don't know why or how. That's unfortunately what you're left with in the real world."

To better understand Connor's motivations and history, Faist spoke with suicide attempt survivors and discovered the website LiveThroughThis.org, which features interviews with people who have tried to take their own lives. He learned that common coping mechanisms of many living with depression and suicidal thoughts include hiding who they really are from the world and battling the stigma of how others perceive them, as Connor does. "I think Connor is a person who feels too much," Faist says. "And he doesn't know how to express it."

In order to get into character, Faist initially devised a pre-show ritual that would take him to the dark place he needed to go. While his castmates would gather for pre-show dance parties in Platt's dressing room, Faist says, "I would be alone in my corner listening to Chet Baker, the Gorillaz, the Smiths, and a little bit of Marilyn Manson, or just not listening to anything at all and constantly telling myself terrible, terrible thoughts in order to get me to that moment."

The emotional cost of this approach—after his scenes in Act One, he would run up to his dressing room and collapse on the floor—finally became too high. "I had to start not allowing it to hurt so much," he says. "I had to get better at my technique, and commit to the text more, and stop beating myself up." (Now, Faist allows himself to join in on the dance parties and let loose.)

Stepping into Connor's military surplus boots has been a formative personal experience for Faist, who considers the role a "gift." "What I've learned is that I need to trust myself more, and love myself more, and know that it is all good," he says. "I am here. I am finally here. I am doing this. Success is defined by oneself. People call this successful. I consider this work. I am okay. I'm beyond okay."

(above) Faist paints his nails black, ∧
Connor's signature color,
before a performance.

MICHAEL PARK

LARRY MURPHY IS THE TYPE OF MAN YOU might expect to find in a boardroom of executives or on the fairway, playing eighteen holes. The cold, stern, stoic-to-a-fault patriarch in *Dear Evan Hansen* deals with his son's suicide by burying his grief beneath an armor of anger and resentment. But Michael Park, who plays Larry, is open and inviting, ruggedly handsome with a shock of silver hair, and he radiates a warmth that is a far cry from the father he plays onstage.

"When I go to sign autographs at the stage door, people say, 'Wonderful job, will you be my dad?'" says Park. He typically responds that they want Act Two Larry, not the shell of a person from Act One who has no idea how to relate to his children. "I would never want a parent to ever have to go through what we as actors perform onstage every night."

Park knows all too well the pain that Larry and the rest of the Murphys go through in losing a child and a sibling. When he was 16, he lost his 14-year-old sister to leukemia. Park says he relates to Zoe, the younger Murphy daughter, as he too had trouble talking with his friends and coming to terms with his sister's death, which he sees as a defining moment of his high school years. Because he was navigating such a terrible loss and so much family grief, he didn't have time to rebel, and he feels like he missed out on being a lost and struggling adolescent.

Looking back on that time, he realizes how much of his performance as Larry Murphy is shaped by his memories of observing his father struggle to cope with his sister's death, and how deeply his father's tenacity seeped into his development of the character. "My father was the first one to get into these ruts, like I imagine Larry Murphy would, where he would be wrong about a subject and he wouldn't let it die," he says. But, unlike Larry, his father worked hard to keep everyone okay instead of retreating: "The person I knew I could always turn to for the strength was my father."

Park grew up in Canandaigua, New York, south of Rochester, part of a big Italian family, with an older brother and two younger sisters. Theater came to him by accident; on a whim, he auditioned for *Bye Bye Birdie* in high school and wound up getting cast as the rock star Conrad Birdie. He calls it his Evan Hansen moment, one in which he felt "seen in a different way." Still, he had no intention of pursuing a career on the stage. During his sophomore year at Nazareth College, though, his now-wife, Laurie Nowak, asked him to join her in auditioning for *Guys and Dolls*. He agreed, primarily as an excuse to sit in the back and do homework with her. Things didn't work out precisely as planned—he was cast as Sky Masterson, and she didn't make the cut—but an actor was born.

Park's career has taken him from the Blackfriars Theatre in Upstate New York to Off Broadway (*Hello Again*) and Broadway (*Smokey Joe's Café*). He also spent thirteen years playing good-guy cop Jack Snyder on *As the World Turns*. "I had to wait twenty-five years to be in a Tony award-winning musical," he says with a laugh.

And Park will be the first to tell you how wonderful the musical is—as he is the only original cast member who has actually sat and watched the show from start to finish. Park, while performing in Broadway's *Tuck Everlasting* during *Dear Evan Hansen*'s run at Second Stage, attended the Off-Broadway opening night. "I was sitting by myself weeping, just in tears, so proud of these people, so proud of the story," says Park, who remembers praying that the show would move to Broadway and that he would be able to play the part again. (John Dossett, who played Larry Murphy at Second Stage, is a good friend of Park's, and agreed to fill the latter's shoes Off Broadway, before going off himself to do *War Paint* on Broadway, also directed by Michael Greif.)

Park has been with the show since the beginning, and he knew from the minute he read the script that it was something he desperately wanted to be a part of. "You know, it's rare when something like this happens." He

> **I would never want a parent to ever have to go through what we as actors perform onstage every night."**

(below) **Park and Carolee** ∨
Carmello in rehearsal for *Tuck*
Everlasting **in February 2016.**

worried for a while that his character would be cut, as the story became more and more about Evan's journey and less about those on the periphery. So he poured himself into working on his second act solo "To Break in a Glove," a pure moment of bonding, where he attempts to heal the fractured relationship with his own son through showing Evan how to turn a stiff baseball mitt supple, a metaphor that could be used for Larry's own journey as a character. Park considers the song his character's "high point in the show," but it's also a crucial moment for Evan, who admits that his rosy picture of having a great dad was a lie. Evan's confession creates a moment in which he and Larry are able encounter more honest versions of themselves, and each other. "It's the first time Evan really tells the truth to anyone in the show," Park says. "It's the first time he's copped to a lie that he's just told."

And in the same way that Larry learns to connect with Evan, Park has learned a thing or two about parenting his own children through playing the role, which has helped him become a more "open communicator." He recently took the time to apologize to his now 19-year-old son for an incident from his childhood when Park scolded his boy for crying after a baseball game. While his son didn't even remember the moment, the parenting failure had continued to haunt Park over a decade later.

His 17-year-old daughter has even used the show as a way to connect with her dad. Instead of coming to Park and saying "I'm depressed," she confessed instead, "Sometimes I feel like Connor." Park remembers feeling so grateful that the musical had given his daughter a vernacular to be able to better express her struggles. But inhabiting Larry Murphy has also led Park to some dark places of his own. "I've gone through bouts of depression, too, dealing with this show," he says. In times like that, it's important for him to "remember the good that has come out, the conversations that I've had with my kids because of it. I remember all these wonderful things, the letters that I'm getting, and the thanks that I'm getting from parents outside, and the kids that are helped, and it all makes me feel better. Those bouts of depression are becoming fewer and fewer."

But for the 49-year-old actor, it continues to be an experience that connects him more deeply to his own humanity and his own family. While Larry comes around on honoring and mourning his son, Park never wants to be in that position and looks to his son and daughter for encouragement and inspiration. "How could anyone not want to celebrate their children? It doesn't matter what they're wearing or who their friends are, what their interests are," he says. "They're there to be celebrated."

JENNIFER LAURA THOMPSON

CYNTHIA MURPHY WOULD DO ABSO-lutely anything for her children. So, when she's faced with a struggling son, her inability to help him—no matter how many books she reads or programs she tries—causes her seemingly perfect world to crumble. Jennifer Laura Thompson would also do anything for her son, and while, thankfully, she doesn't face the realities of her character, she does imagine every night: *What would it be like to lose a child?*

"The most important thing is that I remember at the end of the show that it's not real, but I do allow myself to go to a very real place," she says. As a result, playing Cynthia has reaffirmed her "mama bear tendencies," she adds. "Mama bear" is a spot-on way to describe Thompson, whose kind eyes and warm embrace could make a total stranger divulge their life story to her. Watching her play a character with a shattered heart is devastating for the audience, and portraying her is difficult for Thompson as well. "It would

be too much for me. It would be too much for me to recover from the loss of my child," she says. "However, I had to find a way to get past that."

Like all the cast members who have been with the show since the beginning, Thompson had no idea what she signed up for at the first table read or even what character she would be playing. She did know, after she read the part and heard the songs, that this show was different. "The emotions that it conjured were so utterly natural; there was no question in my mind as to the importance of this piece," she says.

But much of Cynthia's role has been reworked. In early readings and workshops, Thompson had her own song and a duet, both of which have been cut. Thompson understands that sometimes edits need to be made—she does still long to sing a Pasek and Paul solo—and reshaping Cynthia's part over the course of the development process has helped build a backstory and an acting approach for Thompson. "In some ways, it was really cool to go with putting it all out there and then reeling it back in and still having it inside your soul," Thompson says. "It's impossible to play her without knowing everything."

∧ (above) **Thompson in *Wicked* at the Gershwin Theater in January, 2005.**

My poor kid never experienced love with a girlfriend or boyfriend.... It breaks my heart every night."

One of the backstories that was important to Thompson was the relationship between Cynthia and her husband, Larry. The rancor in their marriage, as a result of the ongoing family struggles, becomes magnified in the wake of their son's suicide, and nagging and bickering seems to be the only way either of them knows how to cope. Thompson talked with the writers and director Greif, and together they filled in the missing details of her and Larry's relationship, deciding that the pair met in college and married soon after. "It was a fiery relationship, but it was also one with great mystery," she imagines. Cynthia never actually worked and instead started a family, but she craved an outlet for her intelligence and drive, to "fill the void of whatever intellectual inspiration she needed." Her daughter, Zoe, jokes:

ZOE: That's sort of what she does. She gets into different things. For a while it was Pilates, then it was The Secret, then Buddhism. Now it's free-range, Omnivore's Dilemma . . . whatever.
EVAN: It's cool that she's interested in so much different stuff.
ZOE: She's not. That's just what happens when you're rich and you don't have a job. You get crazy.

In the scene at the principal's office when the Murphys meet Evan and assume the letter they found with their son is Connor's suicide note, all of the latent tension between Larry and Cynthia is on full display. For Thompson, the friction between her Cynthia and Park's Larry comes naturally in that moment. "It's not that we work together to get it to work," Thompson says. "It's that we are so divided and invested in our own agendas that the volatility of it is very real."

Thompson fell in love with theater in high school. Her first musical was *Barnum*, which she auditioned for

because she had a crush on an older student, becoming from that point on "that girl that got all the leads," starring in *Guys and Dolls*, *My Fair Lady*, and *Once Upon a Mattress*. She eventually studied musical theater at the University of Michigan, in the same program that songwriters Justin Paul and Benj Pasek attended years later.

Her first professional job was playing Julie Jordan in the tour of *Carousel*, and she made her Broadway debut in *Footloose*. She earned a Tony nomination for her performance in *Urinetown*, and many fans remember her for playing Glinda in *Wicked*, the first show she did after taking time off following the birth of her now-13-year-old son. "My child needed me to be home," she says. "Your maternal instincts don't really give you a choice. You just are driven to do whatever you know you need to do."

As a mother, Thompson still finds many of the lines and lyrics in the show heart-wrenching, even after saying and hearing them countless times. For example, she points to the moment when Cynthia gives Evan the tie she bought Connor to wear to all the bar mitzvahs he never got invited to, as well as a lyric Evan sings in "For Forever":

There's nothing that we can't discuss
Like girls we wish would notice us
But never do

"My poor kid never experienced love with a girlfriend or boyfriend, whatever it's going to be. It breaks my heart every night," she says of Cynthia's sadness, adding, "I don't think Connor really gave a shit about it, but as a mom, you want there to be so much happiness and joy in your child's life." This feeling makes the climax, when Evan reveals he's been lying, all the more devastating for Cynthia.

Thompson has a tight-knit relationship with her own son, who hasn't seen the show yet. Some of his classmates have gone and many have listened to the cast recording, but Thompson says it might kill her to perform the role knowing he's in the audience. "I didn't feel like it would be beneficial for him to see me portray this character, because she goes through such dark emotions, specifically about losing a son," she says.

Thompson admires Cynthia's stubbornness and her "endless effort to help her son," and she prays she never loses the special connection with her own. "If I were stripped of that, that would be devastating," she says, adding that the lyric in "For Forever" about Connor and Evan telling "jokes that no one understands" is difficult to listen to for Thompson because "that's everything about my relationship with my son," she says. "We understand each other in a way that nobody else does."

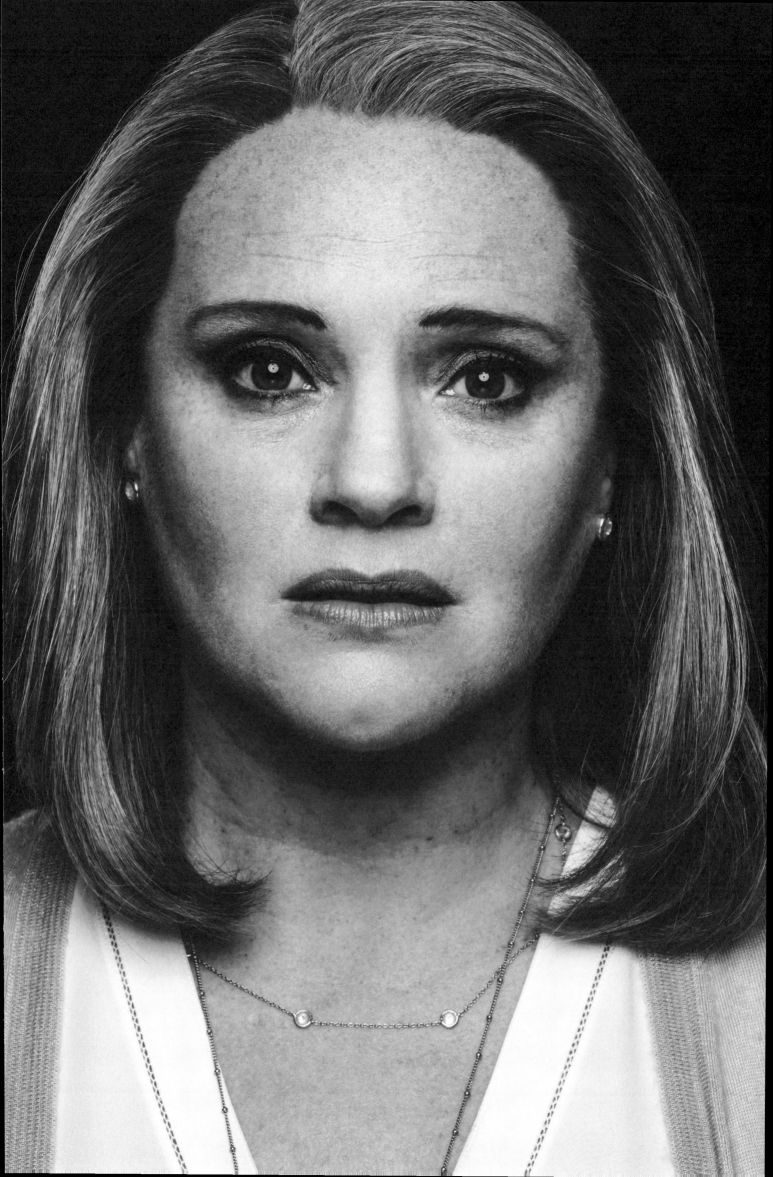

NO ONE DESERVES TO DISAPPEAR

The fans share how the show has affected their lives

WHEN STACEY MINDICH TOOK THE STAGE TO accept the Tony Award for Best Musical, she mentioned three people whose names aren't in the playbill: "From Martha and Julie in California to Kaho in Japan, you have been seen and heard and found. You matter," Mindich said, naming three of the musical's most devoted fans. While many producers thank the audience when taking home the top prize, Mindich knew that the profound impact the musical has had on people of all ages called for something more personal. "I couldn't stop laughing from happiness," says Kaho Kidoguchi, a Japan-based musical theater superfan, who first heard about the show in early readings from following Benj Pasek and Justin Paul on Facebook. "It made me feel like I won a Tony!"

Twin sisters Martha and Julie Stroud were watching in tears before Mindich even said their names. "To feel the love I have given to the show being reciprocated in that way—especially because, in being named, we were representing the whole 'Fansen' community—was a feeling I will never forget," Martha says.

In the same way that "*Rent*-heads" slept on the sidewalk outside the Nederlander Theatre for the *Rent* lottery, and "Hamilfans" flooded 46th Street for the daily Ham-4Ham show, crowds of "Fansens," their self-designated moniker, gather outside the Music Box Theatre each night after the curtain falls, hoping for a moment of connection with the company.

Many of the show's most passionate fans have been following the musical since its early days. Kelly Myslinski traveled to D.C. for the show's second preview at Arena Stage, after reading about it in an email newsletter. "I just remember sitting in the theater and feeling that I was finally being seen and understood," she says. "I went up to Benj Pasek during intermission, tears streaming down my face, and just thanked him for creating something so beautiful, honest, and raw."

After Julie Stroud saw the show at Second Stage for the first time, she tweeted, "Thank you for the gift of @DearEvanHansen, healing my adolescent heart 30 years later. I'm changed by experiencing your show." "When I rooted for Evan to forgive and love himself, I discovered that I still needed to forgive and love a part of myself I didn't realize I was still hiding and hating," she says.

When Kidoguchi visited New York and saw the show, the cast and Michael Greif took her backstage and talked with her about her experience. "I was really surprised that the cast knows me! They even thanked me, what?!" Kidoguchi says. Michael Park has also invited supporters backstage, including Myslinski, and uses the opportunity to open a conversation. "One teacher sent me a letter, and I was so moved by it that I picked up the phone and called him immediately and said whatever you guys need, let me know," says Park. When the teacher and his students eventually made it to the show, Park organized a post-show discussion for them with several of the other actors and himself.

For Mindich, it is essential to consider the show's fans in each of her marketing decisions. "I always say things like, 'What would Julie, or Martha, or Kelly think about that?'" she says. In fact, the Fansens have gradually become part of the fabric of the show itself, as many of them actually appear in the production. Fans, including Myslinski, submitted videos to be used in the projections during "You Will Be Found." As soon as she saw the call to action for videos, she says, she rushed back to her freshman dorm room and had her roommate record a video, with the camera balanced on textbooks and journals. "'You Will Be Found' is a song that I wish I had when I was in high school, because maybe it would've made things a bit easier," she says. Her clip features prominently during the number and even appears in one of the widely circulated production photos.

Fans have also made their way into the show's branding materials and merchandise. The pictures in the mosaic of faces on the front of the theater and on the souvenir brochure are of real fans (Martha and Julie Stroud and Kelly Myslinski are all there), and the show now sells a tote bag featuring fan art, the proceeds of which go to nonprofit partners the Child Mind Institute, Crisis Text Line, the JED Foundation, the Trevor Project, and the Born This Way Foundation.

Through their dedication to the musical, the fans have formed a community both online and in real life. They've recognized each other from social media waiting in line for tickets or at the stage door, or at events like the first Broadway preview. "It meets the very human needs and desires illuminated by the show," says Julie Stroud, "the need to connect, to belong, to be accepted, to be encouraged, to be loved, to matter, and ultimately to be supported in accepting and loving ourselves."

CHAPTER 15

ALL WE SEE IS LIGHT

The show transfers to Broadway

N MAY 25, 2016, WHILE the musical was still playing Off Broadway, Stacey Mindich made the announcement she had been waiting eight years to make: *Dear Evan Hansen* would be on Broadway in the fall. At the time, the casting was not publicly confirmed and the press release simply stated that the show would open at an unspecified Shubert Organization theater, but all systems were a go for the Great White Way.

After the production closed at Second Stage, Mindich announced that the show would be at the Belasco Theatre with the cast still intact (plus Michael Park back in as Larry Murphy) and performances starting in November. But after *Shuffle Along* closed over the summer, Mindich negotiated with the Shubert Organization to move *Dear Evan Hansen* into the Music Box Theatre.

The writers, as always cautious, took the summer to think through the creative implications of a move to Broadway. "We left Second Stage with some trepidation," Paul says. "We thought, *How can we maintain the intimacy of an Off-Broadway experience in a Broadway house?*" Beyond their concerns about the physical production, the writers still had a list—though shorter than ever—with tweaks left to implement. "Every sentence has to matter. If something isn't moving the story forward, or elaborating more about the character, it has to go. There's not room for just chatter," Steven Levenson says of writing for musical theater, explaining that he

meticulously went through the script line by line after Second Stage, asking: Do we need this? "In plays, you can have a *lot* of chatter, and I love that about plays. I like settling in with characters, and the rhythms of their speech, but you can't really do that in a musical."

While the writers and Michael Greif worked out the bulk of the changes Off Broadway, the team still wanted to fine-tune how Connor reappears in the show after his death, as a reflection of Evan's internal emotional state. The final scene in the orchard also needed to deliver just the right emotional uplift without veering into sentimentality. Levenson combed through the dialogue between Zoe and Evan, and adjusted the final monologue over and over.

There was one change, though, that wasn't made to the final scene. One of the show's producers continually asked Mindich for the writers to add a moment at the

If something isn't moving the story forward, or elaborating more about the character, it has to go."

end of the orchard scene for Zoe to turn to Evan and say, "Call me." "That was never, ever going to happen. It became a running joke," Mindich says. She did agree with the producer's underlying concern, however, that the show close on an optimistic note. "I knew that ending with hope was an incredibly important thing."

It was also important that Evan remain a sympathetic and relatable character, and Benj Pasek, Justin Paul, and Levenson continued to build his empathic qualities by showing the attempts Evan makes to get to know the "real" Connor. In the revised final scene, Evan talks to Zoe about finding Connor's eighth grade yearbook page. While most students, Evan says, used their pages for "collages of their friends," Connor's instead listed his favorite books. Evan has spent the last year reading them. Initially, Levenson named three of Connor's favorite books in the script, but upon realizing that every audience member would have a different opinion of what books Connor would and wouldn't choose, he axed the titles. "We prefer to let the audience imagine what Connor liked to read because in the end, he is kind of this mystery," Levenson says.

The actors relished the rehearsal process for Broadway, enjoying the space to dig deeper into the scenes and work on these characters in a way they might not have been able to at Arena Stage or Second Stage, when new songs and changes were coming their way so frequently. "In a lot of ways, it wasn't until we were all really settled on the script that everyone could commit," Greif says. "Rehearsing was a real joy because you got to go back in and really carve out moments."

A large part of the rehearsal process for Broadway was focused on putting Park back into the show. He was tasked with incorporating a number of major changes that had been made since he'd last performed the role at Arena Stage, including the addition of the song "You Will Be Found." In addition, in the climactic section of the song, Larry experiences an emotional breakdown—a major new facet of the role for Park to assimilate. "To be honest, the new arc was not clear to me at first," he says, though with time, he gradually found his way back into the character.

When it came time for the musical to begin loading in at the Music Box, the cast and crew were relieved to find themselves with significantly more stage space than they had at Second Stage. But set designer David Korins wanted to make certain that the larger venue did not alter the audience's experience of the show. Though he tries not to spend much time considering what reviewers might say, in this case, he didn't want any critic who had praised the show for its intimacy at Second Stage to lament that the Broadway production felt cavernous. In order to prevent this, Korins made a series of small changes to the theater. He covered the orchestra pit, since the band sits on an elevated platform onstage, and removed the front row of seats, from which audience members would have strained to see any of the action. He further raked the stage, meaning he gave the surface a slight slope tilting up away from the audience, making it easier for theatergoers to see the projections in their entirety and the performers from head to toe.

AS KORINS REEXAMINED THE PHYSI-cal production, Mindich went about scrutinizing every aspect of the show's marketing campaign. In the same way that the writers didn't want backpacks and lockers onstage that screamed "high-school musical," she was exceedingly careful not to brand the show as something strictly for teenagers. Nor did she want potential audience members to be scared away by the darker themes of the musical. Mindich had been scrupulous about the look and message of the show from the beginning, "right down to matching everything." The show's blue hue has now become synonymous with its title and is consistent on everything from the marquee to the playbill to the Bloomingdale's-sponsored "Blue Room," a converted dressing room in the Music Box Theatre where the cast meets friends, family, and celebrity guests after shows.

In addition to traditional print and online marketing, Mindich also decided to stream three tracks from the musical on the *Dear Evan Hansen* website, in order to further drum up excitement for the Broadway production. In the weeks leading up to the show's first performance, fans eagerly played and replayed the songs "Waving Through a Window," "Only Us," and "If I Could Tell Her," which music supervisor Alex Lacamoire recorded at album quality.

"[Mindich] was…careful not to brand the show as something strictly for teenagers."

The fans may have been eager to see the show—but the writers were nervous. "The last time I had real doubts about the show and its viability was the dress rehearsal for the Broadway production. It was that late. We had an audience the next night," Levenson says, noting his and his fellow writers' persistent worry that the larger space might diffuse the emotional intensity of certain moments.

"As writers, we are always doubting ourselves. I have a hard time imagining that most writers feel satisfied," Paul adds. "You always feel like there's something else you can do and that's why they always force you to stop working on the show at a certain point."

THE FIRST PREVIEW ON NOVEMBER 14, 2016, instantly allayed their concerns. It began with Greif delivering a curtain speech. The presidential election had left much of the country feeling lost and uncertain the week before, and Greif spoke in moving terms about using theater to bring light to dark times. The show itself went off without a hitch, and after the final bow and a sustained standing ovation, audience members leaving the theater were handed commemorative hats with the date of the first preview embossed on them. A sea of hats poured onto 45th Street, practically covering the block in *Dear Evan Hansen* blue. When Pasek, Paul, and Levenson went downstairs and through the stage door to investigate the scene, they were greeted with overwhelming screams. "I'm a playwright—no one has ever 'whooped' upon seeing me before, I can assure you," Levenson says. "That was just a crazy moment. I didn't quite realize until that night, I think, what a deep, personal connection people felt to this show."

As previews went on, and the seats were filled increasingly with more typical theatergoers rather than die-hard fans, the fervent response never dipped. In fact, it only escalated, as new fans were created every night. The show opened on December 4,

< (left) Paul tours the
Music Box Theatre.

2016, and that night, Pasek, Paul, and Levenson sat in "real seats," as opposed to their typical position pacing at the back of the theater. "There is this sense of feeling very exposed—that for the first time people can see your reaction to your own work," Pasek says, but notes that the audience on an opening night is full of friends and family and people who have worked on the show. "So, it's a really beautiful thing."

After the overwhelming ovation at the Music Box, the cast, creative team, crew, industry members, family, and friends celebrated at The Pierre hotel. "I remember being huddled around a phone to read the *New York Times* review with two of my friends," Pasek says. "The tone of those kinds of parties changes really, really quickly and everybody starts looking at their phones and you can kind of see people start leaving if the reviews aren't good, or there will be a sense of euphoria."

It's safe to say that *Dear Evan Hansen* experienced the latter. "This gorgeous heartbreaker of a musical, which opened at the Music Box Theatre on Sunday, has grown in emotional potency during its journey to the big leagues, after first being produced in Washington and Off Broadway. Rarely—scratch that—never have I heard so many stifled sobs and sniffles in the theater," wrote Charles Isherwood in *The New York Times*.

The reviews were exciting, but for the songwriters they represented—more than anything—confirmation that the show wasn't going anywhere soon. Pasek and Paul's only previous Broadway opening was *A Christmas Story: The Musical*, which opened to raves but had a limited run as a holiday musical. "There was a sense of, 'Hey, given what the reviews seem to be like and the way people are talking about the show, it looks like we're gonna be around for a little while,'" Paul says. "That's the goal."

After the party wrapped up around 2 a.m., Levenson and his wife went to the diner around the corner

from their apartment and ate pancakes. "Sitting there, it just felt like Benj and Justin and I had somehow gotten away with something," he says, "because, when we started working on this musical, we had no idea that it would ever reach this far. Broadway was such a distant, improbable dream. And suddenly it was reality."

While critical praise is flattering, Mindich was most interested in listening to audiences, which continued to flood the Music Box night after night, and to the friends and family she trusts above anyone. "My husband has never liked any of the shows I've ever done. He loves this one, and he invited everyone we know," Mindich says, adding that upward of 500 people from her social and professional circles have seen the show. Many have since opened up to her and her husband about their own stories. "People we knew all the years we've been married would come up to us and say, 'We never told you this: Her sister committed suicide.' 'Our son has Asperger's.' People's deepest, darkest secrets would not only come up, but then they'd want to have dinner with us and talk about it even more." These conversations sparked the idea to launch the marketing initiative We Are Evan Hansen, a series of online videos highlighting all of the many individuals who make the show possible night after night, from Ben Platt to the understudies and musicians.

For Greif, the universal appeal of the show is not just that we identify with Evan and the rest of the cast of outsiders, but that we want to believe that forgiveness and acceptance is possible. "I feel like a lot of the unspoken success of *Dear Evan Hansen* is about the generosity inherent in it," Greif says. "That last scene is so unbelievably generous. The Murphy family's behavior is so generous. Everything that Zoe says in that scene is so generous. I just think that we want to see people behave that way, and we want to behave that way ourselves. In times of terrible crisis, when you could imagine people acting appallingly, they act magnanimously. That gets me. And I think it gets all of us."

∧ (from left) Pasek, Levenson, Lacamoire, Paul, and Greif attend opening night at the Music Box.

CHAPTER 16

YOU GOT YOUR DREAM COME TRUE

Will Roland and Kristolyn Lloyd make their Broadway debuts

**HE SAYING GOES, THERE** are no small parts, only small actors. But no part, nor actor, is tiny in *Dear Evan Hansen,* as the tight-knit ensemble moves with the precision of a well-oiled machine night after night. And while many actors first enter on the Great White Way as an ensemble member, it's a rare thing to make a first Broadway bow as a featured player in a hit show with a dedicated following. Of course, an actor never knows it's going to end up that way when he or she signs on, whether joining the project in early development stages, as Will Roland did, or later on in the process, like Kristolyn Lloyd. But for both newly minted stars, *Dear Evan Hansen* has proven to be the ride of a lifetime.

Kristolyn Lloyd and Will Roland > take their bows after the Broadway opening night performance.

It's a rare thing to make a first Broadway bow … in a hit show with a dedicated following."

WILL ROLAND

IF YOU CATCH WILL ROLAND EMERGING FROM the Music Box Theatre stage door, you might start to wonder if Jared Kleinman has come to life. Roland's daily uniform usually includes glasses, a graphic tee with a short-sleeved button-up layered on top, and sneakers, so, he must have at least stolen the costumes, right? In fact, the opposite occurred: The Adidas shoes he wears in the show come from his own closet, and one of his character's shirts even features the logo of his girlfriend's brother's company. Jared is stealing from Roland.

But the endearingly goofy actor, who at 28 hasn't lost his baby face, doesn't seem to mind. After all, imitation is the highest form of flattery. And playing the quip-as-crutch-wielding Jared, Evan's "family friend," isn't the first time he's suited up as a sidekick to an anxiety-ridden leading man played by Ben Platt. They co-starred in a production of Joe Iconis's *The Black Suits* at Massachusetts's Barrington Stage in 2012.

The show was Roland's first Equity job as an actor, and while Platt left after the Barrington run, Roland remained with the musical through its production at Los Angeles's Center Theatre Group. The producers hoped the show might move to Broadway, and when that didn't pan out, Roland returned to New York discouraged and depressed.

About six months later, he received an appointment to audition for a reading of *Dear Evan Hansen*, an opportunity that Roland, who spent most of his early career performing in projects with and by friends, describes as one of the few times he's auditioned for a group of strangers and landed the job. Little did he know, not everyone would be a stranger. "I walked in the room on the first day for the reading," he recalls, "and I thought, *Oh thank God, Ben Platt is here.*"

Though Roland has been involved with the show from that reading forward, the character he plays has undergone a number of changes along the way, most notably in the excision of Jared's big Act One song, "Goin' Viral." When Michael Greif called to let Roland know that the writers were cutting the number before Arena Stage, he was sure that it was a prelude to being fired. It wasn't, of course, and as a result, Roland focused more on the scenes, deepening his relationship with Steven Levenson, who shaped much of the character's humor and demeanor around Roland's inclinations as both an actor and a person. "For me to have that kind of hand in this process, it's not how many people's first Broadway show or second big job go," he says. "Steven and I have developed a really close collaboration. It is truly the most fulfilling and enriching thing to get to say his words every night."

Though Jared often functions in the musical as much-needed comic relief, Roland sees the character as more complex than he appears at first glance. Jared's participation in the deception, by helping craft the fake emails, is a way for him to get closer to Evan, Roland argues, but the character can't admit, even to himself, that he craves this friendship. "Jared gets his jollies making Evan feel bad," he says. "Throughout the play, the opportunity presents itself for him to forge a real

"Jared feeds off that same positive energy that comes from making people laugh....and that sabotages him from making genuine connections with people."

GOIN' VIRAL

The lyrics for Jared's cut song

PASEK AND PAUL MAY HAVE FIGURATIVELY BROKEN the internet, at least among musical theater nerds, when their song cycle *Edges* took then-nascent YouTube by storm in 2006, but in 2017, it's not such a novel concept. Everyone knows how memes, gifs, and cat videos spread online, so in the interest of not dating the show—and since the number slowed down the action—Jared's Act One song about how things go viral hit the chopping block.

JARED

Now there's a lotta stupid shit that hits the internet / But if it's funny or embarrassing then you can bet / It goes viral / That shit goes viral / Ooh whoa-oh / Ooh whoa-oh

When a cat can play piano or a fat girl falls / Then your friends are gonna share it on their facebook walls / And it's viral / Fuckin' viral / Ooh whoa-oh / Ooh whoa-oh

Once your letter first gets tweeted / That shit never gets deleted / One kid clicks / Then two, then six / And oh, you know

It's goin' viral, viral / You'll be an internet celebrity / 'Cause it'll spread like fuckin' H.P.V. / Now ev'rybody knows your shit / It's goin' viral, viral / You'll be the posterboy for 'gay and lame' / So either kill yourself or change your name / 'Cause it's goin' viral, viral, viral

ENSEMBLE

Like, share, like / Like, share at reply / Like, share, like / Like, post a comment

JARED

You'll see it blowin' up on youtube as a hip-hop song / And ev'ry soccer mom in Omaha will sing along / 'Cause it's viral / Va-va-va-va-va-va / Viral / Ooh whoa-oh / Ooh whoa-oh

First you'll see your face on gawker / Soon you'll be the new chris crocker / Just sit back / And watch this fucker / Grow, grow, grow

Oh, it's goin' viral, viral / You're poppin' up on ev'ry laptop screen / And kids'll dress like you for Halloween / Khakis and those fucking shoes / It's goin' viral, viral / I'll get to say i knew the youtube star / That people laugh about in kandahar / 'Cause it's goin' viral, viral, viral

ENSEMBLE

Like, share, like / Like, share at reply / Like, share, like / Like, post a comment

friendship with Evan, which he embraces as much as he knows how to, still sort of woefully inadequate."

As their friendship falls apart, Jared laments his outsider status in "Good for You":

And you say what you need to say
And you play who you need to play
And if somebody's in your way
Crush them and leave them behind.

This verse is one of Roland's few solo moments, even though he studied vocal performance at New York University Steinhardt. The New York native was born at the school's medical center and lived in the West Village before moving to Locust Valley on Long Island when he was 8. His family owns Roland Auctions in downtown Manhattan, and he continues to work for the business between, and sometimes during, acting gigs. His talent for auctioneering came in handy during a three-month period when he auctioned off Evan's cast every night post-show for Broadway Cares Equity Fights AIDS, an organization that partners with Broadway shows twice a year to raise money in support of

LGBTQ and women's health initiatives. (The highest price he commanded was $12,000 for two casts.)

As a teenager, Roland hid his own insecurities in much the same way that Jared does—by covering his fear and anxiety with witty comebacks and jokes. "I was probably a bit of an asshole, not unlike this character," he says. "Jared feeds off that same positive energy that comes from making people laugh or feeling like you're so smart, you're so clever, you're so funny. It's the thing that drives him—and that sabotages him from making genuine connections with people."

Theater ultimately saved Roland from succumbing to the Jared-like cynicism of his younger self. He remembers coming into the city to see shows like *Cats* and *Saturday Night Fever*, and when he demonstrated an inclination for performing, his acting teacher at Friends Academy—where he attended middle school and high school—became a mentor. He started working at the summer camp she ran at the school and participated in leadership training with her, which changed his life. "That was super invaluable to me in terms of learning how to be a good person in addition to being sort of clever," he says, "which has served me much more than being clever ever has."

KRISTOLYN LLOYD

NO ONE WANTS TO BE THE LAST PERSON to arrive at the party, and stepping into an established group—from a Girl Scout troop to a Monday night book club—can be daunting. So when Kristolyn Lloyd joined the already tight-knit cast of *Dear Evan Hansen* at Second Stage, she had every reason to feel intimidated by the chummy ensemble's inside jokes and shared history. But Lloyd instead felt welcomed with open arms. "Stacey is always, like, 'I feel like you've been a part of this family the entire time,'" Lloyd says. "I felt like that kid who got adopted by the really cool family.'"

Lloyd was called in for the role of Alana while she was performing in *Invisible Thread* at Second Stage, the show that brought her permanently to New York after spending six years in L.A. working in theater and filming the soap opera *The Bold and the Beautiful*. She didn't know anything about *Dear Evan Hansen* at the time. A few days before her audition, though, she was hanging out at a friend's place when Ben Platt and Laura Dreyfuss, both of whom she was meeting for the first time, walked through the door. "It had a serendipitous feel to it," Lloyd says. Dreyfuss told her that she was going to get the part.

While bonding with the cast was easy, figuring out the character of Alana, the socially awkward overachiever who clings to Evan's fictional relationship with Connor in her quest for meaning, was more difficult. The writers were still working on the character after D.C., and when Lloyd received the offer, she waited two weeks to accept.

She wanted to see the script, which she hadn't read yet, and to speak with Greif about the role, since she isn't typically cast as the "nerdy" character. She didn't know what she had done in her audition that stood out to the director, and Greif told her that he responded to the way that she portrayed Alana with a certain determination and tone-deafness. Highlighting those characteristics helped clarify the part for her. And since Lloyd didn't have the same prep time as the rest of the cast, she had extra rehearsals for two hours every morning while the show was in technical rehearsals Off Broadway. "It was a matter of getting her into my body and understanding the energy at which they needed her to be, because she operates at such a high intensity," she explains.

Lloyd recognizes now that some of the early difficulty she had in connecting with the character stemmed from the fact that she was "not like Alana at all" in high school, noting that she didn't have the same academic determination or social awkwardness as the character. (She thinks Alana probably ends up working in the White House one day.) One thing with which she did connect was Alana's busy schedule—Lloyd participated in student council, speech and debate, choir, track and field, and swimming in high school, a list of extracurriculars that even Alana might envy.

Ultimately, Lloyd found her own way to connect to the character, seeing her "as a young black girl in a world where she doesn't really see a lot of her type around her." Like Alana, Lloyd knows what it is like "to feel lonely and invisible." She grew up in Houston, and her church, where she sang in the choir, had a mostly white congregation. "I can relate to growing up in a predominately white community, just wanting to have a relationship with other people of color," she explains. "But feeling this fear and insecurity because I don't sound like them when I talk. I don't sound like them

> **"I can relate to growing up in a predominately white community, just wanting to have a relationship with other people of color."**

"

Each night as she prepares to go onstage, she repeats inside her head: Tell her story."

when I sing. I didn't grow up in the same environment. How am I supposed to relate to my people?"

Aiding her in her discovery of the character, Lloyd created a rich backstory for Alana based on some lines in the script. Her grandmother has just died, and Lloyd imagines Alana was close with this relative and would be internally grieving this death, noting that "a lot of times African-Americans aren't really allowed to show vulnerability or emotion." She also imagines Alana had a crush on Connor, which motivates her to dive head-first into preserving his memory.

Though she now feels an undeniably strong connection to the character, Lloyd admits that putting on the emotions of a teenager every day can be exhausting—"Do I have the energy to be 17?" the 32-year-old asks herself some days, but each night as she prepares to go onstage, she repeats inside her head: "Tell her story."

"When I leave the stage, I don't have to live in that world, but when I'm onstage, I get to be that person," she explains. "There's something very empowering about it."

E

VERYTHING IS BLUE.
Blue donuts, macarons, and gummy bears line a blue-lit candy bar. Upstairs, blue lights illuminate the rooftop patio, while downstairs, a neon sign reading, "You will be found," greets guests who have found themselves at the *Dear Evan Hansen* Tony Awards after-party. Waiters dressed in striped blue polo shirts deliver appetizers to partygoers, many of whom, including newly minted Tony Award winners Stacey Mindich and Rachel Bay Jones, are dressed in, you guessed it, blue.

But the energy at the Empire Hotel rooftop is far from blue. Just hours before, the unlikely tuner about the underdog in all of us received the 2017 Tony Award for Best Musical. "At its core, our musical is about wanting to belong," Mindich said from the stage. "It's been an honor to belong to a season filled with such fantastic work." The award brought the show's tally to six. Unlike the previous year when *Hamilton* was a surefire lock, the *Dear Evan Hansen* team was less certain what the outcome would be. "We were really, really nervous," Justin Paul says. "We really didn't expect all that happened." Hours later, standing twelve stories above the street, the earlier events of the evening have already taken on the feeling of a dream.

Benj Pasek and Paul were the first to accept an award for the show, receiving the Tony for Best Score. Taking the stage, giddy like teenagers, and tag-teaming their speech, they eloquently tallied off a list of thanks. "We hoped to write a show that people who were looking for a home could find one," Paul said in their acceptance speech. "And we are so grateful to everyone who gave us the opportunity to try and do that," Pasek added.

Minutes later, as the two navigated the press rooms, Steven Levenson rounded the corner with his Tony. "We didn't know he had won!" Pasek says. "Getting to see him win was honestly more exciting than winning ourselves."

After they completed their press rounds, the three walked back to Radio City, awards in hand, but when they arrived at the door, security wouldn't let them through. They had Tonys—but not tickets. "After the insane high of winning a Tony, that really returned us all to reality," Levenson says. "But, I have to admit, it didn't last very long."

Back in the theater with help from Cynthia Nixon—the security guards recognized her from *Sex and the City*—

the writers watched Alex Lacamoire, Ben Platt, and Jones win, before joining the *Dear Evan Hansen* family onstage when the show was announced as the winner of Best Musical. Platt ended his speech with a rallying cry for the next generation of Evan Hansens—or rather, for the children who might become like the eponymous character. Platt encouraged all the outsiders looking in to embrace their own oddities. "To all the young people watching at home," Platt said, as the orchestra started to play, "don't waste any time trying to be like anybody else but yourself, because the things that make you strange are the things that make you powerful."

For many people at home, watching the Tony Awards was their first taste of *Dear Evan Hansen*. While about a thousand people see the show on Broadway each night, six million people watched the cast perform and heard the acceptance speeches. And for Pasek and Paul, knowing that the show is connecting with audiences at the Music Box and reaching people miles away from the bright lights of Broadway is the greatest gift.

"I don't think that the show offers a cure for loneliness, but I think there's some kind of cure in knowing that we're not alone in our loneliness," Paul said backstage after accepting the Tony.

"We want kids to know that that loneliness or the sense of isolation is a temporary thing and whatever pain you feel, you can use it to make something that can help yourself and save yourself," Pasek said. "So many shows did that for us, and to think that this show might have the potential to do that for someone else, that's the most meaningful thing of all."

This book was produced by

◇ MELCHER
  MEDIA

124 West 13th Street
New York, NY 10011
www.melcher.com

President and CEO: Charles Melcher
Vice President and COO: Bonnie Eldon
Executive Editor/Producer: Lauren Nathan
Production Director: Susan Lynch
Senior Digital Producer: Shannon Fanuko
Project Editor: Victoria Spencer

Stacey Mindich would like to express gratitude and admiration to:

Benj Pasek, Justin Paul, Steven Levenson, and Michael Greif—the dream team, who made my dreams come true; DEH's uber-talented creative team; the extraordinary forever original Broadway cast; the one and only Alex Lacamoire; Judy Schoenfeld, Bob Wankel, Phil Smith, Dessie Moynihan and the Shubert Organization; Pete Ganbarg and Craig Kallman at Atlantic Records; Susan Mindell and Kim Schefler; Second Stage and Arena Stage; the ever-supportive DEH co-producing family; SMP—my amazing team of Caitlin Clements and Lynn Matsumoto; a most passionate and devoted core team—Serino/Coyne, O&M, Situation Interactive and the other "dream team"—101 Productions (Jeff Wilson, Chris Morey, Kate Elliott, and Katie Titley, in

particular); Wendy Orshan, who was there from the beginning; Eric, Russell, Danny and Charlie, my beloveds, who were there before that; Marcia and Arthur Okun, even before that; and…the show's self-proclaimed "Fansens." Where would we be without you? We are all Evan Hansen.

Special thanks from the authors to:

David Berlin, John Buzzetti, Joe Machota, Whitney May, Asher Paul, Jordan Carroll, Ari Conte, and the many unsung heroes of *Dear Evan Hansen* who do not appear in this book, without whom none of our work would be possible: Judy Schoenfeld and the rest of the indefatigable stage management team, our covers and understudies, the run crew, dressers, musicians, house managers, and the staff at the Music Box Theatre, Second Stage, and Arena Stage.

Melcher Media would like to thank:

Chika Azuma, Jess Bass, Emma Blackwood, Renee Bollier, Jeremy Boxer, Tova Carlin, Amélie Cherlin, Karl Daum, Barbara Gogan, Ashley Gould, Emily Kao, Aaron Kenedi, Samantha Klein, Karolina Manko, Emma McIntosh, Founder and CEO of Show-Score Tom Melcher, Josh Raab, Ben Sevier, Gabrielle Sirkin, Megan Worman, Gretchen Young, Gabe Zetter, Retoucher Peter James Zielinski, and Photo Assistant Evan Zimmerman.

Image credits

Matthew Murphy: pp. 32–35, 45–47, 51, 54–183, 188, 190 (bottom), 192, 197–198, 200 (bottom), 201–202, 204 (bottom), 205 (top), 207, 216, 219–222, 224.

p. 2: courtesy of *Dear Evan Hansen*; p. 6: Kyle Dorosz; p. 9: Damon Winter/*The New York Times*/Redux; p. 11: Jesse Dittmar/*The New York Times*/Redux; p. 12: Austin Hargrave/AUGUST; p. 13 (bottom): Peter Smith, (top): Kerry Long; p. 14: Mark Seliger; p. 15: courtesy of Stacey Mindich; p. 17: Brad Barket/Getty Images; p. 18: Tony Cenicola/*The New York Times*/Redux; p. 20: Linda Davidson/*The Washington Post* via Getty Images; p. 21 (top): Chad Kraus, (bottom): Caitlin Clements; p. 26: Mike Cohen; p. 27 (top): Sara Krulwich/*The New York Times*/Redux, (bottom): *New York Post* Archive/Getty Images; p. 28 (top): Sarah Krulwich/*The New York Times*/Redux, (bottom): Mia McDonald; p. 29: David Korins; p. 36: Mark Peterson/Redux; p. 37: Nathan Johnson; p. 38: Mike Cohen; p. 39-40: Situation Interactive Engagement team; p. 42 (top left): Mia McDonald, (top right and bottom): Benj Pasek; p. 43 (top): Gibney Dance Center, (bottom): Karly Beaumont; p. 48: Nathan Johnson; p. 49 (top): Mike Cohen, (bottom): Kyle Dorosz; p. 50: David Korins; pp. 52-53: Emily Rebholz; p. 184: Ben Platt; p. 186: VIEW Pictures Ltd/Alamy Stock Photo; p. 187: Joan Marcus/Arena Stage; p. 190 (top): Chad Kraus, (middle): Kristolyn Lloyd; p. 195: Benj Pasek; p. 196: David Gordon; p. 199: Nathan Johnson; p. 200 (top): Andrew White/*The New York Times*/Redux; p. 204 (top): Slaven Vlasic/Getty Images; p. 205 (bottom): Bruce Glikas/FilmMagic/Getty Images; p. 209 (from top left): row 1: Amy Cash of Storied Script Calligraphy, Amy Cash of Storied Script Calligraphy, H. Delaney Wiggins, Kelly Myslinski, Desiree Nasim; row 2: @DammReen on twitter, Laura Bonacci (@Laurabonacciart), Anna Noran Rogers, Dan Lee (@dandrawnwords), Felice Falk, @hamiltongeek; row 3: K. Dunleavy, A.G. Cooper @dearevanhandsome, John Carter Wolfe, Laura Bonacci (@Laurabonacciart), Kelly Myslinski; row 4: Katie Zhang, Laura Bonacci (@Laurabonacciart), Alexandra Dukes (prabbeli.tumblr.com), Kelly Myslinski, Illustrated by Victoria Berger; row 5: Andrew Garrett, alyona11, Kendall Wood, Laura Bonacci (@Laurabonacciart), Sarah Heise; row 6: Laura Bonacci (@Laurabonacciart), Laura Bonacci (@Laurabonacciart), Jessica VanGiesen, Kelly Myslinski, Kelly Myslinski; row 7: Amy Cash of Storied Script Calligraphy, Kelly Myslinski, Laura Bonacci (@Laurabonacciart), by Emma Marshall, Sam Kerrigan; row 8: Eric Marquez, Kelly Myslinski, Addina Izam, Amy Cash of Storied Script Calligraphy, Tali Natter; row 9: Laura Bonacci (@Laurabonacciart), Amy Cash of Storied Script Calligraphy, A. Conner @monzellious, Alex Graudins, and Laura Bonacci (@Laurabonacciart); p. 210-212: Mia McDonald; p. 213: CC/Situation Interactive; p. 214: Chad Kraus; p. 215: Walter McBride/WireImage/Getty Images; p. 217: Kevin Sprague; p. 223 (bottom left): Jenny Anderson/Getty Images for Tony Awards Productions, (all other images): Chad Kraus.